MADNESS AND SUBJECTIVITY

This crucial new work draws on empirical findings from rural North India in relation to madness and subjectivity, revealing the different structures of subjectivity underlying the narratives of schizophrenia, spirits, ghosts, and deities.

Unravelling the loose ends of madness, the author explores the cultural differences in understanding and experiencing madness to examine how modern insanity is treated as a clinical disorder, but historically it represents how we form knowledge and understand self-knowledge. The author begins by theoretically investigating how the schizophrenic personifies the fractures in modern Western thought to explain why, despite decades of intense contention, the category of schizophrenia is still alive. She then examines the narratives of people in the Himalayan Mountains of rural India to reveal the discursive conditions that animate their stories around what psychology calls psychosis, critiquing the monoculturalism in trauma theory and challenging the ongoing march of the Global Mental Health Movement in the Global South.

Examining what a study of madness reveals about two different cultures, and their ways of thinking and being, this is fascinating reading for students interested in mental health, critical psychology, and Indian culture.

Ayurdhi Dhar, Ph.D., is an instructor of psychology at the University of West Georgia. She has taught psychology in the United States and in India, where she also worked as a psychotherapist. Her research interests include the relation between schizophrenia and immigration, discursive practices sustaining the concept of mental illness, and critiques of acontextual and ahistorical forms of knowledge. She spends her time negotiating the guilt of being an ardent animal lover and meat eater.

CONCEPTS FOR CRITICAL PSYCHOLOGY
Disciplinary Boundaries Re-thought
Series editor: Ian Parker

Developments inside psychology that question the history of the discipline and the way it functions in society have led many psychologists to look outside the discipline for new ideas. This series draws on cutting edge critiques from just outside psychology in order to complement and question critical arguments emerging inside. The authors provide new perspectives on subjectivity from disciplinary debates and cultural phenomena adjacent to traditional studies of the individual.

The books in the series are useful for advanced level undergraduate and postgraduate students, researchers and lecturers in psychology and other related disciplines such as cultural studies, geography, literary theory, philosophy, psychotherapy, social work and sociology.

Most recently published titles:

Rethinking Education through Critical Psychology
Cooperative Schools, Social Justice and Voice
Gail Davidge

Developing Minds
Psychology, Neoliberalism and Power
Elise Klein

Marxism and Psychoanalysis
In or Against Psychology?
David Pavón-Cuéllar

MADNESS AND SUBJECTIVITY

A Cross-Cultural Examination of Psychosis in the West and India

Ayurdhi Dhar

LONDON AND NEW YORK

First published 2020
by Routledge
2 Park Square, Milton Park, Abingdon, Oxon OX14 4RN

and by Routledge
52 Vanderbilt Avenue, New York, NY 10017

Routledge is an imprint of the Taylor & Francis Group, an informa business

© 2020 Ayurdhi Dhar

The right of Ayurdhi Dhar to be identified as author of this work has been asserted by them in accordance with sections 77 and 78 of the Copyright, Designs and Patents Act 1988.

All rights reserved. No part of this book may be reprinted or reproduced or utilised in any form or by any electronic, mechanical, or other means, now known or hereafter invented, including photocopying and recording, or in any information storage or retrieval system, without permission in writing from the publishers.

Trademark notice: Product or corporate names may be trademarks or registered trademarks, and are used only for identification and explanation without intent to infringe.

British Library Cataloguing in Publication Data
A catalogue record for this book is available from the British Library

Library of Congress Cataloging in Publication Data
A catalog record has been requested for this book

ISBN: 978-0-367-19569-4 (hbk)
ISBN: 978-0-367-19571-7 (pbk)
ISBN: 978-0-429-20323-7 (ebk)

Typeset in Bembo
by Swales & Willis, Exeter, Devon, UK
Printed by CPI Group (UK) Ltd, Croydon CR0 4YY

CONTENTS

Preface *vi*

1 Introduction 1

2 Inside schizophrenia: a house of mirrors 12

3 The "unalienated" alien: the schizophrenic as a hyper-modern subject 46

4 Deities and desire: an analysis 83

5 The slip and the sane: an analysis of subjectivity 128

6 Case and point: the girl-child's story 147

7 No country for psychology 160

References *170*
Index *178*

PREFACE

What is distinctively "modern" about madness? The discipline of psychology attempts to answer this question, repeating normative psychiatric conceptions of madness as something irremediably other to subjectivity, as if insanity were a weird wild kind of subjectivity beyond the bounds of what the human subject really should be at its core. Madness as something other threatens the dominant image of the rational unitary subject that holds modern psychological conceptions of the individual together, and then the discipline of psychology insidiously couples that image of the subject to an account of what it is to be modern. The underlying problem, of course, is that psychology is a profoundly modern discipline, and so is implicated in the diagnosis it makes of what is abnormal and, by implication, pre-modern. As Michel Foucault pointed out, as the urban centres become marked out from the countryside, forms of discipline and surveillance become the hallmarks of modern life.

Ayurdhi Dhar takes Foucault as her guide in this book to explore the way the separation between what is "modern" and what is "rural" are mapped onto the modern separation between normal subjectivity and madness. And, since this book is as much about the marking of territory as it is about the marking of concepts, she subverts those oppositions through a process of deterritorialization, now with Deleuze and Guattari as our guides. Along the way, and with India rather than Europe as the setting for this analysis, her book neatly critiques and extends Foucault's own analysis, showing us something more of the global context in which he situated what he called the monologue of reason about madness. We should recall that Foucault, in a preface to his mammoth history of madness in the West, points out that he could have studied other constitutive divisions in culture, but chose to focus in that book – a book that was the reworked publication of his doctoral thesis – on the division between reason and madness, a division which made reason the core of modern subjectivity. He could, he points out, have written about the constitutive division between the "West" and the "Orient", or he could have written about the constitutive division between heteronormative sexuality and what we push out into the shadows as perversion. There have, of course, been later "Foucauldian" studies of orientalism and sexuality, but now in this path-breaking book, we have an analysis of madness and subjectivity that takes us into those conceptual territories.

In place of the monologue of reason about madness we need a quite different approach, the kind of approach to madness that was charted by Foucault's colleagues and friends Deleuze and Guattari, an approach that deterritorializes subjectivity in such a way as to create quite new, we might dare to say "dialogical" connections between what is usually taken to be normal and what is routinely shut out of rational discourse as pathological. *Madness and Subjectivity* shows us that we need to move beyond the stark oppositions that underpin modern discourse, including the discourse of psychology. Instead of simply reversing the oppositions, and thereby reinforcing them, and instead of pretending that we can speak from outside rational "normal" subjectivity, we need to speak in and against it, "outwith" it.

Ian Parker
University of Manchester

1
INTRODUCTION

A 2001 article in a leading Indian newspaper *The Hindu* reported that India's Union Ministry has decided to map out the various faith-healing sites while also initiating a 155-crore mental health project ("Faith healing centers", 2001). Two days later, in a separate piece eerily reminiscent of Pinel's legendary "unchaining of the mad", *The Hindu* ran another article about the release and unchaining of 22 mentally ill patients in South India, complete with a photograph of a frail old woman being unchained by a man ("Patients freed", 2001). The officials involved condemned the mistreatment of the inmates while the reporter wondered with some urgency about how "ironically, the accompanying relatives did not allow the chains to be removed even in the hospital as they believed that the shackle was sacred and healing" ("Patients freed", 2001). The article further reported on the closure of 16 local sites, the now-required licensure of existing asylums, and the welcome introduction of other mental health programs. The stories of horrors at these faith-healing sites along with the bizarrely cruel behavior of accompanying relatives are a popular rhetoric for the educated, elite, upper-caste modern India that prides itself on its pro-science, pro-progress leanings. Experts insist that the irrational must be stamped out of our psyche and the superstitious explained away.

In 2010, National Public Radio (USA-based) ran an article with the headline "India's Mentally Ill Turn to Faith, Not Medicine". In classic NPR style, brimming with appropriate political correctness, the article never censures the East on their non-rational ways but instead presents a seemingly unbiased view of the dearth of mental health access – "only 1 psychiatrist for every 400,000 people" (Kennedy, 2010). The description of Dama Laxmi, "a tough, wiry woman in her 60s who talks nonstop, even as she slurps her plastic cup of chai while squatting on her haunches" (Kennedy, 2010), whose husband abandoned her and who is there to cure her daughter of spirit possession, delivers the perfect candidate ripe for mental health intervention – a wronged but strong woman seeking help for her child. The "women in trance" tableau is positioned against that of a well-meaning social worker who "spends hours trying to cajole the mentally ill to visit a nearby psychiatric clinic" where Dama Laxmi's daughter promptly gets diagnosed as schizophrenic. The article quotes Oxford professor of psychiatry Chris Fairburn whose journey through rural hospitals along bumpy roads leads him to profess that to increase access to these countries with limited resources, the Western experts don't have to approve or condone what we do, only acknowledge our existence. How kind.

Expecting any of these authors, reporters, or social workers to question the implicit assumptions behind concepts like "mental health" or "mental illness" would be foolish. They briefly allude to the subjective experience of the family and the individual; they marvel at their lack of chagrin at these terrible conditions and their strange complicity in these inhumane ways. The only thorn in their narrative of benevolence is that these assertions of abuse do not necessarily resonate with the population they deem as limited and wanting. Moreover, as we will later observe, the universalized understandings of mental illness and the validity of diagnoses like schizophrenia, are themselves under harsh scrutiny in the West. In my interviews with people who had experienced *hearing voices* in rural North India, the subjective experience of such phenomena was vastly heterogeneous – from fear and concern to celebration and boredom. One person noted how in response to hallucinations of a wedding procession (*baraat*), her mother would join the festivities and dance along. How are we to resolve the absence of their horror with the presence of our terror?

Psychology made its way into the Indian culture and psyche by throwing down its colonial roots deeply and silently. While there is psychological literature that explores faith-healing sites, spontaneous psychosis/possession, and indigenous cures, their aggressive theoretical orientations usually distort descriptive narratives. Psychology has long bullied the language of the other – deity attacks become spontaneous psychosis and wandering spirits are just conversion symptoms. There is a perverse contortion of the descriptive to the interpretive, of the material to the mental, and of the appearance to the meaningful. There lacks a framework that neither reduces these experiences to interpretation, nor to superstition. This book responds to these fissures in knowledge and more, and it achieves this through a cross-cultural examination of the structure of subjectivity as revealed by a culture's narratives and experiences concerning madness.

An interrogation of madness

The madman is proficient in laying bare the strangeness of the other; he reveals this other in all its absurdity – impossible to ignore, unbearable to contain. Madness has been romanticized through its associations with wisdom, creativity, and passions; madness has been demonized when positioned along irrationality, violence, and weakness. How can a single entity come to be associated with such drastically diverse experiences? We can tentatively guess that maybe madness exposes something essential about us, not some grand truth about the universe or hidden realities of the self; not even some profound intelligence that discerns what others cannot. Rather, madness can be compared to both weakness and strength, unreason and wisdom, deficiency and creativity, because even in its absurdity it is uniquely tethered to the structure of the subject. It thus permeates all great human experience – love, pain, violence, beauty, desire, suffering, rage. What is certain is that madness as a theme has occupied the minds of Sufi poets, English playwrights, priests, shamans, and doctors alike. It is as if this phenomenon that we repeatedly attempt to isolate in hospitals, temples, clinics, and couches, escapes each time, and shamelessly displays itself through our great sciences and sublime arts. This ubiquity of interest in insanity through the ages has been most famously charted by Michel Foucault (1967) who traces the trajectory of madness from a vice to a weakness, pointing to our desire to exclude and enclose it at the same time. He suggests that knowledge constituting madness might have changed in accordance with the epistemological matrices of different times, but its centrality in the modern world persists as strongly if not as openly as it always did; our interest in the mad changed in valence and quality, but its importance hasn't faded.

At points in Western history, madmen were coupled with the poor, the criminal, and the "deficient" – the undesirables. They have been occasionally worshipped and strategically hunted. Despite this, the traditional documentation of historical shifts bursts with optimism pointing to progress. To survey this incongruence, any attempt to explore madness requires an acknowledgment of contributions by different discourses that have informed our comprehension, ranging from treatments that focused on moral control to a purely physiognomic understanding of insanity that reduced it to neural correlates. Thus, to understand our current conceptualizations, we have to place them in a historical context, which is a task I will undertake in the second chapter.

Amongst the numerous theories that literature points to, there are two significant iterations informing contemporary Western narrative around madness – a reductionist biological understanding that assumes there to be a neurotransmitter imbalance at the heart of the disorder which in turn is guided by preordained genetic structure, and a meaning-based model that relies heavily on trauma theory (Romme & Escher, 2012). Both of these models are profoundly guided by the Western historico-cultural context that assumes either significant life events or biology as the essential starting points of psychotic experiences. They thus ignore the effect of a socially constructed discourse of insanity on the meaning-making experience of an individual. What is left unexamined is whether the psychotic experience can hold its own ground without being pathologized to assuage the discomfort that it produces in the hearts of others. In short, most of our current understandings of psychosis require it to be a pathology (even if a meaningful one) and are equally value laden, and all phenomenological explorations to understand it begin with an assumption of distress, thus ensuring the need for a benevolent clinician. The clinician is neither benevolent nor very brilliant.

Why another book about madness?

To be able to legitimately interrogate the relation between madness and subjectivity, especially in an inter-cultural context, I must make clear my aims and rationale in order to render transparent my assumptions. The modus operandi of this book is to peel back at the raised edges of subjectivity, those raised edges being madness. While criticisms of modern madness (schizophrenia) are galore, few theorists analyze its resistance to extinction in a historical and epistemological framework. Most interest in schizophrenia is reserved to its position as a clinical entity waiting to be explained away by the flavor-of-the decade theory. Similarly, while there are writings that scrutinize academic imperialism and blind exports of knowledge, most remarkably the work of Bhargavi Davar, none look past socio-cultural variables and into the construction of subjectivity and the implicit *styles of thinking* that animate it.

The theoretical assertions and critical stances presented in this book will of course attract those who find mainstream psychology alienating, but they are also vital to our understanding in the West so that we may make strange the familiar, gain appreciation for the historicity of knowledge, and understand that "culturally sensitive psychology" is at times just as problematic, even if it sounds ethical enough. To truly contextualize knowledge without necessarily invalidating it, we must move past arguments restricted to the sociological, cultural, and personal, and begin to analyze the very constitution of the subject — the institutional and the discursive. These concerns are imminent and must be addressed before critique of the discipline feels like an afterthought and phrases like "cultural fair assessment" begin to sound practical.

Throughout these endeavors Michel Foucault's writing will be a constant companion to provide framework, theoretical support, and methodological tools. My choice to lean on Foucault's work is partly based on his exhaustive investigations of madness and Western subjectivity and in part because he skillfully collapses the artificial binaries of individual psyche and social influences in his nuanced presentation of epistemic shifts, the power/knowledge dynamic, and the interdependence of discourse and subjectivity. Despite his vast qualifications to speak on the subject of knowledge and madness, Foucault never really formulated a concrete theory of subjectivity. Thus, later in the project I will rely on Gilles Deleuze and Félix Guattari's writings to help conceptualize a tentative account of how different subjects are structured in relation to the procedures of desire. To be clear, I will not simply import Deleuze and Guattari's theoretical formulations, but instead use their work concerning forms and permutations of desire generated through non-nuclear family matrices to point at something possibly similar in our population. Further, I will build on Louis Sass's (1994) assertions based on his phenomenological study of schizophrenia, and Foucault's (1994) determinations about the defining epistemological features of the modern era to explore how schizophrenia is not only a modern product but also an odd and radical form of modern subjectivity which has been co-opted by the human sciences to be presented as a disease entity. It is important to note that while Sass has already contributed to this discussion, his unique focus is on a thorough analysis of modern literature and art; I, on the other hand, develop a dialogue about schizophrenia and modern forms knowledge, knowing, and self-knowing.

Throughout the book I will critically observe the discourse of the Global Mental Health Movement, trauma theory, and the bio-medical model. The diagnosis of schizophrenia which is increasingly being used by mental health examiners in India is under scrutiny across the world (Bentall, 1993). In light of this import of psycho-pharmacological treatment that has witnessed an astronomical rise in Indian cities but is concurrently under attack in Europe for its ineffectiveness and life-threatening side effects, these concerns are deeply relevant. Even psychoanalytic and humanistic traditions which delve into the content of psychosis eventually focus on the distress that it seems to necessitate, but cross-cultural studies show that this isn't applicable to many across the world — definitions of distress are culture-centric and suffering is molded by the horizon of our social perception.

While critical theory and social constructionism have questioned the ahistorical and apolitical nature of mental illness in the West and brought to light its contextual conditionality, one has to be cautious with their application beyond a Euro-centric context. As Gayatri Spivak (1988) has brilliantly articulated in her canonical work "Can the Subaltern Speak?", even radical theories of subjectivity (her critique is directed at post-structuralist French thinkers like Michel Foucault and Gilles Deleuze) create the colonized world as its Other – as Europe's Other, and can never speak about the post-colonial subaltern subject without instead speaking *for* them. Spivak asserts that, irrespective of how revolutionary and radical an idea is, it is still in the service of bolstering the Western subject, or the West as a subject. More importantly, she declares that the most oppressed, *the subaltern*, have no voice and no place in revisionist history, and that there is a lack of a structure where this voice can emerge. Her warnings ring true, as I observe that, in psychological research across India, it is mostly the upper-caste, educated Hindu subject that is the object of most examination and theoretical formulations. This is unsurprising because, as is true for this book, the researcher himself/herself tends to be from a similar background; this makes it especially important to maintain a descriptive level of analysis.

As I unravel the relevance of Global Mental Health Movement, attempt to discover the implicit discourses behind the indigenous stories of spirits and psychosis, and unpack some of the structural conditions that inform ways of speaking – Spivak's warnings caution me to not place my understanding where the other's voice could be, which with my caste and class background are easy traps to fall in. At the same time, her writings also encourage me to *exploit* my position as a post-liberalization, post-colonial Indian subject, a woman, a researcher, a reluctant academic, and a Harry Potter fan to take up the "circumscribed task" that I must not "disown with a flourish" (p. 104).

The scope of the book

This book begins by observing the rise of modern madness "schizophrenia" in the West, the historical conditions that sustained it, the contentious nature of its conceptualizations, and its strange resilience in the face of constant criticism. I will firstly engage with Foucault's analysis of the history of madness to reveal social conditions that made a certain type of knowledge possible. I will then move through a succinct history of schizophrenia where focus will be laid on *conditions of possibilities* that created and managed schizophrenia from its conception until now. As we observe the revolutions in language, classification, and science around the concept, it will be glaringly evident how schizophrenia is not only the most problematic diagnostic category in psychiatry, but also critical to maintaining the continued authority of the discipline (Woods, 2011). At the same time, one mustn't assume that its weed-like persistence to survive in the face of consistent and harsh critique means that the historical forces supporting it were only deliberate and diabolical. Instead, the schizophrenic subject, as I would demonstrate, is an almost organic, if extreme, product of the modern episteme.

In Chapter 3 I will attempt to explain this resilience by positioning schizophrenia as an epistemic emergence, one that was imminent and that makes absurd the fractures within the modern turn in knowledge. In other words, this book will investigate schizophrenia, its emergence, possible decline, and dependence on modern Western epistemology. I will undertake a theoretical investigation of the discursive history of schizophrenia and its relation with these forms of knowledge to answer what, if any, is the relation between the tensions of modern epistemology and the schizophrenic subject?

I will then take a geographical leap to examine the dialogue around madness in rural North India, to observe if there is a relation between event trauma and psychotic symptoms, and eventually excavate the implicit discourses that inform these discussions. Through an examination of *styles of thought* that animate the narrative around madness, I will explore the corresponding subject positions and contributing institutions in rural North India. I chose Uttarakhand as the area of research because it is rural and remote enough to preserve the uncontaminated indigenous discourse around psychosis, and also because mountains in India are popular for their stories of the anomalous and the exceptional. It did not hurt that the breathtaking beauty of the Himalayan range made data collection feel like a vacation.

The mainstream understanding of psychosis has a narrow focus on finding its causes and correlates with neurological dysfunction, sometimes causing a psychiatric dehumanization of the psychotic. But my attempt is to take the psychotic episode on its own terms – not as a symptom, not as a metaphor. An examination of the local forms of meaning construction brings forth cultural discourses and traces how they influence the experience, course, and content of psychosis. How does this understanding effect the treatment, prognosis, or the lack of it? How does this way of thinking inform people's subjective experiences of distress? Using Foucauldian archaeological analysis on these narratives of madness I answer the question: What conditions – discursive, cultural, epistemological, social, or hermeneutic – make the rural Indian subject possible?

This empirical analysis allows me to thoroughly inspect the peculiarities of the rural Indian "psychotic" subject, what conditions make him possible, and how they preclude his downfall into full-blown schizophrenia. I will partially carry out this deconstruction through an exploration of the Indian female subject as I reveal her split position built through incongruous social and familial messages – how does she not sacrifice her sanity while decoding this communicative discordance as Gregory Bateson's double-bind would predict? Overall, towards the end, this book will respond to the question: What does the discourse around madness in India reveal about the structure of the subject and how are these two co-constituted? Chapter 5 then aims to bring together these conceptualizations around madness to inform a tentative theory of subjectivity, that is, if and how the modern Western and post-colonial rural Indian subject vary in their structures, and the implications this difference has for an unthinking import of Global Mental Health Movement. The works of Sigmund Freud, Jacques Lacan, Gilles Deleuze, and Félix Guattari will help to theorize about the structure of the subject of Western thought, the arrival of the *unthought*, the cut of the symbolic, and the different trajectories of desire.

The theoretical and empirical investigation provides us with sufficient evidence to subvert ideas suggesting inherent distress in psychotic experiences, and we can then begin to question the aims and efficacy of the Global Mental Health Movement. One of the central aims of this book is to explore this difference in the structure of subjectivity as exposed by insanity, and the repercussions these differences have towards decolonizing psychology. Thus, in the last chapter I will employ the understanding of two different forms of subjectivities in the West and in rural India to wonder whether these structural differences render the Global Mental Health Movement ineffective, or even dangerous.

Me and my measuring stick

This book is an empirico-theoretical endeavor; while I begin with a theoretical inspection of the schizophrenic subject, in the second half I lean on my empirical research, which uses the dual methods of thematic analysis and Foucauldian archaeological analysis to care for the above-noted concerns. In 2016, in Uttarakhand, I conducted interviews with six participants, and sometimes their families and friends (in turn expanding it to 15 participants), and asked them questions concerning their personal or anecdotal experience with *seeing things and hearing voices* that others around them do not. I probed their subjective responses to these events, the content and nature of the voices, the contribution of their family and community in meaning-making, their own etiological understanding of these experiences, and their methods of resolution.

I needed to study how we understand, experience, and produce the complex world around us, and I required methods that were deeply flexible, contextually sensitive, and devoid of theoretical baggage. I trusted thematic analysis to allow me to conduct such nuanced interrogations. Braun and Clarke (2006) credit thematic analysis as being one of the most flexible qualitative methods, especially because of its non-allegiance to any epistemological or theoretical position and its compatibility with both "essentialist and constructionist paradigms" (p. 78). A thick analysis with rich details and an appreciation for appearances is imperative to answering questions about madness, magic, and meaning. I do not subscribe to a naïve realist view that assumes that the researcher is only there to "give voice" to the participants because every thematic edit, every choice of data extract, and every seeming regularity that "presents itself" has been funneled through my socio-cultural subjective position. Thematic analysis was the method that allowed me to maintain theoretical distance, which is essential because I was performing this analysis in rural parts of India – far from the birthplace of most psychological and methodological theories. It helped me seek regularities through a bottom-up approach and understand these regularities as socially constructed and discursively sustained.

Staying at the level of description in the thematic analysis was essential to conduct a Foucauldian archaeological analysis. This form of analysis primarily concerns itself with the relationship between language and subjectivity, that is, how do discourses expand, restrict, and define what can be said and who says it (Willig, 2003)? The concept of a discursive economy, i.e. discourse as a resource, is important to this project as it aims to study narratives of the rural and lower-class population with great heterogeneity in their educational levels, gender demographics, and caste realities. Thus, the louder (not dominant) discourse of medicine and psychiatry which is usually embraced and advanced by the cosmopolitan, educated, upper-caste, upper-class Indian elite dominating the academic discourse is entirely absent. I used this method to take statements from thematic analysis and physical practices from institutions like healing/haunted temples, and to discover the different subject positions that are sustained by these statements and visibilities (Kendall & Wickham, 1998). This eventually led to the development of a theory of differences in types of subjectivities in the West and in post-colonial rural India as revealed by the narrative around madness in both cultures.

Conclusion

In 2016, the British Psychological Society released a public information report that undermined the monopoly of the bio-medical model on schizophrenia. It did so by partially subverting the prescription that all *voice hearing* is indicative of illness and further adding that the evidence supporting the efficiency of antipsychotics is inconsistent. The report presented psychosis as being caused by personal and social factors like deprivation and trauma. One can sense that a massive change is underway in how we understand schizophrenia and psychosis, and the conversation around it is ripe for a historically nuanced and culturally contextualized debate. Here I pose the difficult question of whether a culturally relevant approach is ethical or even possible. Can a knowledge so deeply rooted in the Cartesian divide be applicable to those whose implicit discourses are thoroughly material?

My aim in this book is not to come up with any form of a universal theory or to demarcate the essential features of madness in order to bring a forced cross-cultural coherence. Rather, I am wary of any imposed consistencies because of the repercussions of such formulations. The dualities of local versus universal, indigenous versus external, have informed many recent attempts to do psychology, but, contemporaneously, psychologists and activists alike are also probing the increasing globalization of mental health as a concept and calling for its decolonization (Mills, 2014). The export of mental health from high-income countries to low- and middle-income ones has raised questions about the psychiatrization of human distress, "problems of living, conflicts in relationships and social suffering" (Mills & Fernando, 2014).

While the World Health Organization has called for a reduction in the treatment gap in poor countries, this call carries with it an assumption that problems of human suffering are apolitical since they adhere to a biomedical model of mental health. Recent research problematizes these assumptions by showing that the phenomenological experience and the content of hallucinations in a psychotic episode varies considerably across cultures (Luhrmann, Padmavati, Tharoor, & Osei, 2015; Watters, 2010). Thus, distress and pathology might not be the natural bedfellows of psychotic symptoms after all.

Understanding how suffering and psychosis unfold in a culture that produces different types of subjects sheds light not only on those cultures, those experiences, but also on how we conceptualize and essentialize these pathologies in the West. At the same time, it is important not to romanticize the local. Since local treatments and responses to suffering in India are facing rampant eradication by the state and other agents of modern knowledge, this has led to a knee-jerk reaction of unthinking veneration of everything native (Dhar & Siddiqui, 2013), usually co-opted by religious fundamentalists. Instead of a blind glorification of the indigenous, the purpose here is to chart the nature and course of these local responses to socio-political issues of disability and to not indulge in a narrative of progress or regress. This will widen our current understanding without privileging either the homogenous global or the heterogeneous local.

2

INSIDE SCHIZOPHRENIA

A house of mirrors

> MAGIC THEATER
> ENTRANCE NOT FOR EVERYBODY
>
> *Hermann Hesse*, Steppenwolf

The history of madness is littered with stories of passions, tortures, and occasional kindnesses. Despite our endeavors to define, control, and understand it, many realize that we are ramming our heads against an enigma that eludes all description and still permeates all experience. In using the term madness, I tentatively refer to a large array of phenomena marked by psychosis, folly, depersonalization, dysfunction, mania, delusions, and rage. In this chapter I will briefly go over the historical conditions that birthed and sustained schizophrenia, the modern madness. A look at these causes and conditions will allow me to undercut psychology's narrative of progress and reveal it to be fictional. Exposing the historical context that nurtured this narrative will help set the stage for a dialogue that places schizophrenia in a larger epistemological framework rather than reducing it to a narrow medical one. I will explore how madness came under the authority of medicine, and how these circumstances were essential to Emil Kraepelin's conceptualization of dementia praecox and later Eugen Bleuler's "discovery" of schizophrenia. If the reader is someone who is well versed in writings that subvert schizophrenia's clinical status, then s/he may skip this chapter. My aim in the following pages is to summarize the literature that undertook this critique in order to subsequently present my own conceptualization of how studying madness can help reveal the structure of subjectivity.

History of madness in Foucault's *Madness and Civilization*

Any attempt to historicize madness in the West is never complete without the mention of Foucault's (1967) groundbreaking work *Madness and Civilization: A History of Insanity in the Age of Reason*. Foucault's interest over time transformed from an existential inquiry into the nature of madness to an archaeological examination of the objective conditions that triggered this discourse; essentially, he was interested in the structures that made it possible for every episteme to talk about insanity in the way that it did.

Foucault's archaeological explorations painstakingly unearthed how madness was experienced, understood, and managed in different epistemes in Europe. The treatment of "madness" – of those who were mad, the concept itself, and its management as an object of knowledge changed sharply in these times. While the Renaissance saw madness as a challenge to reason, it nevertheless gave it space and allowed it to co-exist with reason. Exclusion, both physical and conceptual was never complete: "This world of the early seventeenth century is strangely hospitable, in all senses, to madness. Madness is here, at the heart of things, and of men ... " (Foucault, 1967, p. 37). A sudden development across Europe in early seventeenth century, which Foucault refers to as "The Great Confinement," witnessed a change in the tolerance towards unreason, leading to physical exclusion of wanderers, idle men, criminals, and the mad. While the initial impetus for this confinement might have been economic and political, Foucault (1967) insists that under these economic reasons and administrative control lay moral condemnation of unreason – the fact that anything that threatened reason and rationality (whether idleness or madness) had to undergo societal and psychical amputation.

Interestingly, madness was "othered" even from other forms of unreason – while criminals and delinquents were merely confined and even hidden, the mad were put on display. The madman was anti-nature, and this is evident in the ascription of animality to him; the remedy consequently was hard labor – to treat him like an animal, a beast. When in later chapters I speak about the mad in India putting hot coals on their tongues or dancing naked in brutal winters, some might attribute this to a similar animality, but that would be erroneous. A more refined glance could reveal that it is not animality but instead divinity that explains their abnormal strength and resistance to pain, but even that explanation would be premature. As I will later show, these phenomena might borrow meaning from the divine, but that divinity is conditioned upon materiality.

Foucault's archaeology reveals the structures underlying these beliefs about madness, for example, the division between mind and body was non-existent as madness was thought to be an affliction of the whole personhood. The Cartesian divide, while present, never truly took hold until the modern period. Thus hallucinations and delusions were considered a dissociation between the mental and physical, but never really broke this said unity. Madness was essentially a delirium – a perverted form of reason.

Due to increasing psychologization, things changed at the end of the eighteenth century; for example, the genesis of hysteria shifted from the body to the mind. It went from being an organic issue with women and their not-dense-enough inner organs to being caused by luxurious living, thus reflecting the time's relation to morality and psychology. Another important change that anticipated psychiatry was that the concept of cure replaced the idea of a panacea. Schizophrenia, interestingly, has a special place in psychology as the incurable illness, and anyone who claims to have been cured is treated with suspicion (Yelich-Koth, 2017). The mind–body unity broke around this point and madness as an object of knowledge became increasingly psychological. Foucault undermines the objective existence of mental illness and reveals how its emergence at the end of the eighteenth century has more to do with the essential features of the modern society itself and less with discovering better understandings of an already existing phenomena. Resultantly, he brought under harsh scrutiny our ideas of a value-free approach which is simply a product of scientific curiosity and compassion and insisted that our treatment narrative might have been languaged medically but was "animated, basically, by a moral myth" (Foucault, 1967, p. 202).

Madness, instead of being a choice, became an affliction that a person had no control over; this humanized the mad man and exposed him to correction and reformation which further instilled unconscious feelings of guilt. Fluctuations in the way madness was understood went hand in hand with the way it was treated; for example, the mad were now isolated from others accused of unreason. This was partly because confinement became economically unfeasible, and since criminals and madmen were not clubbed together anymore, the hospital arose as a setting for their care and control. Thus, contrary to common belief, it wasn't that the mad were confined to hospitals because it was therapeutic, but instead hospitals came to be seen as therapeutic because the mad had to be confined there. Foucault was also skeptical of the mythology behind modern psychology's birth, which forwarded the idea that it was Samuel Tuke's humanitarian intentions and Philippe Pinel's gracious gestures that led us into the golden era of the psychological science. While seemingly benevolent, their methods aimed to inculcate guilt and internalize responsibility in accordance with the tenets of bourgeois morality. This moral and social authority was soon accompanied by a fierce investment in scientific progress and an increasingly positivistic science that designated madness to be mental illness. Thus, around the nineteenth century, moral authority came to be replaced by ideas of medical authority – that the patients were helped not by the personage of the doctor but by his medical skill – "It is not as a scientist that *homo medicus* has authority in the asylum, but as a wise man" (Foucault, 1967, p. 270). The birth of psychiatry wasn't marked by the treatment of madness as an object of value-free scientific study; instead it was grounded in preserving the moral values of bourgeois society as symbolized by medical authority.

Writing about the relation between knowledge and power, Foucault (2006) in *Psychiatric Power: Lectures at College de France, 1973–1974* further suggests that knowledge about madness was based *on* power relays and networks of asylum discipline. This kind of "tactical arrangement" that comprised of servants, supervisors, and the supreme non-reciprocal and asymmetrical authority of the doctor, was a result not of knowledge, but of a dangerous threat that had to be mastered – the madman – who was no more defined by his mistaken beliefs (as in the eighteenth century) but by "insurrection of a force, of a furiously raging uncontrolled and a possibly uncontrollable force within him" (Foucault, 2006, p. 7).

Foucault's historical examination subverts the legend that knowledge around modern madness is based on objective truths and benevolent concerns, and thus is essential to historicize insanity, contextualize its management, and understand schizophrenia's rise and probable imminent decline. Keeping in mind due consideration of the enigmatic nature of madness and the persistent creation of knowledge around it, I now present the circumstances around the conceptualization of modern madness – schizophrenia. While it is a daunting task to study an experience that has been repeatedly researched and has a mammoth body of knowledge around it, one can hope to learn something new if we examine it on its own terms. It is essential to remember that this summarization of writings on the subject is vital to resolve the paradox regarding schizophrenia's persistent yet elusive existence.

Mad doctors and medicine

Theorizing about madness has been the prerogative of doctors, shamans, and priests among others. Over time this burden shifted from "mad doctors" to "medicine men", but how and why this happened is a story with more plot twists than a daytime Indian soap opera. It also uniquely exemplifies Foucault's concept of "accidents of history". In his genealogical period of writings, Foucault studied smaller accidental causes that were independent of each other, and how these "accidents of history" unknowingly informed formations of thought and influenced social control. An example is the scandalous madness of King George III and his attempted murder by James Hadfield (Porter, 2002). In England this "event" brought into spotlight questions about who was the lunatic and what is to be done with him? Hadfield was proclaimed insane and thus the problem of what insanity meant and how to deal with it stood stark in the public's mind. In 1990, there was a similar incident in America where the mental stability of the DuPont family's heir became a matter of public scrutiny; this time it was psychiatrists' diagnostic decisions which led to legal ramifications for the family and defined the discussion around what constituted insanity (Kirk & Kutchins, 1992).

Mary Boyle (2002) in *Schizophrenia: A Scientific Delusion* conducts a historical analysis of the social, political, and linguistic circumstances in which schizophrenia emerged as a scientific concept and a medical condition. Boyle and Andrew Scull's (1975) theoretical explorations create a picture which reinforces Foucault's claim that traditional understandings are only manifestations of truth appearing under specific regimes of knowledge and practices, and both Boyle and Scull implore us not to employ the narrative of progress which presumes solely humanitarian intentions under these changes. Scull (1975) in *From Madness to Mental Illness* insisted that between mid-eighteenth to early nineteenth century the concept of madness transformed in many ways. For one, the responsibility of the deviant shifted hands from the family and community to authorized state asylums. This was partially a result of shifts in the understanding of madness from an ill-defined and imprecise concept to something that was diagnosable by experts with legal authority. At the same time, the "discovery" of schizophrenia was preconditioned by a preoccupation with the classification of insanity that had started many decades early. Significantly, Boyle insists that while in those times it was no more than an academic exercise that had little practical consequence, soon it was to become the focal center of the project.

The Reform movement had begun advocating for better conditions for the insane, and according to Scull (1979) it was informed by two distinct philosophies: Evangelicalism, which focused on kindness, discipline, and moral control, and Benthamism, which focused on centralization, visibility, and efficient control. William Tuke, the most influential leader of the Reform movement had opened a retreat in New York in 1792 where the mad were seen as those who needed to learn self-restraint, which he believed could be slowly inculcated in them.

Scull points to change in other social conditions that would bolster the emergence of the Reform movement. The agrarian and industrial revolution brought with it a desire to think of man as one who has control, and consequently led to the suspicion of superstitious, external factors. Man could change his destiny, in the factory or in the asylum; it only required hard work and training. This alteration in the concept of madness reflected a larger change in man's role in the world. Numerous theories have alluded to the implicit relationship between schizophrenia and Western values. For example, Burnham, Gladstone, and Gibson (1969), in theorizing about schizophrenia as a need-fear dilemma, define the disorder as being a dysfunction in autonomy, organization, linear causality, and internal control – all values that form the foundation of modern Western ethics.

A similar conclusion about the importance of the modern industrial subject in the conceptualization of schizophrenia is posited by Angela Woods (2011) in *The Sublime Object of Psychiatry: Schizophrenia in Clinical and Cultural Theory*. She asserts that it is essential for psychiatry to maintain the linear historical narrative of discovery of dementia praecox to bolster its scientific stature. For that matter, one of the most important conditions that made Kraepelin's discovery possible was how his concept depended on "a grand narrative of modern Western selfhood" (Woods, 2011, p. 40). Kraepelin, in a manner similar to the moral managers who implicitly subscribed to the idea of upward class mobility as part of modern selfhood, thus positioned the person who suffered from dementia praecox as the opposite of the ideal, modern, rational, productive self whose goal was self-mastery (Boyle, 2002). This person was not only "antithetical to this ideal of bourgeois selfhood capable of and committed to the perpetual labor of self-improvement" (Woods, 2011, p. 41) but, more importantly, he did not want to participate as this subject. In their book, Kraepelin and Diefendorf (1904) clearly stated that moral laxity and "above all an unnatural satisfaction with their own ideas and behavior" (p. 158) were one of the foremost symptoms of the disease.

Building on Foucault's assertion of labor being the panacea for the mad due to society's condemnation of idleness, Woods (2011) uncovers that

Kraepelin's disease entity had a similar moral undertone which considered labor as a constitutive element of the modern subject. This perception of madness as the "Other" of the modern self is reflected in Kraepelin and Diefendorf's (1904) statement that the patient "may neglect his duties and sit unoccupied for the greater part of the day, though capable of doing good work if persistently encouraged" (p. 159) and that his/her capacity for employment is severely compromised.

It is possible that Kraepelin envisioned no complete recovery because even those who became better could never contribute in terms of labor and employment, were unproductive, unable to hold down an occupation, and "spend much time in reading, evolving impractical schemes, and pondering over abstract and useless questions" (Woods, 2011, p. 42) thus marking the diseased as strange and beyond understanding. This positioned those afflicted with dementia praecox as the perpetual unproductive Other of the ideal modern industrial selfhood.

Scull (1979) insists that for many it was lucrative to believe that the most unproductive members of the population could be turned around using moral control. Underlying the changing concepts of insanity was a larger cultural shift that witnessed a change in the relationship between man and his environment; this was essential "to justify the demands made on the new industrial working force to adapt to an alien environment" (Boyle, 2002, p. 22). Amidst these demands, moral management, through manipulation of environment and inculcation of emotional regulation, was deeply attractive because of its promise to take the deviant and unproductive and turn them into rational and productive individuals.

Boyle's interest is mostly restricted to social and conceptual revisions in England but the reverberations of these changes were felt across the West including the United States. Before the birth of mandatory state asylums, private madhouses flourished in Britain. The aforementioned industrial and agrarian revolution changed the way people thought about the poor and deviant, and the importance of segregating the deserving and undeserving took precedence; soon workhouses that required intense labor and discipline mushroomed. It is of importance to note that while there were an increasing number of people who required poor relief, the initial response to all of these demands was not centralized but localized; for example, smaller almshouses, charity hospitals, and workhouses. Thus, we can observe that from the very beginning, the understanding of schizophrenia was premised upon larger social values and not merely scientific advances.

Economic decisions were just as important as social values. At the end of the eighteenth and beginning of the nineteenth century, with increases in the number of for-profit private madhouses which had loose admission policies and bred appalling conditions, the question of who was the expert, and the requirement for humanitarian treatment that came to define the Reform movement arose. Unlike the hospitals that emerged later, these could be run by clergymen, laymen, or physicians. The reformers, who arose in response to these conditions, eschewed medical authority to care for the insane, advocated the segregation of the mad from other deviants, argued that current conditions of the mad were not only cruel but also theoretically unjustified, and demanded from the government humane county asylums which were not to be run by doctors (Boyle, 2002). At this point, it is important to recall Foucault's critique of the seemingly benevolent Reform movement and the oversimplified understanding of its humanitarian concerns. The beginning of medical authority on madness represented by the experts who had the *right to speak* was just around the corner.

Porter (2002) explains that private madhouses were a natural consequence of increasing somatization. From the focus of locating mental functions in brain regions by the likes of Thomas Willis (who coined the term neurology) to the work of Richard Mead, somaticism was essential in establishing the authority of medicine over madness. Blood, fiber, nerves, and pores – all were implicated as causes of madness and made treatments like blood-letting reasonable. As insanity began to be considered a nervous disorder, the idea that psychology was instead a philosophy of mind gained traction; consequently, psychiatric publishing and private madhouses thrived (Porter, 2002).

Medical interest in theories of mind wasn't new, considering Hippocrates's well-documented beliefs regarding bodily humors, but Boyle (2002) contends that theorizing about human nature and the nature of madness wasn't restricted to medicine men. Instead, writers and philosophers had equal expertise and interest and their views did not necessarily clash with those of medical authority. It was the rise of highly profitable private madhouses in Britain that inspired the physician's interest in madness as a medical condition (Boyle, 2002). The transition was in its early stage and as Scull (1979) shows, even now, more than medical authority it was legal expertise that defined who was mad and where to detain them. It was around the late eighteenth and early nineteenth century when, according to Boyle (2002), "the medical profession had begun to take a far greater practical interest in the management of those labelled insane" (p. 26) and a pedagogy around insanity began to develop.

The move from moral to medical management of insanity was not without hiccups and was eventually reduced to physicians furiously protecting their interests in increasingly secular times. They supported the moral managers' argument for increasing the number of state asylums, all the while persuading the government and people of their authority and expertise without the help of empirical evidence (Boyle, 2002). This required them to convince the public that successful non-medical intervention did not preclude the fact that insanity was a medical ailment and soon "somatic interpretation of insanity would place it beyond dispute within medicine's recognized sphere of competence" (Scull, 1975, p. 251).

By the mid-nineteenth century, most asylums in Britain were under medical authority, which had convinced everyone, including itself, that medical expertise was indispensable to any cure. Kirk and Kutchins (1992) assert that despite this, psychiatric expertise was and remains precarious due to two reasons: competition from social workers, nurses, psychologists, and counselors; and their low-status in the medical profession. They believe that the resolution to both these problems was the emergence of biopsychiatry. By the 1900s, the optimistic glow of Pinel's benevolence had dissipated and the late nineteenth century was marked by cozying up with the hard sciences like neurology and shedding connections with embarrassments like spiritualism (Porter, 2002).

To consolidate legitimacy, the medical profession used a number of means to establish somatic theory, the first of which was "forming professional organizations and by publishing specialist literature not easily available to nor comprehensible to lay people" (Boyle, 2002, p. 34). They also had to resolve the paradox of using behavioral therapy, i.e., reward and punishment, while advancing the opinion that since insanity is a brain disease and beyond the control of the inmate, he should not punished for it. The physician class did so by ensuring that the term "medical treatment" constituted all actions utilized in order to maintain control – all cure was medical cure.

The medicalization was furthered when the second half of the nineteenth century observed the introduction of laboratories and microscopes in asylums that helped "mad doctors" imitate medicine and solidify their precarious status as doctors in the first place. According to Porter (2002), it was neurology's newfound interest in deviant behavior and the newly established connections between dementia paralytica and syphilis that altered the relation between medicine and madness forever. Neurologists who held more prestige than mad doctors were openly critical of the latter and of asylums as curative institutions, and instead they brought the patients to them. Soon, across the US, psychopathic hospitals that included outpatient clinics and psychiatric wards in hospitals rapidly increased in numbers. The most pertinent consequence of this was that people began to bring in their less-deviant relatives who did not warrant asylum admission to these outpatient clinics, and neurologists began to diagnose and treat milder cases of abnormal behavior, further widening the boundaries of madness (Boyle, 2002). Kirk and Kutchins (1992) remark on how the mental health set-up shifted in three decades from public hospitals to "an array of public, not-for-profit, and for-profit inpatient facilities and an explosion of clinics and private psychotherapists from many disciplines" (p. 9). The social conditions in Germany were different than the United States and Britain. The idea of madness being a brain disease was thus long established in Germany and it is from this theoretical soil that Kraepelin's dementia praecox germinated.

By the end of the nineteenth century, somatic theories of madness were the norm, and moral management was on a steep decline. One of the important prevailing conditions that accompanied this was a huge rise in the number of inmates in state asylums, which Scull (1975) states was a result of widening the definitional margins of madness. He points to the numerous vague definitions of insanity in the nineteenth century, which were unproblematic since the public was assured that the incoherence of the concept was inconsequential because in the end "clinical judgment" was objective. For example, Pinel had divided mental alienation into five categories: dementia or abolition of thought, mania with delirium, mania without delirium, melancholy, and idiotism or abolition of intellectual and affective faculties (Berrios & Markova, 2017). The concerns regarding accurate classification and definition were about to get more prominent, but much like sand, the more tightly psychologists tried to hold on to static classifications, the more swiftly they eluded them. This was especially true for schizophrenia, where physicians were trying hard to consolidate a true definition, but these failing attempts only made the plot holes in their scientific narrative more glaring. These were some of the social and physical conditions on which schizophrenia was premised: a deep connection to morality, economic shifts, establishment of medical authority, and, most important for our later discussion, a relation to modern selfhood.

Capricious classifications

Kieran McNally (2016) in *A Critical History of Schizophrenia* performs an investigation into the fluctuations in definitions, symptoms, mythologies, and misconceptions that came to constitute modern-day schizophrenia. He traces the trajectory of this disorder and its incessant modification beginning with Kraepelin's dementia praecox up until its current avatar, and resultantly scrutinizes the operationalization of schizophrenia to reveal an unstable concept that was neither ahistorical nor objective. McNally (2016) claims that problems regarding the definition did not become apparent to the professionals until the second half of twentieth century when they were already knee deep in its treatment. An exploration of these insecure but rigid categorizations is necessary to later study their stark difference from how the rural Indian subject treats madness and thus slips through its permutations and contradictions with ease.

Kraepelin and Diefendorf (1904) had pointed to a distinct looseness and incoherence of thought and associations seen at the beginning of the disease, and when Bleuler first introduced schizophrenia, splitting of the psychic functions was a primary marker. Later, the tearing up function which concerned itself with associations was demoted and the splitting of personality introduced (McNally, 2016). It was soon recognized that Bleuler's schizophrenia was a much broader concept, incorporating many other pathologies (like hysteria and paranoia) than earlier thought; consequently it was met with both enthusiasm and criticism in the psychiatric community. Further attempts at definition were carried out by various theorists of different schools of thought. There was ample ambiguity around what schizophrenia meant, and for many it was merely synonymous with dementia praecox. While schizophrenia won in the end, the definition continued to be in flux.

The operationalization of schizophrenia became an immediate priority to mitigate the threat its ambiguity posed. The 1952 *Diagnostic and Statistical Manual (DSM-I)* focused on the psychogenic factors of schizophrenia; it considered "schizophrenic reactions" as synonymous with dementia praecox and defined it as "a group of psychotic reactions characterized by fundamental disturbances in reality relationships and concept formations, with affective, behavioral, and intellectual disturbances … emotional disharmony, unpredictable disturbances in stream of thought, regressive behavior, and in some, a tendency to 'deterioration'" (American Psychiatric Association, 1952, p. 26). Despite the definition and sub-types, there was a widespread lack of consensus on what constituted these factors. Thomas Szasz controversially implied schizophrenia to be a catch-all amidst this definitional chaos. Kraepelin and Diefendorf (1904) right from the beginning had pointed to the problem of recognizing fundamental symptoms in the face of a diverse and ever-changing disease picture. Questions about the very existence of mental illness were raised by other psychologists, sociologists, and the 1960s counter-culture. Others were concerned about the iatrogenic effects of diagnosis, and lawyers were regularly pitting psychiatrists against each other in courtrooms; their contradicting testimonies belied their outward confidence and expertise (Kirk & Kutchins, 1992). These circumstances led to the demand that operational definitions must obtain consistency and objectivity, but once a search for operational definition began, the absence of consensus or precision over the concept of schizophrenia became visible. Soon, descriptive definitions were discarded and operational definitions with checklists came to become the norm.

Other approaches turned towards adopting biological markers to surpass the need for a definition. *DSM-II* in 1968, still avoiding "disease" for "disorder" to describe schizophrenia, brought the concept of "thought disorder" to the forefront. Old categories were sub-divided to form new ones like the sub-division of catatonia into excited and withdrawn types. Moreover, it could not reconcile differences with international manuals like the *International Classification of Diseases (ICD 8)* which did not categorize any set of symptoms as "schizophrenia childhood type" as the *DSM-II* did (American Psychiatric Association, 1968). Regarding schizophrenia it stated that delusions and hallucinations might have a protective element and that "disturbances in thinking are marked by alterations of concept formation which may lead to misinterpretation of reality ..." (American Psychiatric Association, 1968, p. 33). While debate over the utility of operational definition continued and thought disorder came to be a primary symptom, there were also those who argued over the benefits of not having a static definition.

The 1970s witnessed, among some attacks by the anti-psychiatry movement, a constant dissonance in conceptualization. It was *DSM-III* that reintroduced to the psychiatric profession the neo-Kraepelanian idea of schizophrenia being a disease entity. It also introduced check-list oriented operational definitions. New and influential genetic and biological research was cited as the underlying criteria for this change because it implied better knowledge, but this assertion was undermined by accusations of circularity in operational definitions. McNally (2016) asserts that this tabulation, interest in taxonomy, and the urge to classify can be traced to Foucault's claim that there was an institutional desire to count and classify madness, to standardize the population through examination, and to tabulate and record their movements.

Recognizing the contentious conceptualization of schizophrenia for over a century, Woods (2011) also explores what makes schizophrenia so notoriously difficult to pin down. Building on philosopher Emmanuel Kant and art historian Mark Cheetam's notion of the sublime, she identifies schizophrenia to be the sublime object for the discipline of psychiatry. Many theorists have unfailingly admitted that no one really knows what schizophrenia is, whether it is a single disorder or syndrome, whether its etiology is neurological, psychological, environmental, or genetic, or even whether one can be tested for it and how. Shrouded in these unanswered questions, schizophrenia threatens to delegitimize psychiatry as a discipline and at the same time, as we will soon observe, is the gift that just keeps giving. According to Woods (2011), psychiatry tolerates the problem child that is schizophrenia because it has deliberately construed it as a mystery to elevate it to the level of sublime. It might be elusive and unknowable but as Parnas (2011) observes, schizophrenia also represents the "zenith of psychopathologic research, creating conditions for the first major scientific accomplishments".

The concept of schizophrenia as a homogenous entity has been questioned repeatedly over the past few years. Richard Bentall (1993) has famously called for its abandonment, insisting that the diagnosis only impedes the understanding of psychotic behavior: "'Schizophrenia' appears to be a disease which has no particular symptoms, which has no particular course and which responds to no particular treatment. It is therefore not surprising that aetiological research has revealed that it has no particular cause" (Bentall, Jackson, & Pilgrim, 1988, p. 314). Bentall argues that the concept of schizophrenia as a diagnostic category has outlived its usefulness and resorts to scientific grounds instead of ethical or philosophical arguments to prove his point. He calls schizophrenia a "disjunctive concept" as it has been used for so many behaviors and symptoms that any two individuals who get the diagnosis might not have anything in common. Additionally, multivariate statistical tests of the internal validity of the concept have revealed no set cluster. While schizophrenia research has seen a surge of neurological, genetic, and neuropsychological theories that focus on cognitive deficits and attribute them to biological dysfunctions, the abnormalities found are "so diverse and yet also so nonspecific that they provide further evidence against the existence of a single, discrete 'schizophrenia' disease entity" (Bentall, 1993, p. 228). As recently as 2016, Robin Murray, who received a knighthood for his services to medicine, states that the end of the concept of schizophrenia as a distinct entity is near. In charting schizophrenia's capricious etiology over the years, from a neuro-degenerative disorder to a developmental one, he muses over his own disregard for causal social factors and study of epidemiology, and expresses his desire to have done differently. Conflict has followed schizophrenia well into the present.

In line with the obstacles encountered in ascertaining a stable definition and etiology, even in the area of classification, psychiatry was in trouble. What is relatively unknown is that it took fair inspiration from botanical taxonomy to classify and categorize disorders, only to realize that madness did not map out its course in a manner similar to slowly evolving plants

(McNally, 2016). This attempt at classification was intended to inaugurate psychology as a science by establishing better communication around disorders. The botanical taxonomy, as seen in suffixes like "oid" and "mitis" (e.g. schizoid), entered the language of schizophrenia but could not capture the nuances of insanity because most patients showed diverse symptoms over time to create a profile that resisted the clear boundaries of botanical classification. This dependence of the human science of psychology on the constituent models of biology was earlier observed by Foucault (1994) in *The Order of Things* where he suggested the importance of organizing principles as opposed to basic elements that came to define psychology and its attempted classifications.

In the 6th edition of *Psychiatry: A Textbook for Students and Doctors* Kraepelin introduced the sub-types of hebephrenia, paranoia, and catatonia. Bleuler in 1911 had classified schizophrenia into four groups: schizophrenia simplex, the paranoid group, the hebephrenia group, and the catatonic group. Schizophrenia simplex was intriguingly class-specific in its symptom presentation; it was mostly found in the lower social classes like laborers, and if ever found in higher socio-economic strata, it presented in eccentrics and nagging wives. As for the intentions and consequences of developing classification systems, McNally (2016) proclaims that "Taxonomy, consequently, made visible to science, in a ceremonial space, categories of people who were not in fact there" (p. 95), a fact which was obfuscated by reports that mischaracterized the therapeutic effects of recognizing subtypes. The boundaries of schizophrenia remained blurred; they extended and attenuated regularly, like the temporary inclusion of schizophrenogenic families. Regionalism made attempts to point to the core of schizophrenia even more difficult. What further destroyed any illusion of consensus was that many individual researchers were using self-made classification systems that existed alongside organizational manuals.

The classification of insanity witnessed many ups and downs and there were many systems in conflict with one another. While some wanted to focus on singular symptoms, others made groups of symptoms their basis for classification, and others still focused on etiology of the behavior under consideration. The difficulties and clashes, says Boyle, led many to suggest abandoning the pursuit of classification completely, but the desire to stay in step with others in medicine who employed groupings of diseases emboldened psychiatrists to continue looking for efficient classificatory systems. The need to develop a scientific theory of behavior pushed them more towards medicine, and since there was no evidence of physical lesions or other somatic markers, they had to conjure the idea that some phenomena occurred only when the physician was present, or could only be ascertained as a symptom by experts (Boyle, 2002). The theorizing around what constituted abnormal behavior in the absence of somatic markers was done retroactively – since people in mental hospitals were assumed to be insane, all their observed behaviors were characterized as symptoms of insanity.

Foucault (1994) had not only noted the affinity, or rather dependence, of psychology on biology in the modern era but also claimed that the former is based on the "constituent models" of the empirical science of biology. Further, dementia paralytica was common in Germany, and influenced Kraepelin's ideas on insanity. Kraepelin's dementia praecox was influenced by his work on infectious diseases and his approach was descriptive (Kirk & Kutchins, 1992). Porter (2002) maintains that his descriptions also ignored the subjective experience and favored the course and core of the disease through a longitudinal approach. Boyle's (2002) scathing critique of Kraepelin's theoretical work does not just concern itself with the validity of his descriptions, instead she upends his whole scientific premise and methodology to reveal a lack of empiricism and an absurd claim to authority that he used to ground his work. According to her, Kraepelin was unable to find diagnostic reliability in his patient group and failed to ascertain biological markers like change in brain structure (to which he admitted), but instead of interpreting that as a problem in his theory, he instead appealed to his authority over empirical evidence. He stated:

> Although I must doubt that all of the disease pictures of Kahlbaum actually belong together, I nevertheless feel that my extensive experience justifies the recognition of the great majority of these cases as examples of a single characteristic illness form.
> *(Boyle, 2002, p. 62)*

She upsets his claims to objectivity by pointing to his lack of scientific rigor, his reliance on personal experience over objectively gathered data, and even expresses amusement that his work was enthusiastically accepted without much critique, so much so that later even Bleuler was to take the existence of the disease entity dementia praecox at face value.

An increasing pressure to reclassify and re-envision psychosis was reflected in the *DSM-V* initiative "Deconstructing psychosis" that was held in Feb 2006. It is intriguing to observe that Kraepelanian dichotomy still informs how we look for genetic markers of psychiatric ailments (Gaebel & Zielasek, 2008). Over the years, various revisions of the *DSM* and *ICD* have led to greater standardization of frames of reference but the manuals have only been able to provide weak evidence on how their operationalization of schizophrenia reflects the "true construct" (Gaebel & Zielasek, 2008). This has brought diagnostic discrepancies of other major disorders into sharp focus as it exposes the lack of strong evidence or clear natural differences between each of them (Jablensky, 2005). Along with schizophrenia, the operational definition of psychosis in the *DSM* also faced accusations of vagueness; it mostly focused on reality testing and erroneous evaluation of perception and thoughts. Further critique over the homogeneity of this disorder is reflected in studies that point to increasing biologization – there is a push to segregate and identify the biomarkers of schizophrenia but research lags due to "a lack of sensitivity, specificity, and predictive value" (Gaebel & Zielasek, 2008).

Over the years, other reclassifications have emerged, with many calling for a division between "general affective syndrome" and "general psychotic syndrome", or even "dopamine dysregulation disorder", or "neuro emotional integration disorder". The lack in consensus points to the fact that we are looking at an entity that is at best ill-defined, and at worst, completely ridiculous. More recently, even in *DSM-V*, psychosis and schizophrenia remain deeply provocative, especially due to the inclusion of "attenuated psychosis syndrome", which many claim was just another name for the controversial "psychosis risk syndrome".

In the end, classificatory chaos, difficulties in definitions, misdiagnosis, hasty operationalization, elusive etiology, and dependence on a biological model that just would not lend itself to psychological constructs were some of the prevailing conditions contemporaneous with the birth of schizophrenia.

Semantically schizophrenic

The words surrounding schizophrenia have proliferated across a century. The following incomplete list is an example of this and also an attempt at mockery: synchronous-syntonic schizophrenia, catastrophic schizophrenia, catatonic parergasia, constitutional schizophrenia, hebeodophrenia, five-day schizophrenia, three-day schizophrenia, larval schizophrenia, nuclear schizophrenia, post-emotive schizophrenia, true schizophrenia, situational schizophrenia, pseudoneurotic schizophrenia, and schizophrenia restzustand, among others (McNally, 2016). This excess in jargon and transience of subtypes belies dissonance and instability, but the first of many such linguistic transitions was the move from Kraepelin's dementia praecox to Bleuler's schizophrenia. This change was neither innocent, not inconsequential. According to McNally (2016), the use of the term "schizophrenic", which was later discarded in favor of "people with schizophrenia", was at least partially deliberate: "Bleuler, doubtless thinking of the adjectival challenges presented by 'Dementia Praecox' – had deliberately chosen it" (p. 13). He further clarifies that language surrounding the concept was of prime importance and changed the way it was conceived scientifically. The lexicon, of which the term "schiz" was of defining importance, referred to schizophrenic traits and created an "unassailable body of knowledge" (McNally, 2016, p. 17) around it. The term schizophrenic entered the clinical and popular usage with force; there was "schizophrenic body type" and "schizophrenic smell" as clinical markers, a schizophrenic style in art, and even a schizotoxin or schizovirus that reinforced the theories of biological etiology. The development of highly specialized terminology helped establish and claim new knowledge. This proliferation of a lexicon gave an impression of progress into which clinicians were initiated, and eventually led to psychology deceiving itself about its own proficiency.

It is Boyle who carefully explores the discursive conditions that have made schizophrenia possible, in turn implying that schizophrenia, at least partially, is a historical construct that requires certain conditions and causes to make it reasonable. Of the many ways this was achieved, language played the most important part in portraying it as a naturally occurring entity. She conducts an expansive breakdown to chart how the discourse of science and medicine has maintained the concept. Building on Foucault's notion that discourse is a way to construct reality, and resisting a simple representational view of language, she discusses how the words we use influence our thinking about it and also create social and institutional ripples. Boyle (2002) divides the "forms of language" that have conceptually sustained schizophrenia primarily into the two systems of science and medicine where the latter is at least partially subsumed under the former. The scientific discourse helps establish discipline-specific repute by allowing it to appear objective and legitimate.

The first common type of such discourse is empiricist discourse, discussed by Potter and Wetherell (Boyle, 2002), which involves the use of passive voice ("the work done by", "the figures showed") and language that points to the objective existence of facts which are devoid of personal agenda and preference, and are only discoverable by an expert. This strain of discourse that uses phrases like "scientific", "research-based" etc., has helped schizophrenia achieve scientific validity without actual empirical evidence. An example is the usage of phrases that imply discovery, for example, "the results showed that", "the research found that", "it was discovered that".

The second type of scientific discourse is the technical-rational repertoire discussed by Kirk and Kutchins (1992). Instead of implying the separate, objective nature of things, this way of languaging leads to a mystification of concepts under scrutiny. Typical applications are usage of overly technical terminology not easily accessible to others, and characterization of problems as technical issues that can only be resolved through the work of specialists and their rational expertise. For mental health professionals, diagnosis is the beginning of the application of such a repertoire and the rhetoric of science uses this language and its set of specific codes to turn everyday behavior into objective symptom criteria (Kirk & Kutchins, 1992). These two types of scientific discourses have been used to make reasonable the preferred form of reality and can lead to loss of curiosity, reduction in critical thinking, and eventually absence of questioning because the ideas either seem self-evident or too specialized to interrogate.

Consistent with the empiricist and technical predilections of institutional science, schizophrenia is deeply woven into the fabric of a medical discourse that allows it to flourish – words like diagnosis, clinical, symptoms, treatment, all point to this discourse; "symptomatic behavior" points to the presence of a disease behind the symptoms, and "diagnosis" implies the existence of a real thing. Fortunately for the discipline, medical language skillfully hides these problems to garb schizophrenia in the prestige of science. Observing this turmoil in language is critical because it helps to later address not only the relationship between modern epistemology and schizophrenia, but also notes the unique role that language has to play in its experience and expression. In more ways than one, it is the disorder of language.

There are many other ways that scientific discourse and medical practice have together maintained the validity of schizophrenia, the first of which is by creating a *narrative of progress*. A narrative of progress is the idea that each new discovery is an increment in knowledge about something, and it is inherent in other sciences except psychiatry, where it had to be conjured through legends and mythology. For example, concepts like "clinical utility" and "clinical judgment", and specific to schizophrenia, "diagnosis through intuition", "atmospheric diagnosis" that are inane in other hard sciences find glowing acceptance in psychiatry. Take for example the assertions of William Carpenter who chaired *DSM-V*'s psychotic disorder work group. On being asked about clinician training to differentiate between primary and secondary negative symptoms, he noted that "Hopefully, clinicians who are evaluating a patient who doesn't express much emotion in their face have to figure out if this person is depressed, if it's akinesia caused by a drug, or if it's a primary lack of emotional experience" (Koola, 2009, p. 2). Kenneth Donaldson (Peterson, 1982) in his book *Insanity Inside Out*, presents some cringe-worthy, horrifying, and almost Kafka-esque examples of his interaction with physicians that exemplify just this. In each conversation one can observe his physicians' dependence on fragile authority and flimsy clinical judgment, something they were later sued over and paid damages for.

Foucault (2006) himself suggested that psychiatric knowledge and power intervenes and exists at the juncture of a decision between reality and fiction; unlike other medical differential diagnoses where the doctor has to respond through specification and characterization to the patients' symptoms, the psychiatrist instead has to answer the question of whether the patient is mad or not in the first place. Thus, according to him, even though "psychiatric knowledge really tried to construct itself on the model of medicine observation, inquiry and demonstration" (Foucault, 2006, p. 251), it was all the while situated in segregating reality from fiction.

The spin of discourse also spills into the sublimity of the concept as described by Woods (2011). The incomprehensibility of madness is displayed in the fact none of the theories explaining it have been remotely conclusive in shedding light on its nature or etiology: "it remains hidden from the psychiatric gaze while being constantly under the scientific spotlight" (Woods, 2011, p. 32). The sublime, she says, is not a property of the object but an experience produced in the encounter between the subject and the object in a social, spatial, and temporal context. Woods proclaims that in the discipline of psychiatry, if we are too close to schizophrenia, it is far too terrifying and overwhelming, but if positioned too far (studying only neural correlates) "apprehension itself becomes strained" (Woods, 2011, p. 29). The perfect distance is maintained through discursive practices – a medicalized professional gaze produced through a rational-empiricist discourse that labels and probes. Intimacy generated with the schizophrenic object in the asylum or therapeutic[1] practice, and remoteness created via scientific methods of classification allow schizophrenia to be both shrouded in mystery and appear accessible through reason at the same time – "it functions as a limit point for this discipline, a potentially daunting unknown, which perpetually spurs greater efforts at analytic conquests ... destabilizing the very discursive structures whose expansion it enables" (Woods, 2011, p. 31). The delight in reason's triumph is evident in the numerous increasingly refined treatments and theories that have proliferated around the disorder, including this very work.

Invigorated by institutions

The conceptual authority of schizophrenia has been under fire since its origin, but it refused to falter under the critical gaze of many theorists, and by the close of the twentieth century, its legitimacy was firmly established.

According to McNally (2016), one of the prime reasons behind this turn of events was the burgeoning involvement of powerful institutions like the American Psychiatric Association and the World Health Organization as they started to conceptualize and export classifications; earlier this task had been restricted to individual researchers and theorists who had guided descriptions and definitions for a century. North America's increasing influence across the world, coupled with its ability to financially sustain research, gave it the edge that Europe didn't have, and it went on to universalize and export its vision. A strong focus on taxonomy and the need to tabulate and count rather than describe symptoms preserved these classifications, so much so that methodology became the central focus instead of being a tool that facilitated consensus and communication. Faith in quantitative analysis, new statistical technology, and specificity in classification and definition witnessed an exponential increase. It is both amusing and horrifying to note that while these powerful institutions push for export of knowledge to address the "treatment gap" in poor countries, they have neither the stability nor the lucidity they claim to possess. An investigation of their own shortcomings is imperative to destroy their claims of objectivity, universality, and expertise.

The *International Classification of Diseases 6* and the *Diagnostic and Statistical Manual-II* were forced to bring similarity and coherence in their classifications as political international treaties required them to be in agreement. This obligatory coherence "contributed to disruption, distortion, and, in addition, to a modicum of farce in the classification of schizophrenia" (McNally, 2016, p. 173), not to mention that is was eventually a failed attempt. *DSM* preferred schizophrenia over dementia praecox and divided it into nine sub-types. It further came up with 13 divisions but as American Psychiatric Association Chairperson E.M. Gruenberg wrote in the preface of *DSM-II* in 1968: "Even if it had tried, the Committee could not establish agreement about what this disorder is; it could only agree on what to call it" (American Psychiatric Association, 1968). Intriguingly, on one hand he commented upon the importance of labels in defining attitudes and subjective experience, while on the other he said that the change in name for schizophrenia did not bring any change to the disorder (American Psychiatric Association, 1968). Gruenberg's comments are still relevant, as William Carpenter, the psychiatrist who chaired *DSM-V*'s psychotic disorder workgroup noted that, "There is substantial dissatisfaction with schizophrenia treated as a disease entity; its symptoms are like a fever – something is wrong, but we don't know what" (Yuhas, 2013, p. 1). The lack of unity of thought had insidious repercussions as the language surrounding *DSM-II*'s paranoid schizophrenia was also responsible for the disproportionate diagnosis of schizophrenia in black men who participated in the civil rights movement (Metzl, 2009).

There was growing interest in using quantitative, scientific, and empirical research over theoretical deliberation to develop diagnostic criteria. Multivariate analysis and cluster analysis were utilized to discover what were assumed to be four stable sub-types of schizophrenia, but the 1974 international pilot study showed that glaring inconsistencies still existed in sub-typing schizophrenia across the world. The years preceding *DSM-III* saw a neo-Kraepelanian revival that repositioned schizophrenia yet again as a disease entity that was biologically rooted. As Metzl (2009) found, many who would have received the diagnosis of schizophrenia is *DSM-II* now fitted in other categories like brief reactive psychosis, and a diagnosis of schizophrenia required active psychotic symptoms of hallucinations and delusions. The new, operationalized schizophrenia revealed itself in 1980 with the sub-types: catatonic, disorganized, residual, paranoid, and undifferentiated.

It wasn't only the early *DSMs* that faced a rough time with schizophrenia. Maj (1998) reported on numerous issues with *DSM-IV*'s schizophrenia criteria: the absence of schizophrenia as a syndrome with any characteristic clustering, equal weight for symptom groups problematizing diagnosis in community mental health settings, poor inter-rater reliability of what "bizarre delusions" meant etc. This eventually turned schizophrenia diagnosis into a "diagnosis by exclusion" since there was no underlying binding character, only a set of symptoms. One of *DSM-IV-R*'s focus points was on theoretical neutrality but its first of the three sub-types (paranoid, disorganized, catatonic) only regurgitated Kraepelin's dementia praecox sub-types; it was yet again mute on the question of what caused schizophrenia (Woods, 2011).

Currently things do not appear great for APA's *DSM-V* either. More recently, *DSM-V*'s attempted addition of "Psychosis Risk Syndrome" has been called "the most dangerous of all suggestions" (Frances, 2010, p. 9) as it would invite unnecessary misdiagnosis, stigma, and a deluge of false positives. This diagnostic category received widespread critique when the early draft of *DSM-V* was released, so much so, that it seemed the APA would back off from its inclusion. But as Frances (2013) notes, it crept its way in under "Other Specified Schizophrenia Spectrum Disorder/Other Psychotic Disorder".

Despite the APA's institutional diagnostic authority, critique of the concept never died. As recently as 2019, the contention around psychiatric diagnosis can be seen in cases like that of Kamilah Brock, a black female banker arrested and institutionalized for eight days (and given a diagnosis of bipolar disorder) after she appeared delusional and manic because she said Obama followed her on Twitter and that she became a banker without a college degree – both facts were true (Morgan-Smith, 2019). Brock recently lost the case against her doctors and as one juror explained "That's not the first thing I'd say to somebody – that Obama follows me on Twitter. It's the way she's saying it – that she's important – the grandiosity". The jurors believed that the three doctors and an NYPD officer were more credible than a black woman who had spoken truth at every step. The case has received widespread publicity and questions about validity of psychiatric diagnosis and racism in psychiatry are rightfully back in the public's mind.

As the uselessness of stringent categories for psychiatric diagnosis becomes evident, a shift from categorical to dimensional models has been proposed. Since categories work so well in the medical discourse and are useful in carrying out treatment, their appeal to psychology is natural. But the exclusiveness required by a categorical model does not translate to psychological ailments which tend to occur together, disappear at will, and change whimsically in form and intensity. As Jablensky (2010) points out, while the categorical model has obvious disadvantages in psychiatric diagnoses, a dimensional model has "the advantage of introducing explicitly quantitative variation and graded transition between forms of disorder, as well as between normality and pathology" (p. 280). But before we get too excited, he adds that dimensional models come with their own set of problems: lack of agreement on variations and gradations; lack of empirical data to ground claims of intensity and severity; and their inherent complexity that makes them difficult to use in clinical practice. Even though Jablensky does not call for dismantling of the concept, he accepts that the etiology, neuropathology, and pathophysiology remain unidentified. It appears that while the institutions of psychiatry managed schizophrenia's survival, they could not ensure its stability.

Mythologies and legends: the split and the stupor

A popular image that seized public imagination and textbook illustrations was that of the catatonic patient in his characteristic stupor, but how real was the quintessential schizophrenic whose awkward posture and half-open hospital robe seemed to reflect his strange otherness? To understand schizophrenia and psychosis, it is essential to pay attention to how deeply historical each iteration of the disorder is, which is reflected in the transience of its sub-types. Parnas (2011) alludes to this transience and differentiates between fundamental core symptoms and fluctuating surface ones – the former representing the essential phenomenological structure of the condition. There are many sub-types that became increasingly popular and then quietly disappeared from clinical literature, the most prevalent one being catatonia. Both Bleuler and Kraepelin and Diefendorf (1904) discussed the rigidity or stupor that marked catatonic patients, a concept first introduced by Karl Ludwig Kahlbaum (Kraepelin & Diefendorf, 1904) as *katatonie*.

While twentieth-century literature regularly reported catatonic cases, the sub-type was already disappearing. Jung, as early as 1919, attributed catatonia reactions to the asylum environment and reported improvements when the patient's surroundings were changed. It was soon agreed that catatonia was at least partially iatrogenic. By mid-century, when cases of catatonic schizophrenia had nearly disappeared, the idea of catatonia remained alive and the image of a patient's characteristic vacant stare still remained integral to literature on schizophrenia. Catatonia was considered to be a characteristic of chronic schizophrenia but around this time even acceptance of chronic schizophrenia was under fire – some considered it iatrogenic and preventable.

The tolerance of such an unstable concept is unsurprising, since reinforcing it was an even more troublesome concept – schizophrenia. It would eventually be in *DSM-V* that the catatonic sub-type would cease to exist. Many have noted the absence of symptoms and sub-types like catatonia in today's population. It is possible that the patients who Bleuler and Kraepelin dealt with were a different set than those currently diagnosed schizophrenic, as their symptoms fit better with what was later discovered to be encephalitis lethargica; Kraepelin and Diefendorf (1904) clearly state how typhoid, scarlet fever, and head injuries could precede the symptoms of dementia praecox and that some patients even presented physical malformations. Catatonia was not the only vanishing symptom; Foucault (2006) similarly stated that in the nineteenth century there was a rise and fall in the cases of dementia in asylums. He noted that this was a result of the intricacies of psychiatric power on one hand, which made madness real in the institution of the asylum, and the disciplinary power of the institution on the other, which flattened out all the symptoms of dementia. Other vanishing disorders have been hysteria, fugue, and dissociative identity disorder, to name a few. As neurology and psychiatry grew into two separate disciplines and many infectious and neurological disorders like encephalitis lethargica began to disappear, the concept of schizophrenia transitioned subtly and uncritically over the years and now bears only slight resemblance to the one presented by Bleuler and Kraepelin.

It is clear that schizophrenia is the core around which psychiatric practice is established as scientific, useful, and relevant. This is because it projects the discovery of etiology into the future, and paradoxically it is one of the few disorders where phenomenological, etiological, and nosological understanding still eludes us. Woods (2011) asserts that the creation of schizophrenia as a sublime object with its "paradoxical legitimization and destabilization of psychiatry's scientificity" (p. 35) began as early as Kraepelin's work with dementia praecox. While others in Germany were looking for somatic markers and the exciting new technology of microscopes was all the rage in laboratories, Kraepelin's poor eyesight limited this endeavor and instead led him to focus on his meticulously descriptive account of the disease's course. Resonating with Boyle's accusation, Woods states that bringing various bizarre behaviors and psychosis under the single rubric of dementia praecox was more a matter of his faith in the scientific authority of psychiatry and less the result of real evidence. Thus the reason for schizophrenia's dual nature as legitimizing and delegitimizing psychiatry's expertise begins with Kraepelin's methodological analysis which instead of focusing on etiology, focused on detailed descriptions of behavior, thus creating a concept that was loose and flexible but also exhaustive enough to be diagnostic and prognostic. This flexibility that lent itself effortlessly to different theories over decades allowed for dementia praecox to survive. It consequently led to the creation of methods and research that accommodated vastly different philosophies – biological, genetic, psychoanalytic, and even existential–phenomenological ones. In the voice of David Attenborough one can almost hear: *Schizophrenia has developed a vast, diverse, and fragile ecosystem of its own; while greatly explored by humans for decades, it also remains mostly misunderstood.*

Schizophrenia: abuse and anti-psychiatry

Schizophrenia reified "moral insanity" into an entity that was more clinical and scientific than ever before, making way for the pathologization of various forms of deviant behavior, familial relations, racial conduct, etc. Needless to say, this had and continues to have immense social repercussions which belie its underlying moral dimension as a disorder. From the early twentieth century Kraepelin and Diefendorf (1904) stated that the inability to make normative moral distinctions were associated with dementia praecox. Herbert Harley (1921) asserted that the disorder actually produced criminals like burglars and pick-pockets who "band together and make a profitable business of crime" (p. 519). He further asserted that dementia praecox was a natural bedfellow of the most brutal crimes like rape and murder and even wrote that, while incorrigible criminal delinquency and intelligence defects were related, it was emotional eccentricities of the type found in dementia praecox that created moral defect for which there is no correctional reform. Thus, he stated, a person with dementia praecox has no moral inhibitions, no sense of right and wrong, and even "corrupts the feeble minded inmate who has normal affectivity" (Harley, 1921, p. 519).

Moral prejudice inundated various sub-types of schizophrenia, for example, "ambulatory schizophrenia" constituted the non-productive, the inefficient, the pervert, and transvestites. Masturbation, especially early onset masturbation in men, was seen as symptomatic of the disorder by Kraepelin and Diefendorf (1904) who associated it with the hebephrenic sub-type. Likewise, other deviant sexual behavior was connected to schizophrenia – latent homosexual tendencies, promiscuity, fetishes – all were fair game for diagnosis. This narrative flawlessly lent itself to the idea of curative sterilization as a radical measure espoused by experts. For someone diagnosed with dementia praecox, sterilization was thus a natural consequence of legal restrictions on marriage; more importantly, it led others to call for castration and even the execution of patients who were untreatable.

Dowbiggin (1997) stresses the overlooked relationship between support for eugenics and a psychiatrist's personal experience; he emphasizes the class dimension of the support for eugenics, which he reminds us was prevalent but not unanimous. According to Dowbiggin (1997), the lack of consensus can partially be explained by the fact that psychiatrists with poor patients were largely pro-eugenics while those with more affluent ones were not. The 1881 assassination of President Garfield by Charles Guiteau led to the psychiatric community labeling Guiteau as a degenerate (in his defense), and it brought to public scrutiny issues of heredity, madness, and criminality (Porter, 2002). A consequence of this was the call for radical measures against the mad – eugenics was made sensible. Despite lack of consensus on whether forced sterilization was necessary, it seemed that for many it was a useful way to cut costs in over-crowded institutions. While, like most other categorizations and definitions of schizophrenia, eugenics saw its ultimate demise, it left in its wake more than 80,000 forced sterilizations and castrations in the United States and inclusion of negative eugenics in the curriculum of college and high school students (Black, 2003).

Racial and ethnic bias pervaded the diagnosis, with famous epidemiologist John Carothers openly stating that there is only a slight gap between the primitive attitude of the African and the schizophrenic (Torrey, 1973): "he theorized that their forebrain was underdeveloped and said that they were similar in behavior to leucotomized Europeans" (p. 55). Unsurprisingly, in Africa and African American communities in the 1960s US, the diagnosis of schizophrenia was disproportionately high, and black men and women's connection to the civil rights movement was considered a symptom of the disease (Metzl, 2009). Families were pathologized and policed, with a special focus on mothers' behavioral and emotional conduct that could far too easily be construed as excessively passive or immensely controlling; women neglecting their motherly and wifely duties were also under the radar. Further, deviance in political beliefs was brought under the rubric of schizophrenic symptoms and etiology.

The prejudice and abuse was not invisible. For that matter, throughout the twentieth century there were many attacks that accused psychiatry of prejudice and claimed it targeted the eccentrics and the disobedient; painters, readers, and outsiders were all accommodated in its fuzzy boundaries. Throughout the conceptualization of schizophrenia, dissenting voices had shown their skepticism, which only increased in the 1960s counter-culture movement. Anti-psychiatrists like David Cooper and other non-traditional thinkers like R.D Laing came to the fore. The term *antipsychiatrie* existed as far back as 1908 when it was first introduced by Bernhard Neyer, and later taken up by David Cooper.

Laing presented the idea that schizophrenia was a coping response to an unsustainable situation in a threatening world. Laing's (1990) work suggested that schizophrenia is the presentation of a schizoid's last line of defense; it is what is left when the veil is pulled off the false self. He characterized the schizophrenic as a man desperately trying to hold his world together – unsure of his alive-ness, doubtful of his real-ness, insecure in his substantiality (ontological insecurity) – who unlike the neurotic is not interested in gratification but absorbed by existential preservation. The schizophrenic psyche's fortress which was built to keep at bay the existential anxieties of engulfment, implosion, and petrification soon turns into a prison, and to his horror, the false-self system that was earlier a protector now turns captor.

Perhaps most famous is the critique by Thomas Szasz (1970) who said that new psychiatric rules produced new classes of the mentally ill in the same manner that new laws created new types of criminals, and that this expansion of categories was essential to maintain psychiatric power. He likened modern psychiatry to the Inquisition, with mere changes in the "vocabulary and social style" (p. 27). According to McNally (2016), anti-psychiatry's criticism was divided in two directions: exposing the contradictions and inconsistencies inherent in psychological concepts, and revealing the ideological construction of schizophrenia. Some of these criticisms led to real and radical changes in the way patients were treated in alternative communities. We can point to Franco Bassaglia in Italy who attempted to replace psychiatric institutions with community centers and Hans Maier who spoke against institutionalization and the harmful effects of isolating psychotics. Bassaglia (Bassaglia & Ongaro, 2018) wrote about rehabilitation from the institutionalized condition and compared the asylum to apartheid by pointing to its desire to "other" those that scare us. Forced isolation, according to him, was at least partially responsible for certain mental disorders. The vehement critiques of classification and conceptualization resulted in the establishment of few alternative therapeutic spaces, of which Laing's Kingsley Hall is probably the most famous. These attempts made the critique of schizophrenia public and accessible to laymen as opposed to being the sole prerogative of academics.

Sociologists also joined the critique and focused on the societal systems of authority and their opportunistic classification of what is deviant (Kirk & Kutchins, 1992). Schizophrenics were on occasion seen as the victims of pressures exerted by the society, and research on LSD and mescaline led others to think that insight into their minds was imminent. The stage was set for R.D Laing and David Cooper's controversial, putatively romanticized, but nonetheless brilliant idea of the schizophrenic as he who is saner than the sane. David Rosenhann's (Rosenhan, 1973) experiment furthered this backlash as it explosively suggested that classification was either simply redundant or downright damaging. The results of his study were important enough to warrant an article in the *American Journal of Psychiatry*, which agreed that the experiment brought into harsh focus the problems of objectivity and validity in diagnosis.

Regardless of these seemingly revolutionary advances, very soon cracks in the counter-culture movement began to appear. From Mark Vonnegut's (son of Kurt Vonnegut) public and vocal disillusionment with Laing whom he had earlier admired, to Szasz's critique of Cooper and Laing, things were under transition again. Laing's work was critiqued for lacking specificity, being self-contradicting and unable to show why schizophrenia and not manic-depressive psychosis would develop as a result of dysfunctional family dynamic, and for claiming that his descriptions made the schizophrenic's behavior comprehensible to others (Rachman, 1976).

The unrest with anti-psychiatry intensified because despite the dissent of the last few decades, faith in the biological etiology of mental disorders had remained strong. The use of neuroleptics and their presumed positive effects, as epitomized in the study by Jean Delay and Pierre Deniker on chlorpromazine in 1952, led to the strengthening of the chemical-imbalance theory. Inspired by pharmacological research and intervention, there was growing interest in biological theories; this would eventually lead to the very influential dopamine-dysregulation hypothesis. New technology helped pave this path, for example, MRIs allowed psychologists to look for anatomical and structural causes. Along with neurological chemical-imbalance studies, genetic studies that looked for the elusive "schizophrenia gene" were being carried out (Gottesman and Shields in 1976). Soon, with the publication of *DSM-III*, the idea of mental disorders as a disease was established. The 1960s dissent was a continuation of unease that had started a long time ago but eventually the voices of anti-psychiatry were smoothly quietened. There were those who worried that *DSM-III* turned human problems into medical ones but the apparent triumph of "fact over theory" was deafening (Kirk & Kutchins, 1992).

Studying the historical ups and downs of schizophrenia helps us neither to romanticize it nor reduce it. Dorothy Rowe (1980) cautions us against reaching such reductive conclusions when she observes the importance of testing psychiatry's underlying assumptions through the lens of philosophy. She states that doing so will reveal that schizophrenia's etiology-of-the-week problem is caused by its dependence on the medical-science model, which seeks to find a single physical cause. Rowe (1980) reminds us that even medical science does not adhere to this simplistic understanding, as exemplified in the finding that tuberculosis cannot be simply explained by tubercle bacillus but is also dependent on a host of social factors.

Porter (2002) concludes that the question of whether there has been any real progress in psychiatry is one with many answers; psychotropic drugs are a success but also a failure because "pacifying patients is hardly a pinnacle of achievement" (p. 216). Similarly, the deinstitutionalization of the 1960s remains a topic of contention amongst psychiatrists, and despite weathering the storm of anti-psychiatry, a general lack of unity in thought mars the profession as it still oscillates between the biological and the social. Eventually, despite mainstream rejection, anti-psychiatry had a lasting effect in several pockets around the world (for example, birthing a collective movement called *survivors of psychiatry*) and for those who seek it, it remains a source of some of the harshest critique psychology ever had to encounter.

Schizophrenia: claims and cautions in current theories

Schizophrenia survives vibrantly in public consciousness and as a diagnostic category. Current mainstream theories indulge in absolute biological reductionism but there are pockets of subversion that aim for a more balanced approach focusing on personal biography and socio-cultural factors. In this section, I will quickly recapitulate recent research in the field and show

how, despite psychology's cool tools and shiny toys, schizophrenia still remains elusive and contentious. This exposes the vulnerability of the concept and the phenomena, and will help to show later that placing schizophrenia in an epistemological framework is the only way to solve the conundrum.

Schizophrenia is now understood to be a polygenic disorder and even then most studies can only speak about genetic and neurological correlates and not causes. This simple difference between cause and correlation is taught in most Psychology 101 classes (I hope) but is conveniently forgotten in real-world research. While the disorder presents a high heritability rate, the concordance rates in monozygotic twins is only 41 to 65 percent (in some studies) implicating reasons other than genetic (Cardno & Gottesman, 2000). This emphasis on genetics exists from the time of Kraepelin & Diefendorf (1904) who pointed to defective heredity as a major factor in etiology.

The excitement around the discovery of a schizophrenia gene (a popular theory for a long time) had already been dampened by whispers of caution by geneticists who insisted that since genes always express themselves in a context and an environment, finding one directly implicated may not be possible. Neuroscientist Robert Sapolsky (2014) suggested that the concept of gene–environment interaction is outdated because it erroneously implies that there is a basic and general way that a gene acts; instead genetic presentation only manifests a certain way in a certain environment. A more recent critique is that of the classical twin method used in most genetic studies of schizophrenia; it questions the underlying Equal Environment Assumption (EEA), which states that the environments of monozygotic and fraternal twins reared together are similar. This assumption is critical because any changes within a twin pair is then attributed to genetic and not environmental causes. Recent meta-analysis by Fosse, Joseph, and Richardson (2015) showed that "schizophrenia related social adversities are more similar in identical than fraternal pairs" (p. 3) thus invalidating the EEA on which the classical twin method is based. Identical twins showed higher similarity than fraternal pairs on "bullying, sexual abuse, physical maltreatment, emotional abuse and neglect, and general negative life events and trauma" (p. 5). Additionally, parents and society treat identical twins in a highly similar manner when compared to fraternal twins.

The first line of treatment for psychotic disorders is neuroleptics. Both first- and second-generation (atypical) antipsychotics have distressing side effects but second-generation ones are often touted to have reduced extrapyramidal side effects and produce better results. Concurrently there is evidence that suggests that there is little if any difference between the effectiveness of first- and second-generation neuroleptics (Jones et al., 2006). Further, clozapine, the only antipsychotic that has shown some degree of effectiveness in the treatment of "treatment resistant schizophrenia" (a problematic term in itself because it is circular) has a potentially lethal side effect – hematoxicity (Miyamoto, Miyake, Jarskog, Fleischhacker, & Lieberman, 2012). The numbers suggestive of effectiveness of neuroleptics are inconsistent, to say the least, and it appears that at this point neuroleptics can't be considered a cure for schizophrenia since more than half the patients post-administration continue to show symptoms of moderate to severe psychosis (Matei, Mihailescu, & Davidson, 2014). A recent analysis of patient data from 16 randomized controlled trials with 6,221 patients showed that no symptomatic remission rate was 66.9 percent, meaning that only one third of patients in the trials experienced full improvement using antipsychotics, and antipsychotic use along with early onset were related with higher nonresponsive percentages (Nilolakopoulou & Laucht, 2018).

Other inconsistencies also point to gaps in knowledge. For example, it is known that NDMA-receptor hypo-function can lead to a spectrum of positive, negative, and cognitive schizophrenia-like symptoms (Miyamoto et al., 2012), and second-generation antipsychotics have on occasion been effective in curbing them, but the mechanism through which this happens is still not understood because none of the second-generation antipsychotics display direct affinity for NDMA-R. There is further conflicting evidence on whether neuroleptics have neuro-protective functions or are instead detrimental. For example, Olanzapine in the long term was supposed to reduce gray-matter loss (Lieberman et al., 1998) – but how this happens is again not understood. On the other hand, a recent study of first-episode schizophrenia has shown that antipsychotics might actually be associated with brain-tissue loss over time (Andreasen et al., 2011). Another similar research done on Macau monkeys (Dorph-Petersen et al., 2005) pointed to antipsychotic use and loss of fronto-parietal volume. Similarly, the belief that larger ventricle sizes had etiological significance in the disorder was later undermined by findings that such anatomical changes were a side effect of long-term antipsychotic use (Murray, 2016).

The culture of psycho-pharmaceuticals is premised upon the idea that schizophrenia is a result of chemical imbalance that has something to do with dopamine. The dopamine-dysregulation hypothesis is called so because over decades both too little and too much dopamine has been associated with schizophrenia (Jucaite & Nyberg, 2012). More recently, it has been shown that long-term antipsychotic use leads to a proliferation of D2R receptor sites, in turn exacerbating psychotic symptoms by creating a super sensitivity to dopamine (a drug-induced psychotic relapse) thus questioning the efficacy of placebo studies (Jucaite & Nyberg, 2012; Murray, 2016). A conclusive investigation of this hypothesis by Jucaite and Nyberg (2012) showed that "Vigorous search for abnormalities in the dopamine system in schizophrenia so far has yielded inconclusive results … it is unlikely a single neurotransmitter system can explain such diverse symptoms" (p. 23).

Current understanding of psychosis and schizophrenia have reached an unprecedented level of biologization which includes biologizing the concept of insight, the lack of which is termed anosognosia – a biological deficit to be treated. Anosognosia is now regarded as one of the primary symptoms of schizophrenia, and calling it a biological deficit disempowers the patient, rendering them unable to form their own medical and legal decisions. An excellent example of the weaponization of insight can be seen in the case of Kenneth Donaldson (Peterson, 1982). Donaldson was the first person to receive damages when he sued the psychiatrists under whose care (or rather lack of care) he was institutionalized for years. The physicians justified his confinement by saying that, among other things, in a psychological test he did not draw pupils on the eyes of stick figures. Further, they stated that his belief and assertion that he will find a job and write a book (about the hospital) after he left the facility displayed a characteristic lack of insight into his own condition. They were later charged with acting maliciously or wantonly or oppressively and Donaldson's was the first such case that made it to the Supreme Court (Peterson, 1982). By biologizing a socio-cultural concept like insight and calling it a neuro-cognitive deficit, freedom of choice is undermined since it is premised upon awareness of one's situation and consequences of acts – "if you remove or pathologize insight by calling it a neurological deficit like Anosognosia, then the legal choices of the patient go away" (Tranulis, Corin, & Kirmayer, 2008, p. 235).

The first-break or early-intervention approach has seen great success over the past few years. This approach calls for professional intervention as soon as the person experiences his or her first psychotic episode instead of waiting for a diagnoses to be administered. Early intervention is premised on evidence suggesting that a high duration of untreated psychosis (DUP) is related to worse prognosis, high remission, and higher chances of self-harm by the patient. It has brought about some much-needed changes, like an optimistic outlook towards psychosis, focus on community intervention, and efforts towards de-stigmatization (Tranulis, 2012). Despite these benefits, it has fallen prey to its own aggressive enthusiasm in many ways.

According to Tranulis (2012), the success of the early-intervention model has led to its acceptance in the mainstream treatment approaches, which has unfortunately increased the chances of involuntary hospitalization and treatment. Evidence of better prognosis resulted in doctors demanding more power in order to restrain patients and the slightest feature of psychosis is to be treated with aggressive antipsychotics (Tranulis, 2012) – the most extreme example of this has been the inclusion of "attenuated psychosis risk" in the *DSM-V* (Frances, 2013). Emerging problems are more ethical and moral than clinical.

An example of a highly successful early-intervention program is Western Finnish Lapland's Open Dialogue approach, pioneered by Dr. Jaako Seikkula. This group acts as first responders and their main focus is on establishing dialogue with the patient and caregivers within the first 24 hours after the psychotic break, de-emphasizing pharmaceutical treatment, and encouraging complete transparency with the patient. A five-year follow-up study showed significantly decreased DUP, reduced number of hospitalizations, and 82 percent of patients showed no residual psychotic symptoms (Seikkula et al., 2006).

Some of the most important and recent research comes from The Hearing Voices Foundation. In their book *Psychosis as a Personal Crisis*, Marius Romme and Sandra Escher (2012) maintain that voice-hearing (they prefer the term compared to auditory hallucinations) is more prevalent in the general population without illness than ordinarily thought (Romme & Escher, 2012). They heavily emphasize the relational aspects of the therapeutic process rather than diagnostic ones, and attach immense significance to the content of delusions and hallucinations. They point to cases where patients experienced their voices as benign, some seem to enjoy them and others even find them helpful – the majority though are tortured by their persecutory nature. Monica Hoffman (as cited in Romme & Escher, 2012) argues against the use of the term auditory hallucinations, insisting that it precludes a genuine, warm, and respectful therapist–client relationship. There is an emphasis on the biography of the patient, examination of the timeline around when these voices emerged, and the relation between these two aspects.

The Hearing Voices network introduced the term *formulation*, an alternative to the concept of diagnosis. While opposed to the stigmatizing and limiting effects of "diagnosis", they recognize a need for language that not only helps professionals talk to each other but actually helps the patient understand their problem while giving them a sense of agency and hope. Formulations do not ignore personal meaning and are drawn up in collaboration with patients; they are not seen as truths but tentative understandings open to change, and their usefulness is assessed by the client and not the putative expert. This approach has caused a resurgence in the interest of assessing the importance of traumatic life experience in development of psychosis and schizophrenia. The content is important; the rant is relevant.

This process emerges from theories of schizophrenia which attribute the origin of psychosis to psychological factors like trauma and dysfunctional childhood relationships. It could be related to traumatic life events, insecure attachment style, and a pattern of communicating with the child that is ambiguous, disjointed, and contradictory (Bentall & Fernyhough, 2008). Research in the field has indicated a dose-response association: while abused children are 10.6 times more likely to develop psychosis than non-abused children, this number increases to 48.4 times for those whose abuse was severe (as cited in Larkin & Read, 2012). Could hallucinations be a way for the individual to cope with traumatic events? Could delusions be adaptive or beneficial? Interestingly, Kellett (1973) once proposed that schizophrenia could even have an evolutionary advantage for the family members of the sufferer as it is useful in maintaining alertness. In some studies, schizophrenics showed higher creativity and intelligence, a better immune system, and even a lower susceptibility to cancer (Van Dongen & Boomsma, 2013). This line of research that implicates childhood trauma in psychotic breaks is important because part of my interest in India involved understanding whether such a connection between suffering and psychosis existed there. The answers were surprising to say the least.

Questions regarding the ethics of forced treatment, the importance of insight, and relevance of the content of delusions are acquiring mainstream importance. In a recent *New York Times* article, psychiatrist Irene Huford (2016) questions her decision to involuntarily hospitalize a patient who thought he was a prophet. She wonders about people's right to choose psychosis if they so desire, how lack of insight is a tricky concept, and how altruistic intentions of the physician can be traumatic to the patient. Huford suggests engaging in people's stories and experiences, and states that meaningful recovery can happen without cure. She points to the 2014 meta-analysis which revealed doubts over the benefits of assisted outpatient treatments. While they appear less invasive than inpatient programs, it was noted that there was no statistically significant advantage of forced outpatient care in decreasing hospitalizations, arrests, homelessness, or in advancing quality of life (Kisely & Campbell, 2014; as cited in Huford, 2016).

Conclusion

We have taken a journey that charts out the historical conditions that birthed and sustained schizophrenia over the decades. While an eternal shape-shifter, schizophrenia still remains a powerful clinical entity and a popular public one. In the next chapter, I attempt to resolve this discordance between its instability and its resilience, its constant critique and its continued persistence. I reveal why the schizophrenic subject is at home in the modern world, and is perhaps even an extreme product of our escapades with knowledge and self-knowledge. It would do us well to investigate the epistemic conditions, for they reveal how the strangeness of the schizophrenic is not so far from our own experience after all, why the schizophrenic might be the *ununderstandable* but is simultaneously, the inevitable.

Note

1 An important element of the sublime is the delight that the subject encounters when reason totalizes the experience of something that surpasses the faculties of imagination – an affirmation of reason's victory. Another important constituent of the sublime is distance between the subject and the object that allows us to negotiate safely with that which produces awe and terror. The object is almost inessential as sublimity is produced in the subject but depends on the subject's position to the object, that is, on the distance.

3
THE "UNALIENATED" ALIEN
The schizophrenic as a hyper-modern subject

From Kraepelin's conceptualization to Laing's disruptions, the story of schizophrenia is replete with contradicting evidence, unstable classifications, and slippery semantics. The previous chapter attempted to provide a history of these ups and downs to reveal the social conditions that sustained schizophrenia in the West. Foucault's (1967) work was utilized to demarcate various forms of madness and their control over the decades as he revealed how humanitarian advances of Pinel and Tuke were more nuanced in their motivations than is acknowledged by psychology textbooks. I used Boyle's (2002) and Scull's (1975, 1979) writings to investigate how historical conditions, like an attempted regicide and private madhouses, partially informed the developing interest of medicine men in madness. Moreover, a larger cultural shift that held productive industrial selfhood as the epitome of health and success assisted the discourse of moral management. McNally (2016) helped reveal shortcomings in the classification and definition of schizophrenia; he provided comically long lists of sub-types that have since become extinct, in effect rendering them absurd. Eventually, Kraepelin's death, a providential translation of Bleuler's work to English, and the inherent pessimism in the concept of "dementia praecox" led to its downfall and the birth of "schizophrenia". There were desperate attempts at operationalization, first based on presentation and then etiology. Similarly, there were failed efforts to achieve international consensus pushed by institutions like the American Psychological Association and the World Health Organization; years later, vast discrepancies still exist in the way psychiatrists diagnose schizophrenia across the world.

In the light of these disputes, Woods (2011) claimed that this consistent fuzziness of the concept contributed to it becoming the sublime of the discipline – both psychology's foremost adversary and its savior. This vast history of the conditions that sustained the sublime of the discipline only discloses how resilient the concept and the pathology have been. This chapter will examine the reasons behind this resilience to reveal whether there is something more about schizophrenia than meets the eye, something that makes it indispensable to modern Western subjectivity. The contentious history of schizophrenia we traversed in the previous chapter will help us stay alert to the pitfalls of scientific knowledge and practice devoid of historical consciousness and thus restrict us from naively engaging in the narrative of progress.

To study the structure of the subject – the thinking, feeling, acting, and desiring product of the numerous epistemic forces of Western modernity – is an intimidating task. It requires an attempt to pull apart an entity whose coherence is precarious in the first place. This holds truer for the schizophrenic subject, a marginalized love child of the self-referential nature of the modern episteme and the inherent contradictions it upholds. In attempting to understand the schizophrenic subject as a peculiar twisted permutation of modern subjectivity I run the risk of pulling at the loose threads of language, speech, knowledge, thought, and the *unthought* to encounter an unstoppable deconstruction which leaves us remorseful and more baffled than ever before; on the other hand it might just explain why Karl Jaspers (Woods, 2011) held "ununderstandability" as the heart of this pathology. How is the schizophrenic subject constituted? Born in misrecognition, sustained through myth (or discourse?), propped by meaning, mitigated by symbols, pinned by power, bent by institutions, brutalized by language, violated by ideology, and the originating condition underlying of all of these – primarily psychotic but only occasionally schizophrenic – what kind of subject is this?

This chapter will investigate the emergence and nature of this marginal subject of Western thought, the forever alien, the inherently *Other* – the schizophrenic. To show that the schizophrenic subject is not only a modern product but a specific and radical form of modern subjectivity, I will use the writings of Louis Sass (1994) and Foucault (1994) to delineate the essential epistemological frameworks of modernity. The central schizophrenic features under scrutiny are an excessive hyper-consciousness and an ability to sustain and even thrive in affective and cognitive contradictions, which I will later show are also the defining markers of modernity. Sass has already elaborated on modern art and literature's deep relations with the schizophrenic consciousness; instead of revisiting those arguments I will use

Foucault's (1994) ideas in *The Order of Things* to develop a dialogue about schizophrenia and modern forms of knowledge and knowing. My central thesis is that the schizophrenic subject erupts as a personification of the cracks in the modern epistemology. I will not take the already explored stances that either ridicule the madman for cognitive weakness and unreasoned ignorance or praise him for his desire for truth and his preternatural strength. Instead I carve out the position that the schizophrenic (the madman of our age) suffers not from truth but from a stubborn and strained recognition of processes that constitute how we think, emote, desire, speak, and behave. He is a de-constructor of form, not content.

In the following pages I present a short description of Sass and Foucault's ideas that are relevant to our discussion, and then dive into how schizophrenia is a marginal form of modern subjectivity by investigating the defining features of modern epistemology: man as a subject and an object of knowledge, the nature of self-referential language and schizophrenic speech, and the emergence of the *unthought* and its negotiations with the *cogito*. These theoretical assertions are brought to life by different autobiographical works.

Sass on modernity and madness

Sass (1994) in *Madness and Modernism* posited that the conceptual and relational inaccessibility of schizophrenia is caused by two factors – the heterogeneity of its symptoms and the "ununderstandibility" (to use Jaspers's term) of its presentation. He brings forth buried connections between some basic features of modernity as seen in modern art and literature, and the defining characteristics of schizophrenia. He further contests that under the diversity of symptoms and within the incomprehensibility of behavior and utterances, lies the common ground of hyper-reflexivity which is a modern style of thinking. Modern (and post-modern) art and literature, Sass insists, has the quality of being unnerving, incomprehensible, and disconcerting – all of which are reminiscent of the "praecox feeling". I believe that this "praecox feeling" the schizophrenic also engenders is due to his extreme personification of the era's epistemological tensions – he does not live in another world, instead he makes strange and inhospitable the world we all live in. Both modernism and madness, as we will later observe, present themselves in contradictions where self-reflexivity and detachment eventually lead modern values and schizophrenic symptoms to turn upon themselves and morph into their opposite (Sass, 1994).

Sass names many features of modern art that are reflected in madness, for example, a non-traditionalism on one hand but also a caricaturized sycophancy on the other. "Derealization" and "unworlding" occur when the external world loses its position as external, as seen in Mallarme' poetry, which was "preoccupied with its own sound and syntax, seeking to negate rather than to evoke a realm of external objects and events" (Sass, 1994, p. 32). These features – unworlding, marked self-referentiality, extreme perspectivism, and a rejection of both convention and representation – define both modern art and modern madness, but according to Sass it is hyper-reflexivity and alienation that mark crucial parallels between modernism and madness. The former is essential to my conceptualization.

Hyper-reflexivity: when process becomes content

According to Sass and Parnas (2003), despite the numerous, flexible, and ever-changing signs and symptoms that have qualified as schizophrenia over the decades, the heart of disorder is a disturbance in consciousness and our experience of our self: what they refer to as ipseity. Their phenomenological analysis reveals two forms of disturbance in the sense of self: hyper-reflexivity and diminished self-affection. Hyper-reflexivity is an enhanced and even bizarre self-awareness where the parts of our self which normally remain in the background come under extreme scrutiny and attention, and eventually become objectified as external to our self. It is not a simple hyper-awareness of our self, image, identity, or an object of the psyche, for example, an obsessive thought. Instead it is a hyper-consciousness of "phenomena and processes that would normally remain in the tacit background of awareness" (Sass, 2007b, p. 69) which now feel strange and alienated.

This disturbance in ipseity leads to problems in maintaining perceptual and conceptual hold (Sass, 2007b). These self-disturbances that underlie superficial categorizations like positive, negative, and disorganized symptoms can also be seen in prodromal phases of the disorder. To exemplify perceptual disorganization in prodromal phases of illness, we can turn to the 1951 autobiographical account of "Renee" (Sechehaye & Rubin-Rabson, 1979) from *The Autobiography of a Schizophrenic Girl*. Renee was six when a feeling of unreality came over her while jumping ropes with her friends, and she found that her friend Alice became larger as she came closer:

> Though I saw her as she was, still, it was not she. Standing at the other end of the rope, she had seemed smaller, but the nearer we approached each other, the taller she grew, the more she swelled up in size.
>
> *(p. 23)*

Normally, when an object comes closer and its retinal image becomes larger, most people are able to contextualize distance and other cues to understand that its literal size has not changed, which is otherwise known as size constancy. But problems in perceptual hold, especially in contextualizing figure and ground, might not allow the schizophrenic the luxury of context. Later, Renee faces a similar problem in drawing class: "I seemed to have lost a sense of perspective. So I copied the model from a school-mate's sketch, thus lending a false perspective from where I sat" (p. 29). Thus, this disturbance is an ineffable alteration in the fundamental starting point which is normally a prerequisite for all our experience, cognition, and consciousness.

Further, phenomenological research with patients subverts our traditional understanding that they mostly experience flat affect and that catatonics are not in touch with reality. The subjective experience of patients differs vastly and many report acute awareness of their surroundings, increased affective arousal, and desire for intimacy despite overt signs of asociality (Arieti, 1961; as cited in Sass & Parnas, 2003). I will revisit this juxtaposition of emotional flatness with emotional reactivity while talking about schizophrenic paradoxes. Thus, in hyper-reflexivity the tacit becomes focal (like anomalous realization of bodily sensations, subtle thoughts, and underlying affects we never pay attention to) due to diminished self-affectation – "the tacit is no longer being inhabited as a medium for taken-for-granted selfhood" (Sass & Parnas, 2003, p. 430). Eventually the fluidity and effortlessness that is inherent in inhabiting our own body schema and the easy felt sense of conscious awareness are all eroded to create someone whose meta-awareness causes them to not inhabit the lived world but instead focus on it.

While Sass outlines various parallels between schizophrenia and modernism, especially in modern art and literature, it is Foucault who has written extensively about modern knowledge. It is essential to revisit his conceptualization of Western epistemology to further our theoretical investigation of the schizophrenic's odd subjective position in the modern era.

The Order of Things: an introduction

In *The Order of Things*, Foucault (1994) attempted to excavate the nature of knowledge through the Renaissance, Classical, and Modern epistemes, and man's relationship to that knowledge. He unearthed the implicit structures and formations of thought that inform what constitutes knowledge in a certain time period. The constraints of rules of thought on every episteme make certain forms of knowledge unthinkable. As a result, unlike man in the modern episteme, the classical subject could never appear in knowledge as men were the locus but not the source of representation, and the questioning of the source of representation was a modern endeavor (Gutting, 1989). Gutting (1989), in *Michel Foucault's Archaeology of Scientific Reason*, states that the absence of "man" in the classical age meant that "there was no way of representing representation itself and therefore no way of knowing representation as one object among others" (p. 199).

What is of most interest to us is the change from classical to modern episteme where Foucault (1994) insists "man" came into existence: "He is quite a recent creature, which the demiurge of knowledge fabricated with its own hands less than two hundred years ago" (p. 308). An intense reflexivity marks the modern episteme where representation becomes representable, that is, the human faculty to be able to represent is no longer tacit, and no longer the only way of constituting knowledge and responding to the world – instead it is just another faculty and becomes an object to be explored. Foucault charts this change to the great turn of modern philosophy where Kant places representation under the epistemological radar as he states that the factors that limit us also make knowledge possible; for example, concepts of space, time, and causality, which were once implicit, now come to the fore and are understood as both ways of thinking/being that limit us, but also at the same time the conditions that make all we can know possible. What is important to note here is man's newfound ability to self-reflect on representation which was impossible in the classical episteme; the representing "man" becomes an object of knowledge – what was once an underlying process of conditions of knowledge is now under inspection. No longer identical to all thought or consciousness, representation is now an object and not just its structure but its origin, and the conditions that make representation possible must be studied. Thus, we must look "beyond its immediate visibility, in a sort of behind-the-scenes world even deeper and more dense than representation itself" (Foucault, 1994, p. 238).

I would note here that it is after all in this episteme that consciousness studies as a field of inquiry arose with its constant tension between understanding consciousness from a first- or third-person perspective. Merleau-Ponty's phenomenological understanding falls in the former category while Crick and Koch's (1998) scientific work on neural correlates of consciousness fits the latter. It is this episteme that made it possible to investigate neurons on one hand, and pure experience on the other, without ever being able to resolve the problem of causal direction, the moment of their emergence, or the nature of their interaction. Seminal essays and theories attempting to untangle this very oscillation between studying consciousness as an object or subject range from David Chalmers's (1995) hard problem of consciousness, Daniel Dennett's (1991) rejection of first-person experience, and Nagel's (1974) pivotal essay "What it's like to be a bat". It is in this episteme that modern philosophy in a positivist spirit reduced consciousness to mere empirical objects.

This and many other questions about the origin of representation were partially made visible by Kant's critique. Knowledge in the modern episteme, then, is forever doomed to oscillate; on one hand it holds "man" as a transcendental object (empirical sciences) defined by language (philology), life (biology), and labor (economics), and on the other, a transcendental subject constituting all these "positivities". It fluctuates between the poles of the *cogito* and the *unthought*, and enters into a doomed pursuit of the origin of the forever-receding "man". Our interest is in this epistemic reflexivity which resonates with Sass's assertion that the defining feature of the schizophrenic condition is hyper-reflexivity where the tacit processes of our thinking become objects of the psyche leading to an awkward deliberation in speech and acts. Human sciences, of which psychology is one type, is situated in this field of modern knowledge, and schizophrenia, the champion of psychology, incorporates in the extreme all the features that inform this knowledge.

The god and the machine: living the doublet

According to Foucault (1994), knowledge in the modern age could be broadly divided into mathematics, philosophy, and empirical sciences (later the human sciences); the latter two are of interest to us as they were to him. The empirical sciences study man as an object, defined and pinned by the historical forces of language, labor, and life. Here man is seen to be constituted by powers/forces outside his control, and studied as an object of knowledge. On the other hand, philosophy (and later human sciences) aims to study man as a subject – the one who constitutes history and the forces that define and pin him in the first place. Foucault emphasizes the importance of history in the modern episteme, where the empirical sciences of philology, economics, and biology are all historicized and fall into the category of transcendental objectivism (as man is constituted by forces of labor, language, life). It is here that man becomes an object as he is constituted by the history he has no control over – the language that that was spoken before him and the burden of older meanings; his economic dependence on the value of commodities constituted by the tools, labor, and forms of production which went into it before him; and his biology, which also conforms to the historical forces of the environment and heredity. He is essentially historical and temporal, and as Gutting (1989) so succinctly paraphrases "Man as an object – that is, of the empirical sciences – appears as a finite being, limited by the environment, forces of production, and linguistic heritage that have formed him" (p. 199).

But while constituted by these forces, he is also simultaneously constituting them – he is the condition of possibility of knowledge and the object of the same knowledge. This oscillation between the "fundamental" and the "positive" is at the heart of the modern project of knowledge: "Man, in the analytic of finitude, is a strange empirico-transcendental doublet, since he is a being such that knowledge will be attained in him of what renders all knowledge possible" (Foucault, 1994, p. 318). As mentioned above, consciousness studies and debates regarding its nature, structure, and emergence are an excellent example of Foucault's observation that the modern episteme experiences a dissection in terms of its management of man as an object of history and a subject of knowledge.

Where then does the schizophrenic subject fit in this epistemological disjunction between transcendental objectivity of the empirical sciences which find the conditions of the subject's experience in the object, and the transcendental subjectivity of Kant that looks in the subject for the conditions of representing the object? The question we need to be asking is – where else has the experience of being all-powerful and all-helpless, being constituted, and constituting, being limited and at the same time limitless existed in the same person if not the schizophrenic? For as man is determined by history, so is history determined by man. The schizophrenic presents himself as the supreme subject and the utterly objectified, violently limited and absolutely boundless – both god and machine. Laing (1990) once said that the schizophrenic lives out his fragile existential position as his real position – "A 'truth' about his 'existential position' is lived as 'really' true" (p. 36). He meant that the charades and delusions presented by the schizophrenic are literal renditions of his dual subjective felt-position as completely exposed, and at the same time, utterly isolated. I would instead say that the schizophrenic lives out his dual epistemological position (in the modern era) as his real position. In other words, "man" (Foucault's modern man for whom representation is but one form of thinking) and schizophrenia co-emerge. Elyn Saks (2007) who spent most of her student life in institutions with the diagnosis of schizophrenia writes in *The Center Cannot Hold* of the forces that controlled her in the form of commands:

> The origin of the commands was unclear. In my mind, they were issued by some sort of beings. Not real people with names or faces, but shapeless, powerful beings that controlled me with thoughts (not voices) that had been placed in my head … It never occurred to me that disobedience was an option … *I do not make the rules. I just follow them.*
>
> (p. 84)

This experience of being slave to powerful forces oscillates with contradictory ideas of all-powerfulness as she screeches to her analyst: "I *am* in control. I control the world. The world is at my whim. I control the world and everything in it" (p. 92) or later: "You *are* under my control. You go where I go. There will be no separation. I have killed people before and I will kill them again. I give life and I take it away" (p. 111). Much like man in the modern age, who shifts between being a historical product and producing history, but in an increasingly bizarre and aggravated manner, the schizophrenic shuttles back and forth between being omnipotent and impotent.

Daniel Paul Schreber's (2000) *Memoirs of My Nervous Illness* is an important first-person narrative that speaks to this. Schreber's work is of historical significance to psychoanalysis as Freud's interpretation of the case allowed him to expound on the nature and cause of paranoid delusions and while the theory itself was heavily critiqued by the likes of Melanie Klein, Gilles Deleuze and Felix Guattari, Freud's work on Schreber's case is still considered his first big statement on what causes psychosis (Zuk & Zuk, 1995). Sass (1994) too interprets this work and points to a dissonance in how the divine rays controlled Schreber's nerves and nerve-language: "At times Schreber believed he was as wide as all space, that his boundaries were coextensive with the universe. Yet he would sometimes maintain that his actions, both physical and mental, were entirely out of his control …" (p. 244). The schizophrenic is therefore captured in the radically lived-out personification of modern man's dual existence as the empirico-transcendental doublet, exaggerated beyond recognition into someone who at the same time objectifies not just the contents of his psyche (thoughts, images) but the processes of his psyche, all the while being the supreme subject – the knower and the known. An example of this is someone experiencing "ideas of reference", a common delusion that he is the *object* of everyone's attention and thought, the center of the universe. I would suggest that the two extremes of the empirico-transcendental doublet converge in this one symptom, where the schizophrenic subject is at once the object of all gazes and glares, which might make him feel small and fearful, but also oddly confer on him a specialness and importance – a grandness.

Eleanor Longden (2013), a popular voice of the Hearing Voices movement, shares her experience of being diagnosed with schizophrenia in a TED Talk. She jokingly cites Oscar Wilde when speaking of her terrifying hallucinations which would pass constant commentary on her actions and thoughts – "There is only one thing in life worse than being talked about, and that is not being talked about". Despite the humorous note, she is alluding to the sense of grandness that the schizophrenic assumes is conferred onto them while also being terrorized by the same attention. Clifford Beers writes in *A Mind That Found Itself* (Peterson, 1982): "For with an insane ingenuity I managed to connect myself with almost every crime of importance of which I had ever read", again pointing to the same paradoxical grandness and terror. This is also reflected in Laing's (1990) assertion about the schizoid person: "His whole life has been torn between his desire to reveal himself and his desire to conceal himself" (p. 37). This strange mix of being pinned by others' thoughts, which is sometimes felt as a reality (they are killing me with their thoughts, they control me with their thoughts), and at the same time being the subject of their thinking can be differentiated like this: "*They* are thinking about me" versus "They are thinking about *me*".

Between certitude and indifference

Sass has rightly pointed to an intriguing element of the way schizophrenics treat their delusions with both certitude and indifference, which explains why most do not act on their delusions despite subscribing to a belief. Thus, the delusions might be "unshakable, and no logical argument or empirical evidence is capable of undermining the patient's commitment to them" (Sass, 1994, p. 274) but despite the certitude, a person who persists that there are aliens inside his head *rarely* drills a hole to drag them out. A similar unreality is prevalent in hallucinations where most patients, while perceiving vivid sounds and visions, are still somehow aware that they lack objectivity "with real-world referents or sources" (Sass, 1994, p. 275).

How can we explain this certitude and the co-existing indifference observed by Sass? I propose that the schizophrenic's position towards his delusions is that he takes them very seriously but not literally. For example, Renee from *The Autobiography of a Schizophrenic Girl* (Sechehaye & Rubin-Rabson, 1979) who on one hand experiences intense terror ("The Fear") as she is sure that the world is ending, on the other hand also says: "Nonetheless, I did not believe that the world would be destroyed as I believed in real facts" (p. 34). While Sass explains this through double-bookkeeping of the schizophrenic mind, we can instead note how the complete *absorption* in both extreme epistemological positions (as empirical object and transcendental subject) make the schizophrenic take his delusions with utmost seriousness (I am absolutely killing babies with my thoughts – Saks), but the constant *oscillation* voids the belief of any sort of objective reality. The hyper-reflexivity that allows the schizophrenic, rather forces them, to deconstruct and focus on cognitive, affective, and linguistic background process thus leads them to recognize their own dual position as both constituted and constituting, and see through the flimsy disjunction that holds the extremes together, which then explains the indifference towards otherwise unshakable delusions. At the same time, the absorption in the dual positions leads to the certitude of the same delusions. In other words, while absorption leads to certitude (taking delusions seriously), the oscillation causes indifference (not taking them literally). How do you strongly believe a belief you don't actually believe? You do it if you are aware of it being a construction, when you feel that you are constituted by numerous forces – rays, thoughts, etc. but are also constituting them as you accurately note that they are constructions of your own mind. Even in the throes of psychosis, Saks accurately perceived that her violent thoughts of having murdered children were only thoughts, but that knowledge did not abate her terror or her conviction regarding the belief.

So the schizophrenic subject might be sure that he is an omnipotent god or dictator, but this belief cannot be taken literally because of the opposing awareness of being completely limited and immobilized by various forces, and vice versa. This explains why Saks, while experiencing overwhelming terror and thinking she was killing babies with her thoughts, still never did anything about it. It should be noted that it is not always that schizophrenics do not act on their delusions, but there is a large number of mostly non-paranoid patients who maintain this peculiar dual position.

As a side note, while explaining the conflict between the empirico-transcendental doublet of the modern era, Foucault (1994) does wonder if there is a form of knowledge that can hold the tension between the two extremes, "a discourse whose tension would keep separate the empirical and the transcendental, while being directed at both" (p. 320). For a moment there, Husserl's phenomenology seems to be the answer but Foucault disregards that as he concedes that even phenomenology eventually reduces man to the empirical. The question that arises is: "Does the schizophrenic, in personifying the schism of modern knowledge, hold this said tension?" Unfortunately the answer is no. This is because in personifying this said ambivalence, the schizophrenic, instead of holding the tension, gets absorbed by both positions – he is inundated by the terror of being a machine and the glory of being god. Reminding ourselves of this ensures we do not romanticize an agonizing experience as some form of ultimate truth.

The un-grounding of language

> I remember as one of my most unpleasant experiences that I began to see handwriting on the sheets of my bed staring me in the face, and not me alone ... On each fresh sheet placed over me I would soon begin to see words, sentences, and signatures, all in my own handwriting. Yet I could not decipher any of the words ...
> *(Clifford Beers in* A Mind That Found Itself, *cited in Peterson, 1982, p. 166)*

To understand the relation between language in the modern era and schizophrenic speech, we have to first observe how the nature and function of language changes over time. Foucault (1994) claims that the sign's sole function in the classical age was representation – its nature was exhausted through directly representing an object. Since representation was considered the origin and background of all thought in this episteme, we could not reflectively shift attention on the background to objectify it, and create knowledge about it. The emergence of language as an object of knowledge, and questions regarding its nature became possible because discourse and representation became detached and "the being of language itself became, as it were, fragmented ... Thought was brought back, and violently so, towards language itself, towards its unique and difficult being" (Foucault, 1994, p. 306).

The simple function of all signs in the classical episteme was direct representation and all consciousness was representative. It is not until the modern episteme that consciousness is "no longer regarded as intrinsically representational and questions are raised as to how the mind is able to form thoughts and represent objects" (Gutting, 1989, p. 151). It takes a turn of events, a different way of ordering knowledge and thoughts – the modern episteme – that brings with it an inward *hyper-focus* on all that made knowledge possible, which then shifts the axis of knowledge to make representation one of the ways man coordinates and organizes sense data. Modern literature doesn't only tell stories about things – it's not just representative – but rather it focuses *on* language, on its nature and structure; it exists and operates for its own sake (Sass, 1994).

This can be observed in other contemporary works of art too, for example, the 1998 song "Teardrop" written and sung by Elizabeth Fraser for the band Massive Attack. The first time I heard the song I was both mesmerized by Fraser's ethereal voice but also flummoxed because the song was entirely incomprehensible. After ensuring that it was indeed in English, I discovered that Fraser had mastered a form of singing that focuses on the texture of the words rather than their meaning. In an undated radio interview, Fraser explains her style and says that her focus was on "sound rather than meaning" (Wilson, 2009) which is why she sometimes uses foreign words without any adherence to their context and signification, based only on their feel and texture when she sings it. Even when in English, Fraser's songs like "Teardrop" are nearly impossible to understand because of her distinctive and odd focus on syllables and sounds. If we consider the fact that her singing is *process-* and not *content*-governed, and that the purpose is not to narrate a love story but to excavate the sound and *feel* of words, then meaning becomes a constraint and the feel of other languages, unrestrained by reference, would indeed provide a certain sense of freedom.

One can similarly observe an intriguing epistemic shift in recent times: the focus on language is no more the lone prerogative of the linguist, the analyst, or the schizophrenic. Words have, in a way, replaced things. The birth of a narrative around the concept of micro-aggressions, verbal abuse, neglect, correct pronouns, verbalization of traumatic event as therapeutics, and appropriate labels (like "neurotypicals") could only have happened in a time where language itself came under the focus of knowledge – an interrogation of word. I do not want in any way to imply that this is progressive or regressive, it just is. What concerns us are the conditions of thought that made these epistemic priorities possible. The explosion of language around things (as seen in schizophrenia too) is not without consequence, it creates different iterations of identity and deconstructs old ones that appeared natural. This emphasis bolsters and is assisted by increasing mentalization, as we live in a world that holds our inner experience as supreme. Often times this translates to words gaining more importance than actions. We are no more in a time where "one good deed equals a thousand words", and again this is not a good or a bad thing – it is a mesmerizing thing. A perfect example is a glance at one of the most popular and populous sources of the written word – the Harry Potter fandom (the author spends an inappropriate amount of time on these forums). Most people in this fandom, which consists of millions, agree that the character of Severus Snape was clearly that of a villain. They point to his verbal bullying and offensive language, and the sacrifice of his life for the right cause does not matter as much as the psychological turmoil he caused his students. The discourse about discourse, the victory (transient?) of language over action, valuing words as much as things – is just one fascinating example of this episteme's style of thinking. Thus the medium is no longer latent, and language:

> becomes the object of knowledge, we see it reappearing in a strictly opposite modality: a silent, cautious deposition of the word upon the whiteness of a piece of paper, where it can possess neither sound nor interlocutor, where it has nothing to say but itself, nothing to do but shine in the brightness of its being.
> *(Foucault, 1994, p. 300)*

It is here that its similarity to schizophrenic signs can be traced.

Foucault states that the function of language becomes more than representation; its study (philology) is enamored by its grammatical system and structure. Yet again, we can observe here an inward turn where the tacit moves to the foreground – the system that made communication possible is made an object of study. If we understand the schizophrenic condition as an exaggerated personification of such epistemic changes, we can see how these changes are reflected here: an awkwardness and tension seeps through the schizophrenic's communicative attempts because consciousness has shifted towards words, grammar, and the inherent processes of language and speaking. As modern empirical science focuses on the formal systems of language, the schizophrenic focuses on the background systems of signs. For that matter, according to Foucault (1994), one of the features of modern language was that it lost the central position that it occupied in the classical episteme to become just another object of knowledge (but not completely reduced to it), implying yet another reflexive turn from the classical to the modern episteme. Similarly, the reflexive inward turn of the schizophrenic consciousness precludes fluidity of being, which then turns rigid under the harsh eye of attention.

The central point being made here is that in an episteme where the focus of knowledge is on the structure and systems of language (as in literature or philology), the marginal and schizophrenic subject in an embellished personification displays speech which is measured, catatonic, awkward – too aware of its own structure. But what about the numerous other explanations of schizophrenic language? While the biomedical model considers schizophrenic speech to be of no prognostic importance or a mere epiphenomena of pathological neural activity, there are other theories which insist that the schizophrenic, through his nonsensical utterances or his absurd word associations, is attempting to represent either his biographical history, like past traumatic events (as understood by the Hearing Voices movement) or his current psychological position (Laing's famous exposition of Kraepelin's patient); he could even be testing others' intention and attention. It is a valid concern to figure out whether hidden in the bizarre words there can be metaphorical meanings but this explanation does not apply to the whole range of phenomena. There are, after all, those who present no history of traumatic events and those who are not undermining their psychiatrist's interpretations. This is especially important to note since we live in an aggressively psychologized time where inner feelings and deepest thoughts, that is, a person's interiority, are constantly under observation and forced into meaning. It is thus difficult to reposition ourselves to notice how some of the ways schizophrenics use language might not have much to do with meaning or representation, but with the nature of language itself – the sound, spatiality, and the concrete nature of the sign. The schizophrenic language, akin to epistemological understandings of language in the modern episteme and the nature of language in modern literature, does not exhaust itself through representational functions – it is more than signification or the communication of ideas, feelings, or experiences for the schizophrenic.

It is not that schizophrenics are incapable of using signs for representation; for that matter, many resort to lucid communication when in preferred company or emergent situations. For example, Schreber's (2000) asylum and district medical officer's report states that "The patient is in command of great many ideas and can discourse on them in an orderly fashion" (p. 343). Further, when the topic of conversation was not his delusions but something that was of interest to him like politics, art, or law, the officer stated that "Doctor Schreber showed keen interest, detailed knowledge, good memory, and correct judgment ..." (Schreber, 2000, p. 343). Amidst his dramatic delusions of controlling rays and divine beings, he could still hold a normal conversation. Similarly, during my clinical internship in Delhi where I was working with long-term rehabilitation-center patients, many of whom were diagnosed schizophrenics, I observed that they displayed selective lucidity. My former schizophrenic patient "X", who showed dramatic poverty of speech and compulsively used repetitive phrases, was on one occasion able to stop his catatonic gestures and in a clear, linear, lucid manner, was able to communicate his feelings by saying "Of course I feel hurt, of course it feels awful". This was in response to my exasperated inquiry "Don't you get sick of people treating you like shit?" Similarly, Elyn Saks, with excruciating difficulty, was able to hold normal conversations at school and with her friends and would only allow herself to *indulge* in her psychosis with her Kleinian therapist Mrs. Jones.

Thus, I am not suggesting that all schizophrenic utterances are devoid of meaning; instead I assert that the usage of signs takes a deeply reflexive turn that is characteristically seen in modern literature (Sass, 1994) and becomes frozen, awkward, and outlandish – "Inside my head, my voice sounded like an old LP record on a very slow speed" says Saks of her perception of her own speech (Saks, 2007, p. 158). Let's consider an example – the word "book" not only represents a book but it has a vocal, visual, and tactile quality, and just as easily could be associated with "hook" or "crook"; sentences could be deconstructed phonetically, grammatically, syntactically; the word could have a taste, a smell (features that are found in synesthetes and not just schizophrenics) and uttering it could induce muscle movement of mouth and tongue that always remained implicit for others. I already noted this style of speech in the music of Elizabeth Fraser, specifically in the song "Teardrop". In a psychotic break in front of her Yale law professor, Saks (2007) chimes: "Because I'm tall, I fall …. Lemons, memos, and mass murders" (p. 139). The most obvious link between "tall" and "fall" is the sound "aal", and between lemons, memos, and mass murders is the sound "umm". Her speech is not just about meaning but also about sound – the form of the words, and the structure of the signs. For that matter, the only time Saks speaks of an inability to track conversation, it is due to a side effect of Trilafon.

What happens when language comes under its own glare? If a swimmer decides to focus intensely on the nature, structure, and/or on the form of his own strokes – he can swim no more. To operate in the world is to forget about the world, at least to some degree. While some schools of thought might consider making the implicit explicit, through meditative states, to be desirable, the schizophrenic has little control over what gets scorched under the heat of conscious thought. Similarly, language, usually a medium of representation, when out under the reflexive glare of consciousness ceases to function as communicative – we witness this in the absurdity of speech or in the complete poverty of it. Signs as they turn inwards (*not* doubling upon themselves as in the classical age where they have to represent themselves) become both heavy, as their construction and texture comes to the center (how does the word "book" feel in my mouth, how does my tongue move when I say it, or sing it – what is its *feel* like?) and turn hollow. It is this dense hollowness that concerns us.

As Foucault observed, language in the modern episteme is not directly attached to things – signs are not incantations that can affect the real world as in the Renaissance; they also don't merely represent things as in the classical episteme. Since it is not a thing and neither does it only point to things (signification as a function), the groundless nature of language becomes evident: what I am calling its dense hollowness. Disjunctive phonemes and meaningless graphemes – language for the schizophrenic subject can have the terrifying and liberating quality of groundlessness, untied to things, unattached from the world and yet at the same time tied to itself and attached to its own presentation (phonetic, visual, structural). It resonates with Elizabeth Fraser's assertion that meaninglessness gave her freedom (Wilson, 2009). As Foucault (1994) says:

> To the Nietzschean question: "Who is speaking", Mallarme replies – and constantly reverts to that reply – by saying that what is speaking is, in its solitude, in its fragile vibration, in its nothingness, the word itself – not the meaning of the word, but its enigmatic and precarious being.
>
> *(p. 305)*

While some may contend that this dissociation with things lets the sign run loose and present itself in the disconnected speech of the schizophrenic who dismantles all syntactic, grammatical, and semantic convention (and indeed this might be the case sometimes), I instead think that it actually reifies under the weight of its own groundlessness, becomes rigid when confronted with its hollow nature, and presents instead as half-eaten sentences, agonizingly repetitive phrases, caricaturizing repetition of others' dialogues (echolalia), dislocated words, and paucity of speech – "the language of modern literature is totally ungrounded and wanders with 'no point of departure, no end and no promise'" (Gutting, 1989, p. 197).

Schreber (2000) alludes to this rigid repetition and half-baked speech when he speaks of nerve-language, vibrations that correspond to words – "for a long time now the voices had consisted only of a terrible, monotonous repetition of ever-recurring phrases" (p. 59). Schreber's asylum and district medical officer points to Schreber having "attacks of bellowing" as he himself called them. The medical officer describes these as "utterings of partly inarticulate sounds ... These noisy outbursts occur completely automatically and in a compulsive manner against the patient's will" (p. 345). Similarly, a six-year-old Renee (Sechehaye & Rubin-Rabson, 1979) describes a trip to the principal's office where she is inundated by suffocating dread caused by the harsh and artificial brilliance of electric light. She feels others around her to be mere puppets with voices that were "metallic, without warmth or color" (p. 26) and words had a life of their own: "from time to time, a word detached itself from the rest. It repeated itself over and over in my head, absurd, as if cut off by a knife" (p. 26). These are not examples of attempted meaning-making or even signs running loose – they are cases where word is free from meaning but enslaved by sound. It now makes sense that schizophrenia itself, as we observed in Chapter 2, has been marked by an almost absurd proliferation of words around it.

We still face the threat of meaning, which is not easy to discard, and rightly so; I am referring to the question of whether schizophrenic speech is meaningful or not. To say "no" is to invite practices that have knowingly or unknowingly been abusive (numerous cases where patients complain of life-threatening injuries but are ignored because the madman speaks nothing of use), but to say "yes" allows the possibility of faulty and flimsy projective interpretations many patients are contemptuous of. Lara Jefferson's (Fadiman & Kewman, 1979) self-disclosure of her madness in a Midwest mental hospital gives us a peek into her thinking. She openly states her disdain for those (including herself) who analyze her behavior, interpret her thoughts, and indulge in "crooked philosophizing", without ever being able to really help – she calls the doctor "too damned wise ... They have got us all analyzed and psychoanalyzed down to insignificant daubs of protoplasm" (p. 24).

My ex-patient X would compulsively smile and ask everyone in the ward: "Hello madam, how are you?" and respond with equal courtesy "I'm good. Thank you". On the one hand, keeping in mind the punitive environment of the rehabilitation center, it only makes sense that he would attempt to ingratiate himself to those in power. On the other hand, there was something sickly sweet about the greeting, which would be awarded irrespective of whether the staff was kind to him or threatening him with various forms of punishment (and there were many). The phrase "Hello madam, how are you doing?" is courteous in a certain context but when repeated over and over, especially in the face of threats and punishments, it turns on itself to become a caricature of courtesy. It transforms into a type of subversion disguised as subservience displayed by some schizophrenics and known in extreme forms as echopraxia, where the patient not only does every little thing he is told but imitates the doctor's every move. The words spoken by X probably represented neither his obsequious nature nor his attempts at ingratiation; when repeated in different ways, with different intonations, they curved inwards to become hollow and caricaturized, devoid of meaning, stubborn in their presentation, and thick in texture – they became autonomous.

The density of one's gaze on those signs turns them into stone, losing their fluidity, ruining the flow of language, and the ease of human communication. Laing (1990) presents the case of Julie, a chronic schizophrenic who calls herself Mrs. Taylor because she insists "I'm tailor-made. I'm a tailored maid; I was made, fed, clothed, and tailored" (p. 192). This small excerpt exemplifies a statement that could be both relevant in terms of what it is attempting to convey (which Laing interprets) while at the same time being tied to the sounds and the structure of words. Where once ordering of the world through relations of identity and difference allowed for representation (Foucault, 1994), now the reflexive turn of the modern era gets condensed in the marginal schizophrenic subject for whom language is no more a justified and unquestioned medium.

Language and the doublet

Foucault pointing to the historical turn taken by language allows us to revisit how life, labor, and language constitute man, and his dual epistemological position. Language as historical implies that the words we speak are not our own but their meanings have been defined and their usage has been predetermined in turn affecting what we *can* say and how we say it (in turn defining what we can be, think, and feel). Language bears the burden of past meanings; it is out of our control, as people express their "thoughts in words of which they are not the masters" (Foucault, 1994, p. 96). As observed in the previous section, which concerned itself with man's dual position and the schizophrenic's personification of the same, man as constituted by the historicity of language points to one extreme of that position. Schreber's delusions regarding nerve-language are an excellent example of being restrained and forced into submission by the external force of language.

Nerve-language for Schreber is an internal form of language that is without the use of external parts like lips; he likens it to a silent succession of words that we try to commit to our memory. While people inscribed in the normal "Order of the World" are unaware of this language, according to Schreber, he is made aware due to his nervous illness. This is reminiscent of the schizophrenic's intense inward focus on background cognitive processes that are invisible to others because others are, in not being aware of them, masters of them. Similarly, he says that others are masters of this language but he is not as his nerves are made to vibrate by *forces outside his control* (and each of these vibrations corresponds to different words) – "my nerves have been set in motion *from without* incessantly and without respite" (Schreber, 2000, p. 55). He calls these forces divine rays, so that now he is no more the master of his nerve-language, which then leads to "compulsive thinking". It is interesting to note here that Sass (1994) compares Schreber's nerve-language to inner speech, for example both Schreber's nerve-language and inner speech have in common the removal of unnecessary words. Such an acute focus on the processes of speech and language, processes that normally remain tacit so language can be used to communicate, points to the same reflexivity referred to earlier. Schreber's (2000) dramatic description of his nerve-language being controlled by exogenous forces other than himself – "the influence of the rays forced my nerves to perform the movements corresponding to the use of these words" (p. 56) – is eerily reminiscent of the modern epistemological strand of language as a historical object impinging upon and constituting the modern subject.

This graphic expression of how language's historicity limits the subject doesn't only correspond to Sass's description of hyper-reflexivity towards inner speech but also to Foucault's assertion of language's epistemological position corresponding with one extreme of the empirico-transcendental doublet. But there is another end to this extreme. Foucault insists that to overcome the loss of control over language, modern thought attempted to either formalize language so that thought would not be dependent on it, or tried to develop a critical interpretation to understand the implicit meanings. In keeping with modern thought's attempts to regulate language, howsoever misguided or brilliant they may be, the schizophrenic situation might involve attempts to gain complete dominion over the realm of the symbolic. An excellent example of this is found in Joanne (Hannah) Green's (1989) semi-autobiographical novel *I Never Promised You a Rose Garden*, where the protagonist Deborah creates her own language, Yri, which is spoken in the kingdom of Yr. Not only does her alternate world of Yr have its own language but more importantly it also has *its own logic*, which is different from "Earth logic". Of interest to us is that Yri allows Deborah to say and feel things that "Earth language" fails to; it has a representation function but is more than that. She has complete jurisdiction over this language which no one else can access or understand. The creation of Yri is not a choice but an obligation:

> In recent years thoughts often came, and happenings also, for which there seemed no sharer on the hard earth, and so the plains, pits, and peaks of Yr began to echo a growing vocabulary to frame its strange agonies and grandeurs.
>
> *(Green, 1989, p. 45)*

The inwardness, intensity, and function of this language can be perceived in the following dialogue between Deborah and her doctor:

> "And it has a language of its own?" the doctor asked, remembering the alluring words and the withdrawal that came after them.
>
> "Yes," Deborah said. "It is a secret language, and there is a Latinated cover-language that I use sometimes – but that's only a screen really, a fake."
>
> "You can't use the real one all the time?"
>
> Deborah laughed because it was an absurd question. "It would be like powering a firefly with lightning bolts."
>
> "Yet you sound quite competent in English."
>
> "English is for the world – for getting disappointed by and getting hated in. Yri is for saying what is to be said."
>
> *(Green, 1989, p. 53)*

These two dialogues present a strange paradox – Deborah did not choose to create Yri; instead it seems something that burst out of her, impinged itself on her, and at the same time there is the reality that she did indeed create this symbolic structure with its own inherent logic out of thin air, and utilized it at times and places when "Earth language" failed her – she was both its slave and its master, immobilized by it and its architect.

Schizophrenic speech is, as we have observed, marred by an inward turn; it is also rife with tensions, and riddled with historical burdens – as is language itself is the modern era. On the one hand, schizophrenic speech is an excellent example of man's objectified reduction in the empirico-transcendental doublet because it twists under its own burden by becoming a mere object – frozen, narrow, and completely constituted by external and internal forces. On the other hand, "Yri" shows us how, when it oscillates to the other end, it can create a supreme subject who can build words, meaning, and logic out of thin air, all-constituting and all-powerful. It again reflects to us Foucault's assertions on the tensions of knowledge in the modern era and man's place in it.

From blinding clarity to clear blindness

The third and last epistemological feature of the modern era observed by Foucault and reflected in the schizophrenic condition is the attempt of modern philosophy to resolve the analytic of finitude through its inspection of the oscillation between the Cartesian *cogito* and the *unthought*. According to Foucault (1994), "the modern cogito does not lead to an affirmation of being, but it does lead to a whole series of questions concerned with being" (p. 325), in effect problematizing a presumption about the relationship between knowledge and being that was once taken for granted. As the *cogito* is confronted with the *unthought*, modern man can no more presume his existence from the fact of his clear consciousness (his thinking). Just as the taken-for-granted existence of being is shattered for "man", so is the grounded self no more an assurance for the schizophrenic. As background processes of thought come under inspection, thinking can no longer sustain being; after all, schizophrenics are known to cast doubt over their existence and point to the fragility of their being – the Cartesian *cogito* does not come to their rescue with reassurances that they think is the proof that they are.

Foucault (1994) expounded that the modern episteme must take into consideration the Other *in* our consciousness. The Cartesian *cogito* defined by its open clarity that makes transparent and accessible even half-baked thoughts, illusions, and dreams, is now incomplete without that which is opaque and unknown in our self, the *unthought*. As Foucault (1994) enigmatically states: "What must I be, I who think and who am my thought, in order to be what I do not think, in order for my thought to be what I am not" (p. 324). This *unthought* of modern philosophy is what will later transform to become the unconscious of the human sciences. What is of significance is that the schizophrenic subject, in his characteristic exaggerated manner, lives out these two polarities in real life. The exaggerated split between the all-seeing conscious *cogito* and the opaque *unthought* that fights inclusion in this clarity can be observed in the delusions of enlightenment. On the one hand, patients vehemently assert that they have the answers to life, the universe, and everything – an aggressive clarity of thought, ideas, and speech, and, on the other, this clarity is met with an utter opaqueness *to themselves*. Thus, at one end, the schizophrenic personifies the *cogito*'s clarity as seen in the quality of enlightenment of some delusions or hallucinations that might appear as visions where the schizophrenic knows how things function, their structure, and essence. It could present as the brilliant knowledge of god who reveals himself to an all clear consciousness, sometimes solving the dense mysteries of philosophy. Kraepelin and Diefendorf (1904) had noted the schizophrenic's predilection towards philosophizing, but this clarity goes beyond the cognitive to the perceptual.

This forceful and violent lucidity of consciousness and perception is exemplified in Renee's (Sechehaye & Rubin-Rabson, 1979) entire experience of a consciousness that is inundated with harsh artificial illumination which makes the world appear unreal. She repeatedly talks about a world too lit, too bright, and it is of interest to us to note that her references to "enlightenment" are both in terms of actual light and intellectual enlightenment – both cognitive and perceptual. Whereas portrayals of madness have concerned themselves with motifs of lost men in search for truth in the darkness of unreason, the first-hand accounts of schizophrenics tell a different story:

> of a noonday rather than a midnight world, a world marked less by the mysteries of hidden depths than the uncanniness of immense spaces and the enigmas of gleaming surfaces and brilliant light ... Often the schizophrenics feel not farther but closer to truth and illumination.
>
> *(Sass, 1994, p. 6)*

This brings us to the other extreme – the personification of the *unthought*. The *unthought* is first of all the "Other" in man, born beside him as the modern man emerged:

> The unthought (whatever name we give it) is not lodged in man like a shriveled-up nature or a stratified history; it is, in relation to man, the Other: the Other that is not only a brother but a twin, born, not of man, not in man, but beside him and at the same time, in an identical newness, in an unavoidable duality.
>
> *(Foucault, 1994, p. 326)*

This opaque, unknown, but forever present within our self, is reified (through reflexivity) and lived-out in the schizophrenic in an alienation with his own thoughts and feelings, so much so that they seem to be originating from others – a cut so thorough that it allows no interruption. Such extreme alienation from his own being presents itself in a manner that he experiences his actions, desires, thoughts, etc. to not be his own – an opposite of clarity, a lack of complete conscious control – impenetrable chaos. The "Other" in one's self, which for the neurotic is a constant presence but not a drastically distanced entity, creates new external realities for the schizophrenic. Everyone in the modern episteme has an opacity at the heart of the self, but the schizophrenic, through the harsh radiance of his consciousness of this opacity, is flooded with the terror of the void.

Let me clarify that I am not suggesting, like some theorists have, that the madman lives out the contents of his unconscious with utter abandon, if the unconscious operates like that in the first place. Instead I am suggesting he personifies the structure and obscurity of the *unthought* (which is a historical emergence), for the only thing we can state with any confidence about the nature of the *unthought* is that it is inaccessible and inevitable (for the modern Western man). It is nearly impervious to interpretations and at the same time given to interruptions and eruptions. To live out the position of the "Other" in one's self is to *be* opaque and inaccessible, or as Jaspers once said – "ununderstandable". We can observe this disdain for understanding, the terror of interpretation, and a dislike for meaning in many first-person accounts. Deborah (Green, 1989) who had created her own language, Yri, in her own world, Yr, experiences psychotic breaks every time a physician attempts to talk about Yr. While Renee's perception of the world is basked in terrifying brightness and clarity, Deborah's world is denuded with murky grayness pointing to real perceptual obscurity:

> And, as the teacher stood by her desk, some nightmare terror coming to life had risen in the day-same-school room. Deborah had looked about and found that she could not see except in outlines, gray against gray, and with no depth, but flatly, like a picture.
> *(Green, 1989, p. 13)*

Lara Jefferson (Fadiman & Kewman, 1979) openly mocks her therapist's interpretations as narcissistic and useless:

> Phobias are sensitive little critters ... he cannot cure them. All he does is go prowling around among them, knocking them over. When he finds an extra fine specimen he is as thrilled with his discovery as some be-spectacled bug hunter who captures a rare type of beetle. He does not know what to do with it.

Joan (Fadiman & Kewman, 1979) similarly displays contempt towards her doctor's theories regarding her illness, while at the same time accepting that they might be true ("you seemed so wonderful, but your words so horrible ... If you forced your words on me, I would usually go catatonic because of the horrible ideas").

As the rein of conscious thought is undermined by the emergence of the *unthought*, the grounded self finds itself unsure in its footing. The Othering is so violent and complete that the locus of control of the schizophrenic's own basic actions, desires, etc. moves away from his lived body. To further explore this un-grounding of self in the schizophrenic condition one has to visit Descartes. The Cartesian assertion, "I think therefore I am" implied that conscious thought is the necessary and sufficient condition for the assurance of an existing self, but with the advent of the counter-science of psychoanalysis that de-thrones conscious thought to focus on the unconscious, and is supposed to lead to what Foucault (1994) calls the death of "man" (as we know him), the self as dependent on conscious thought loses its grounding; just like representation, it no more remains unquestioned. Consequently, this leads to the dislodging of the self (and "man" as center of knowledge) which is played out by the schizophrenic as reflected in his doubts regarding the existence of self, or his accurately assumed fragility of being. Laing (1990) speaks of this fragility as a marker of the schizoid condition where a patient insists that he is made of glass and one harsh look from another would shatter him. Other common statements like "I am dead", "I don't feel alive", "I am a machine", etc. come to mind, and Sass (1994) reports a patient saying "Why do I divide myself in different pieces? I feel that I am without poise, that my personality is melting and my ego disappears and that I do not exist anymore" (p. 15). He further speaks of a patient who describes himself as "dead yet hyperalert – a sort of corpse with insomnia" (p. 8) exemplifying the hyper-awareness which co-exists with a state of suspected non-self. To conclude, whereas Sass contests schizophrenia as a heightening of conscious awareness, I would add that it is equally a heightening of the *unthought* – a drastic resurrection of the Other in one's self while playing out the drama of epistemological tensions of this period.

Airplanes are birds: hyper-cognition

Foucault's assertions imply that there is an underlying interdependence which characterizes the modern era. Man becomes historicized through the forces of labor, language, and biology that constitute him as an object – there is thus a radical dependence on the forces of the past. These range from old meanings and predetermined values of commodities to life itself as determined by forces that lead to its current organic structure. Further, modern man is also the condition for their possibility; it is not a linear chain but rather a grid where to exist is dependent on numerous factors which are then dependent on "man" – the connections are prolific and multi-directional.

In terms of how this feature of modern thought and being translates to the schizophrenic condition, one has to understand schizophrenic thought. Superficially, this dependence is reminiscent of the extreme craving of other people that schizophrenic patients can sometimes display but I am more intrigued by the nature of schizophrenic cognition than interpersonal dependence. This cognition which is a personified exaggeration of the epistemic interdependence is sometimes reflected in schizophrenic speech.

Modern man is dependent on historical forces and in turn constitutes these forces – he is connected and connecting, an essential node in the vast network of associations, of which the schizophrenic subject is one deformed iteration. This subject lives out this epistemological connectedness as real connectedness through a hyper-association between cognitive knots. Research on schizophrenic cognition has noted that compared to the normal population, the schizophrenic has an ability/obligation to make conceptual, semantic, phonetic, schematic and episodic (memory) connections that are vastly disparate, and that they do this at an incredible speed (Spitzer et al., 1994). Yet again, schizophrenic cognition puts up a flamboyant display of the episteme's markers. For example, "M", a brilliant and successful friend who was diagnosed schizophrenic at the age of sixteen writes:

> I let go of all self-control and with that my faculties melted away as well. These moments were probably my first where true freedom of thought was realized. The realization of true freedom of the mind without the constructs of boundaries and possibilities has shaped much of my creative process ....

Schizophrenic patients are also known to show deficits in semantic memory, but only very specific types of deficits. Similar to most research done on the subject of psychosis and schizophrenia, the evidence is scattered. The deficits limit themselves to semantic and not episodic memory and are usually assessed through memory tests of categorization, picture naming, etc. (Laws & Al-Uzri, 2012) There is also some evidence of information loss from the semantic store, but only in patients with chronic schizophrenia (Laws & Al-Uzri, 2012). While this is usually attributed to grey-matter loss or larger ventricle size (which in turn has been recently related to long-term neuroleptic use), I propose that there is also something else that accounts for the loss of semantic store in only long-term patients. Patients suffering from formal thought disorders tend to be over-inclusive in their semantic category tasks, for example, the inclusion of airplanes into the category of birds. This points to a lack of boundaries or blurring of boundaries in categorical thinking (Laws & Al-Uzri, 2012).

The pervasive model of semantic memory consists of the idea that there are memory nodes forming a network and that this background processing effects our conscious and unconscious experience. What is of interest to us is that studies show that schizophrenics could have an over-activation or a dis-inhibition of the semantic network (Spitzer et al., 1994). This is tested through tests of indirect priming, for example, in the normal population the prime "black" could lead to thinking about "white", which serves as a prime for "whale", which further connects to other concepts that are culturally shared or personally relevant – they are connected through meaning. For schizophrenics with over-activated networks, the connections are faster and farther away (semantically, visually, and phonetically). Thus, "black" could serve as a prime for "lack", "sack" (phonetic connections). Semantically, it could serve as a prime connecting seemingly disparate concepts. We already discussed how the schizophrenic can shun meaning for sound. For example, Saks utters the phrases "fresh tasting lemon juice *naturally*" and "*natural* volcano" together. The connections made, due to over-activation or dis-inhibition are greater (hyper-priming), faster and further apart – and could account for what are pejoratively called "word salads". Thus, formal thought disorder patients have overactive or decreased inhibition of the semantic network (Spitzer et al., 1994) and they reach distant concepts faster.

What can account for semantic store loss in patients of long-term schizophrenia (but not short term) aren't just physiological changes like grey-matter loss but a new network of semantics that has reified, thus obliterating older connections – a form of retroactive inhibition. Thus, the loss of information normally attributed to physiological deficit could partially be due to reification and repetition of newer, faster, and more distant connections that most schizophrenics have the ability/obligation to make, which in turn have physiological consequences.

More importantly, the schizophrenic subject seems to reflect an exaggeration of the modern Western epistemological condition, this time that of hyper-connectedness. Reflecting the modern episteme's hyper-connected subject, the intricate and hyperbolic interdependence of schizophrenic cognition and memory creates forms of thought and speech which are nonsensical to others as their cognitive connections are neither over-activated, nor are their boundaries disinhibited. Whereas the neurotic could use language and memory to create a meaningful narrative of personal history (parental unfairness and childhood betrayals), his cognitive associations, whether episodic (life events), semantic, or conceptual, allow him to operate in the world. Instead, for the schizophrenic, the entire gamut of cognitive associations, memory, and schematic connections which normally operate implicitly, come into harsh focus, creating a characteristic tautness in these associations. According to Sass (1994), schizophrenics "often display a more deliberative and ideational rather than intuitive or emotional style of acting and problem solving" (p. 23). Similarly, "M" once described this awareness and inspection of usually tacit cognitive processes through an excruciating procedure:

> That's when I devised what would become the only method by which I would make unmodified memories and hopefully maintain a grasp of reality. Fondly referred to as "the grid" this method involves strict maintenance of nodes and flags of all experiences and has helped me become functional in the sense that I make a decent living.

We can observe an important paradox operating here: schematic associations that are created and move rapidly and without boundaries, and the parallel intransigence of these associations where significations lose their flexible quality.

It was Bleuler himself for whom the loosening of associations was the primary marker of schizophrenia; I posit that associations don't necessarily get loosened but instead, under the forceful gaze of the schizophrenic consciousness, they deconstruct and get reconfigured through the hyper-connections into bizarre, enduring, awkward, and sometimes ingenious formations. Whereas the cognitive associations of the neurotic allow him the privilege to be an economic, biological, and languaged agent, the schizophrenic, not bolstered by the ease of tacit cognitive connections and instead hindered by rigid hyper-connections which have been deconstructed and reassembled in twisted ways, is allowed no such ease of personal narrative and human communication. It may seem then that the only hope for a psychotic is indeed to become neurotic, that is, to use language with ease of representation and action, to enter meaning, to develop a life story. An example is the narrative offered by the Hearing Voices movement which is built around the idea that psychosis is a response to traumatic life events; it emphasizes the biography of the patient and considers delusions and hallucinations to be metaphorical renditions of past experiences, or inner unconscious emotions – in other words, it focuses on creating meaning and entering a personal narrative. One only has to read the autobiography of Mary Barnes (Barnes & Berke, 1971) to understand the importance of faith in meaning, which in her case was meaning in Laing's "therapy", which she clutched on to through intense breakdowns and terrifying delirium. The cutting-edge avatar therapy (Leff, Williams, Huckvale, Arbuthnot, & Leff, 2014), which has seen excellent results in reducing hallucinations, is conceived in a similar vein where patients create a computerized visual avatar of their hallucinations and converse with it. It is then inconsequential whether there is any reality to the narrative (like an actual traumatic event) or any truth to these interpretations; what is of importance is the conjuration of meaning as therapeutic. If the hyper-reflexive glare on the process of cognitive associations, and exaggerations of schematic, semantic, and conceptual connections can cause a breakdown in the meaning-making operations in the lived world, then probably, supplanting meaning from outside (whether it's about childhood experiences or that schizophrenia is a brain disease), might normalize the background cognitive processes through a shift in focus away from process to content.

The schizophrenic and the traumatic

The schizophrenic subject is only one peculiar and extreme form of modern subjectivity. This brings us to another rendition of this subjectivity – the subject of trauma. It should be clarified that the traumatic subject hereon referred to pertains not to an individual who has survived event trauma but instead to the Lacanian barred subject who is "alienated" through language. For Lacan, this modern subject's primary trauma lies in the cut of language, or in other words, in its adherence to "the name of the father". At the heart of this subject lies an injury sustained during its entry into the symbolic; as Fink (1996) paraphrases Lacan, the letter kills the real. This modern subject then is always inherently traumatized as it is always barred or divided, and its bargain with language ensures that it can never "get to" itself, or describe and understand itself, except through language. Thus, at the heart of this subject, true to its historical context (modernity), lies the same opacity I earlier spoke about.

The traumatic subject's inculcation into the symbolic and adherence to the law brings with it a sense of loss – a loss of the direct experience or access to the real. In analysis or otherwise, the chain of signifiers can only circle the real but never reach and totalize it. This basic loss is the foundation of the traumatic subject and this inaccessibility informs the core of the inner opacity. This precludes a direct understanding of experience of one's self and results in an unending chase where word pitifully tries to catch up with desire, and verbalization becomes our savior – a marker of all modern subjects.

In popular art and film, this opacity and its chase is evident everywhere. Akira Kurosawa (1983), the famed Japanese director of *Rashomon*, which exemplifies modern art's perspectivism and relativism, exposes through the movie's narrative this era's ambiguity and diversity of view-points while also forcing the human subject to the center of attention. *Rashomon* tells the story of a murder from the eyes of different witnesses, where each have a contradictory narrative to tell. A tale that focuses on the very nature of the telling and remembering of tales, *Rashomon* inhabits a true perspectivism where our memory and comprehension are influenced by our position and subjectivity. The open-to-interpretation ending annihilates any assumptions of "the truth" and instead creates tension in the viewer for s/he does not have the god's eye view anymore but instead, like much a character in the movie, is oblivious to the truth. Instead of being a peripheral observer, the audience is pulled into the narrative through their ignorance of the facts and through the use of camera angles where the viewer sits in the position of the local court while different witnesses regale their versions of truth. In his memoir *Something Like an Autobiography*, Kurosawa (1983) writes about the circumstances around the movie. He says that Akutagawa's story "In the Grove" which served as inspiration for *Rashomon* was chosen for its harsh insight into the "dark complexities and bizarre twists" of the human heart (p. 183). Kurosawa also recalls his frustration before the beginning of the film's shooting where three assistant directors persistently asked him to explain the nonsensical script. In the end, resonating our assertions about the opacity of the modern era and its subjects, both the traumatic and the schizophrenic, Kurosawa tells them that:

> human beings are unable to be honest with themselves about themselves ... You say that you can't understand the script at all, but that is because the human heart itself is impossible to understand. If you focus on the impossibility of truly understanding human psychology and read the script one more time, I think you will grasp the point of it.
>
> (p. 183)

It is evident how Kurosawa's style of thought subscribes to the epistemic peculiarities of a barred subject forever opaque to himself (the subject of trauma), a fact that also reflected itself in his seminal work.

As noted earlier, the schizophrenic personifies this opacity – instead of the traumatic subject's "I can't know myself", "who am I really", "what do I desire", the schizophrenic experiences "I am not myself, I am a robot", "My desires are controlled by aliens". This cut from one's self isn't just *in* him because through his characteristic extreme personifications of the epistemic fissures, he *becomes* someone/something else. As opposed to the traumatic subject, the schizophrenic is drenched in this opacity; he does not *have* it, he *is* it. Moreover, it is interesting to note that this opacity seeps through the schizophrenic subject to inundate even the concept of schizophrenia, the sublime object of psychiatry for Woods (2011). People's (therapist's, caretaker's) distanced encounter with this utter opacity which is otherwise so close to their own structure but simultaneously also foreign (as the *unthought* is an epistemic reality for everyone but the exaggeration of the *unthought* isn't), their awe and terror at this encounter, and their subsequent attempts to totalize it with reason point to how the schizophrenic subject truly is the sublime – ever-present and always inaccessible.

For Lacan (Fink, 1996), the psychotic never made the cut of language, never adhered to the law ("no") of the father, and while we know that the schizophrenic is assimilated into language, I showed earlier how language could not be utilized by him the way it is by others. This non-adherence to the law of the father follows him even later in life, for example, because he trusts his delusions and not the interpretations of his psychiatrist, he remains "treatment-resistant". He is "treatment-compliant" when he takes his medication but he is only cured when he enters the world ruled by the same laws and logic as his physician who has now replaced the function of the father – he has to at some point make the cut. It is, then, intriguing to note the traumatic and schizophrenic subject's relation to meaning. Jean Laplanche (Caruth, 2001) suggested that the birth of the unconscious lies in the primary trauma of encountering the enigmatic messages of the Other (other's unconscious), pointing to an encounter with the absurd and meaningless (enigmatic). Similarly, Lacan places due importance on the trauma of the child attempting to decipher the desire of the Other – reading between the lines. It is then ironic that the traumatic subject is, at least consciously, so dependent on meaning when it is birthed through a confrontation with the meaningless. He is ripe for therapy and ready for interpretation. As for the schizophrenic, we have already observed his disdain for both.

The first big difference between these two permutations of the modern subject is that while the psychotic subject takes the opacity (and its opposing clarity of the *cogito*) to their caricaturized extreme, the traumatic subject in some ways can sustain that tension – he can even attempt to bring this opacity into discourse. Language then is the prison and the rescuer of the traumatic subject and he can use language to narrate the obsessions, desires, and sufferings of his life. He can use words, without encountering the pitfall of a hyper-reflexive glare that turns language hostile and rigid, to attempt to describe and understand his interiority. In other words, he can be the subject and the object, which Sass and Parnas

(2003) insist is the mark of healthy self-affectation, without having to oscillate and be overwhelmed by the two positions. He might be barred from himself but language allows him to flourish in the flowing (if wounded) nature of his consciousness (J. Roberts, personal communication, September 15, 2017). To have a division, an opacity, and a wound, one must have a self – the self whose contents one can attempt to understand and bring forth. The traumatic subject's glare is merely reflexive and his inward focus (man as an object) stays at the level of content and never freezes the background processes of thinking and feeling. His experience of himself, while always incomplete, begins from a sense of a stable body schema, which we noted was absent for the schizophrenic. For he is the quintessential modern subject – he can objectify himself but never reduce himself to an object. His obsession with his interiority might or might not be "healthy", depending on the school of thought one subscribes to, but it surely is epistemically normal. This subject, instead of oscillating between the empirical and the transcendental position, can sustain the middle ground and thus is the quintessential modern subject. In other words, this subject can treat itself as an object using language to explain "My parents used to …", "I wonder why I …", "I don't know who I am!"

In order to language, this division, or primary trauma, is essential for the Lacanian subject. Thus, in a bizarre way, the modern episteme, rigged with tensions and fractures, *suits* the traumatic subject – the subject of trauma. The "unalienated" schizophrenic, on the other hand, appears alien to the rest of us. He is overwhelmed by the episteme's oscillations or rather is a product of the episteme's extremes, making him the peculiar and exaggerated iteration. The traumatic subject might carry an injury *within* him but the schizophrenic subject personifies the fracture of the episteme. I noted earlier that a mark of modern epistemology is an inward turn which the schizophrenic subject, personifying the fracture, skillfully caricaturizes. The traumatic subject, also a product of the same fissures, thrives instead; instead of wildly oscillating, he painfully survives. Not only is he the product of these ways of knowing but, if the explosion of literature/knowledge around trauma psychology, verbalized analysis, and cure through meaning is any indicator, he most competently sustains them.

Schizophrenia and immigration: becoming unalienated through alienation

Lastly, I want to note here and attempt to explain a pattern that has been observed in the epidemiology of schizophrenia. It has been known for some time that schizophrenia rates are higher than normal among marginalized populations, especially among those who have encountered recent migration. A 2017 BBC documentary *Why Did I Go Mad* (Mendham & Farnham, 2017) which centralizes the trauma narrative in the etiology of psychosis, speaks of immigrant populations displaying higher-than-normal rates (35%) of schizophrenia, which it attributes to a sense of displacement and a feeling of being the constant outsider. Similarly, a meta-analysis conducted by Cantor-Graae and Selten (2005) which investigated studies from 1977 to 2003 to assess the effect size of migration as associated with schizophrenia concluded that "personal and family history of migration is an important risk factor for schizophrenia" (Cantor-Graae & Selten, 2005, p. 12). This has usually been attributed to the stress of migration, higher rates of schizophrenia in sending population, and traumatic experiences of migration (Bhugra, 2000). From what has been observed in the previous pages, it seems that there could be another reason for this surge in numbers, and this is of unique interest to us because it exemplifies the role of hyper-focus in schizophrenia. Being positioned as a constant outsider brings into focus the underlying assumptions and implicit processes governing the operations of other cultures. Immigrants not only confront strange languages and different foods, but the very technology of life they are used to is turned upside down. They thus have the privilege (or the misfortune) to *accidentally* investigate the implicit discourses and unintentionally examine the tacit processes which underlie the shallow differences. When you are continuously confronted with ways of being that are unfamiliar, it is not as difficult to see through the ways of thinking that inform them. One of the consequences of this alienation is that the gaze may turn inwards to examine, at a superficial level, the values and actions of one's own culture, and at a much deeper and reflexive level, the procedures and assumptions that until now had been held as normal and thus seamlessly functioned in the background to inform one's actions, responses, emotions, thoughts, and desires.

My interest in this explanation originated from my conversations with immigrants in the US. Despite leading comfortable lives and coming from privileged backgrounds in their own countries, most people I spoke to talked about a feeling of unreality, the perception of a certain cut or distance from the world, and of encountering a subtle ever-present sense of things being not-real-enough. In effect, being positioned as a foreigner in an alien land or an alien in a foreign land makes obvious the obscure and tacit assumptions (cultural and personal) that allow us to operate flawlessly in the world. The immigrant or any cultural outsider, in being forced to question or even just inspect the conditions of his subjectivity, throws his own consciousness into harsh focus, that is, becomes reflective, and, in some cases, hyper-reflective (Sass, 2007b). At times, especially when intensified by the extreme stress of living because of discrimination and poverty, this may be a few steps away from a psychotic break. For that matter, the "unworlding" as defined by Sass (2007b) and the alienation normally ascribed to the schizophrenic are uniquely similar to the descriptions provided by foreigners in alien lands. Take for example Sass's description of the "truth-taking stare" and "Stimmung" which are features of prodromal phases of psychosis. The patient reports that the world seems alien, strange, and unfamiliar as things take on different meanings or no meaning – a state not entirely dissimilar to auras before seizures and migraines – "everything having undergone some subtle, all-encompassing change" (Sass, 1994, p. 44). This description of a period before full-blown psychosis where the "familiar has turned strange and the unfamiliar familiar" (Sass, 1994, p. 44) strikingly describes the alienation of a foreigner in a strange land.

This "unworlding" that Sass characterizes as typical to schizophrenics also can be encountered in migrants, especially migrants whose host culture differs significantly from their heritage culture. Consider this description of a prodromal phase: "This strange and enigmatic atmosphere, a mood that infuses everything yet eludes description ... the world appears to be, in some sense, quite normal .... Still everything is totally and uncannily transformed: the fabric of space seems subtly changed" (Sass, 1994, p. 44). We can compare this description of an ineffable change in being and perception to a first generation immigrant woman's experience in Jhumpa Lahiri's (2003) novel *The Namesake*:

> Though no longer pregnant, she continues, at times, to mix Rice Krispies and peanuts and onions in a bowl. For being a foreigner Ashima is beginning to realize, is a sort of lifelong pregnancy – a perpetual wait, a constant burden, *a continuous feeling out of sorts*. It is an ongoing responsibility, a parenthesis in what had once been an ordinary life, only to discover that previous life has vanished, replaced by something more complicated and demanding.

One can observe here a similar allusion to feeling akin to a phantom limb, there and not there at the same time – a perpetual discomfort at an absent site. Chimamanda Ngozi Adichie's (2014) award-winning novel *Americanah* about a Nigerian girl in America speaks of a similar subtle and change in one's sense of self and the world:

> It had been there for a while, an early morning disease of fatigue, a bleakness and borderlessness. It brought with it amorphous longings, shapeless desires, brief imaginary glints of other lives she could be living, that over the months melded into a piercing homesickness.

Both the experience of migration and that of "Stimmung" point to a dislocation of being and a simultaneous *heightening of senses* – a change in texture of everything that at one point made sense and was familiar. It is not surprising that so much literature on schizophrenia is dedicated to contradictions which in some ways are the cognitive form of no-man's land. Similarly, T.R., a Pakistan-born friend of mine who had lived in London for eight years described her own sense of distance from the world. It should be noted how her experience largely concerns itself with perceptual oddness:

> It has been eight years and I still never dream about London, I am always back at home in my dreams doing silly things. Sometimes it seems to me that I am dreaming when I go to the store or take M (her daughter) to school … It's not a feeling that is constant but *humesha parde ke peeche rehti hai* (it's always just behind the curtain), the feeling that the world here has a layer over it, a veil of sorts … and that one day if I peel it off, it will feel real and I will feel real. Sometimes people move here move in slow motion or sometimes I feel that I do. I don't think my daughter feels it but I am sure she has her own struggles … I wondered why amidst the beauty that the Scottish countryside is I still could not connect; we went there a couple of years ago. It was really beautiful, like in the movies, but it inspired/touched nothing in me. I felt I was still watching a movie because I felt I was not really there. People think it is crazy that I want to go back especially because R has such a great job here and so do I … The other day I could hear a train on railway tracks and I closed my eyes hard and tried to imagine that I was back – you know the sound. For just a few seconds everything felt like it had substance.
>
> T.R., *personal correspondence*

Thus it is not the merely violence of forced migration that contributes to this experience; instead it is the intense reflexivity towards the other and consequently the self's implicit practices that the migrant is forced to take leading to an awkward sense of perception. When I stumbled upon this narrative in my conversations with other immigrants, most of them either spoke about or recognized the feeling that perceptually and cognitively things often appeared unreal, like houses were made of cardboard and if pushed, would crumble to the ground.

An inspection of the repercussions of the violent India–Pakistan partition of 1947 where about 1 to 2 million people died and 10 to 15 million were displaced, further solidifies this argument. I can even point to the Kashmiri migration crisis of 1981–1989 which forced my family to leave our home. While both events witnessed intense violence, loss of life, and suffering, reports of increased psychotic breakdowns or schizophrenic episodes in these populations are absent. This can be attributed to lack of psychological research in the country but that isn't entirely true since studies have linked Kashmiri migration with slightly increased rates of depression (Banal et al., 2010). I speculate that the reason for this lack of schizophrenia epidemic is the similarity between the heritage and host cultures; for that matter, the similarity between them precludes the usage of terms like host and heritage cultures. Both of these refugee crises happened amongst people who shared most of their culture, values, assumptions, and ethics. Their institutions, discourses, and perceptual frameworks were also almost identical, even if their religion was not. This cultural and societal uniformity protected them from developing a hyper-attentive consciousness towards the social and personal assumptions that formed their lived background. This importance of cultural consistency is evident in Bhugra's (2000) work who identified higher rates of schizophrenia in migrant populations in Trinidad and London and attributed it not just to the stress of migration but rather to social factors like cultural identity. The relation thus is not so much between immigration and schizophrenia but rather in immigrating to culturally alien and unfamiliar spaces which makes people dig into the ground they are standing on.

In the end, it is important to remember that this form of comparison does not imply that modernism is causally responsible for schizophrenia but instead it can shed light on modernity's "more disturbing potentialities – as these are refracted through the most exaggerated or pathological of examples" (Sass, 1994, p. 12). It is also essential to point out that the hyper-reflexivity that informs much of Sass's theory is but an utter objectification of the self by looking inwards, not at the contents of the psyche, but at the self itself – its structure and processes. Hyper-reflexivity, then, seamlessly fits the modern era's treatment of "man" as an object.

Conclusion

In this chapter I conducted an exposition on how no true understanding of schizophrenia, the most mysterious of all mental illness, can restrict itself to biology or even psychology, but instead has to take into account the epistemic position of man as a subject of knowledge and history. Contradictions, dualities, and polarities form an inalienable part of this understanding where unresolved tensions are not so much due to the lack of better drugs or the right therapy, but instead due to the restrictions placed upon *forms of thought* by historical conditions.

4
DEITIES AND DESIRE
An analysis

> I just don't understand you. In our time, *we couldn't even think like that.*
>
> My mother

As I finished my last interview on the edge of a cliff and under the thick tarp of deodars, I watched my interviewee walk back into the guest house a few hundred yards away. Ruskin Bond wrote some magical tales about Himalayan towns but my mind had no place for Rusty's adventures. Sitting there alone, my head instead swimming with stories of ghosts and dead ancestors, deity possessions, and murderous relatives, I heard a rustling above me – crackling branches and whistling winds are all too common in the Himalayan peaks as you are surrounded by dense forests and gushing streams. But this time I felt anxious, which was swiftly followed by self-loathing – after all, what kind of self-respecting researcher takes stories about river ghosts seriously? As I sat there, pretending to be bolder than I felt, several narratives of vanishing apparitions came to my mind along with the repeated plea and prescription of the locals: "Just don't get scared. It attaches to the person who catches fright". It was another two minutes before I packed my belongings and moved away to the safety of my non-rustling room.

The phrase "catching a fright" is important here. Its use, while odd, initiates us into a world where things are first and foremost tactile, and where mind is no more a negotiator between the realms of thought and touch.

Mind, that bridge which holds the weight of psychology, has collapsed under the presence of materiality. Thus, to impress upon us the importance and effect of this materiality, I deliberately liken fright in this context to a virus or a cold that someone might catch or become infected by.

The Himalayan landscape in the state of Uttarakhand, district of Kumaon, is an overwhelming place. Figure 4.1 is an example of this. The beauty is as dramatic as the stories – stories of betrayal, envy, murder, magic, and revenge; stories of vengeful ghosts, pining spirits, and whimsical deities. To the question, "So, has it ever happened to you or anyone you know that they see or hear things that others around them don't?" the answers are many, the explanations are varied, and resolutions aplenty. I made a feeble and misguided attempt to sort them and neatly classify them, for example, classification of types of entities that afflict a person, its expression (or symptoms), and the eventual resolution or cure. It was soon evident that a classificatory endeavor was doomed, not because there aren't any categories but because the categories are porous, ambiguous, and contradict each other consistently. Unlike Charaka's ancient Indian medical text, which features immaculate distinctions between types of insanity, the descriptions here are neither fixed nor trite. People will lucidly explain the difference between hallucinations caused by a ghost encounter as opposed to a spirit possession and 15 minutes later obliterate the same difference. They displayed no discomfort or dissonance in their contradictory statements and were utterly oblivious to my confusion. The trick here was to immerse myself in the chaos, a task not as difficult for me as I am a product of similar upbringing – I just had to, momentarily, discard my measuring stick.

FIGURE 4.1 Uttarakhand: Site of interview

As I got acquainted with the lives and stories of the people in rural Uttarakhand, I consciously avoided looking for "deeper meaning" or trying to understand what they were *actually* saying. I stripped my vocabulary of any and all medico-psychological terminology and restricted myself to a dialogue around the experience of *seeing things* and *hearing things* that others do not. Kendall and Wickham (1998) have insisted that "recognizing the strangeness in all social arrangements is an important part of using Foucault's methods" (p. 8). Thus I made no attempt to "make sensible" the experiences of our participants in accordance with Foucault's claim that the present is as equally strange as the history we use to diagnose it. I was also excruciatingly careful not to imply that these occurrences were in any way pathological. It should be noted that I encountered not a single individual or group that did not want to enthusiastically engage in a conversation about these topics – there was no restraint, stigma, or embarrassment attached to these issues. Thus, tea-stall owners to grocery-shop workers – all with their hole-in-the-wall shops on the precarious edges of rocky Himalayan cliffs – contributed to this book and my understanding.

The previous chapters established the instability and resilience of modern forms of madness by exploring the co-emergence of schizophrenia and modern subjectivity. In this chapter I further investigate this co-dependence, but this time in rural North India and through an examination of the indigenous discourses around madness and what they reveal about local forms of subjectivity. Until now I have inspected the validity of schizophrenia by observing the semantic controversies and classificatory contentions. It has become clear that schizophrenia's sustained presence amongst us belies its existence as a mere psychopathology. Destabilizing the neutrality of schizophrenia discourages us from unthinkingly replacing local conceptualizations with universal truths, since we know now that those truths stand on shaky ground themselves. Through our earlier examination of language and the schizophrenic subject, we observed that meaning/representation did not occupy a central place in modern thought, and this further helped in historicizing the discipline's focus on verbalization, which sustains trauma theory. Since the link between traumatic life events and psychosis is a popular topic of research, placing it in an epistemic framework helps investigate its universality.

As calls for spreading mental health awareness and psychiatric access to third-world nations grow louder by the day, we must know whether the assertions of the discipline translate cross-culturally. Encouraged by the growing critique of those examining the unscrutinized applications of psychiatric models in the global south (e.g. Mills & Fernando, 2014) I utilized the Foucauldian archaeological method to analyze the discourse around psychotic experiences of those in rural North India. This type of investigation helps to problematize the seeming benevolence of academic imperialism, questions the universality of emerging trauma narratives, and most importantly, answers deeper questions about the structure of this rural North Indian subject in relation to its understanding of madness. The earlier theoretical findings have positioned us to not only observe the various local meanings that organize the experiences of *seeing things and hearing voices*, but more importantly, to look *through* those meanings to excavate the thought processes which make them possible, and consequently undermine the dominance of mainstream psychological narrative.

Just as an examination of modern Western subjectivity was shown to have held the possibility of modern Western madness and vice versa, now, by unearthing the implicit discourses about madness, I explore the organization of Indian subjectivity. Akin to the centrality of the *unthought* to modern Western experience, are there any epistemic and structural peculiarities that are vital to the underlying styles of thinking of the rural Indian subject? The question then isn't "why are they thinking this" but rather "how can they think like this and what rules of thinking allow it"? My mother's exasperated statement that marks the beginning of the chapter "In our times we *couldn't even think like this*" captures this difference. What I thought was her general exasperation at my teenage behavior (and there was plenty to be exasperated about) was instead a very Foucauldian statement, for she was right: being subjected to vastly disparate institutions and discourses, the rules of thinking that informed our beliefs, needs, and desires were very different; she literally could not think like I did and the same held true for me where her experience was concerned. Before we find out more about styles of thought and the subjects who sustain them, we must gather a cursory understanding of the history of madness in India. This includes ancient Ayurvedic conceptualizations, the more recent advent of psychiatry, and the place of contemporary indigenous healing spaces and traditions. We do this with the hope that being attentive to history will provide a context to my theorizations while revealing the complexity of structures at play here.

History of madness: India

One of the most definitive ancient medical texts that expounds on the nature and etiology of insanity is the Charaka Samhita, dated loosely between fourth-century BCE and second-century CE. Like many other ancient Indian texts, some historians trace its origins to an earlier time while others wonder if it was indeed authored solely by Charaka. The oratory nature of this Ayurvedic treatise and difficulties in translation from Sanskrit further complicate understanding. For example, some translations confuse "heart" with "brain", which is important to note because for Charaka, mental processes were not traced to the brain like they were for lesser-known physicians like Bhela (Haldipur, 1984). The text divided insanity into being either endogenous (constitutional), that is, produced by disruption in humors/elements; or exogenous (accidental), that is, insanity produced by deities or demons. The humoral theory was triarchic, with wind (vatta), bile (pitta), and phlegm (kapha) playing a central role not just in defining and diagnosing mental processes but also physical ones. Interestingly, instead of affecting the brain, imbalance in humors affected the heart which influenced the mind and led to insanity. Insanity was described as "A clouded or confused understanding, restlessness of mind, anxious glances, restlessness of manner, indistinct articulation, and emptiness of the chest" (Caraka, 1896, p. 1261). Charaka also defined it as:

> A bedimmed understanding, the person that is insane feels neither happiness not misery. He becomes oblivious to conduct and duty. Peace of mind is not his. Destitute of memory and understanding and consciousness, the mind of the person afflicted with Insanity wanders hither and tither.
> *(Caraka, 1896, p. 1261)*

Certain aspects of personality and physical attributes were considered premorbid traits, e.g. not adhering to dietary rules, rules of cleanliness, a wasted body, etc. While the etiology, description, and cure appear psychosomatic, I will soon show how the relationship is not negotiated through a psyche but instead implies a more materialistic ontology.

Of general etiology, Charaka Samhita declares: "Food that consist of hostile or inharmonious ingredients that are vitiated, or that are impure (tainted), attacks on the deities, Brahmanans, and seniors, mental shocks caused by fear and joy, and abnormal efforts are the cause of insanity" (Charaka, 1896, p. 1261). By now the glaring absence of mind–body division should be evident, as mental shocks and impure foods occupy the same explanatory framework. It is essential to note this absence because while Charaka Samhita is an ancient text, its underlying assumptions regularly erupt into the field of contemporary consciousness. They don't lie dormant and neither have they been unchanged through time; instead they

88 Deities and desire

are reflected in local explanatory discourses of insanity and point to the existence of a subject that renders the mind–body dichotomy absurd.

Specific descriptions of khapa-induced, pitta-induced, and vatta-induced insanity reflect how the division between physiological and psychological symptoms is non-existent. This also held true for those I met and spoke to about hearing voices and seeing things others do not. Some listed symptoms included: increased need for sleep, decreased appetite, fondness of women, being quiet, nasal discharge, salivary discharge, desire to be alone, vomiting, and whiteness in appearance (nails, eyes, urine) were symptoms of excited kapha-induced (phlegm) insanity. A person suffering from excited pitta-induced (bile) insanity displayed "impatience, fury, nudity, wrathful abuse of others, running away, heat (of body), rage, desire for cool food and drink, and a yellow complexion" (Charaka, 1896, p. 1262. Lastly, vatta-induced insanity was marked by excessive "laughter and smile and dancing and singing and speech on inappropriate occasion and motions and gestures, and crying, and roughness and leanness of the body and reddishness of the complexion" (Charaka, 1896, p. 1262).

The classificatory system gives further exhaustive descriptions of accidental insanity which is caused by the numerous deities, sages, demons, spirits, ghosts and others, or by "breaches, arising from hypocracy (sic) and falsehood, of religious observances and vows, as also the (evil) acts of a former life" (Caraka, 1896, p. 1263). It elaborates on the type of person who is susceptible to it, and provides lengthy descriptions of the time of year, day, and place a person is liable to get attacked/possessed/attacked by these entities. There are many other symptoms and forms of insanity classified under the actions of different beings and the section on treatment is equally exhaustive, where "verse after verse instruct about various ways of preparing recipes with ghee (melted butter), herbs, and spices" (Haldipur, 1984, p. 337) in order to target each form of insanity. There was also an emphasis on cure through compassion and sympathy, especially when dealing with insanity caused by losing a loved one, and also on restoring balance in emotions to deal with insanity caused by excess of passions like desire, envy, greed, delight, and grief (Haldipur, 1984). Lastly, precautionary measures are ascribed to allay insanity that is both endogenous and exogenous; some include controlling passions, eating right according to one's constitution, cultivating control and goodness. Haldipur (1984) states that descriptions of accidental forms of madness (e.g. the ones caused by deities) have led many scholars to focus on the mystical and disregard the "rational and empirical elements in Indian thought" (p. 339), and translations are often either unable to comprehend or choose to ignore the comments on investigations, diagnosis, and prognosis achieved through a sophisticated classificatory system.

Charaka was not the only one; *Sushruta Samhita* (Sushruta's compendium), written by Sushruta is another ancient Vedic text that forms the backbone of Ayurveda which is still practiced today. While Sushruta does describe and explain insanity, his work mainly focused on surgery. Like Charaka, he divided insanity according to its etiology, the first three being caused by the elements/humors/doshas, and last two being a result of grief (both real and imagined) and actions (Sushruta, 1916). Finally, there was also insanity caused by poisons, which was to be treated differently. What is of interest are his portrayals of the other two types of insanity which incorporate fright, personal loss, shock, obsessions, and even something akin to inappropriate affect:

> A person frightened by a thief, a king's officers or his own enemy or any such person, or suffering from any distracted state of the mind owing to a loss of wealth, or from any grief (Soka) or bereavement or from any disappointed love would likely have an attack of mental distraction (insanity). In such cases he would unconsciously talk incoherently about subjects uppermost in his mind or would sing in a stupid fashion or laugh or weep. (These are the symptoms of Sokaja insanity.)
> *(Sushruta, 1916, p. 387)*

These classical texts on madness informed the import of psychiatry and gave birth to local versions of medical discourse around insanity.

History of psychiatry in India

The history of asylum psychiatry in India can be traced back to the mid-eighteenth century colonial period, where it was first practiced on sepoys and soldiers. This doesn't imply that areas of confinement for the mad didn't exist in pre-colonial India, but the establishment of an organized lunatic asylum that brought with it a different and "superior" discourse of madness that produced new knowledge and was in conflict with the old, was a specifically colonial product. The first lunatic asylum was opened in the back of a hospital in Mumbai in the 1740s, and by the beginning of the early nineteenth century, the British government had opened others in Bengal, and Madras (Crawford, 1915; as cited in Basu, 2004). Amit Ranjan Basu (2004) explores how in the move from lunatic asylums to mental hospitals, the organization of knowledge about the insane underwent a change that was partially a result of the resistance from the native madman himself, but also a pushback inside the culture of colonialism. The new knowledge had to confront not the powers of unreason, like magic and witchcraft (as many assume), but established medical systems like Ayurveda, along with other local but organized practices where the mind–body divide was absent, and interiority wasn't central. As a result, psychiatry was not a natural evolution of medical sciences that reflected post-Enlightenment values; rather its import was already in conflict and had to negotiate "a range of epistemological systems and cultural practices in India" (Basu, 2004, p. 260). To understand how such confrontation occurred and created a system of exclusion and appropriation of local discourses, we must look at asylum psychiatry as more than just a site of repressive and ideological colonial power, because interestingly, their practical conflicts did not mirror conceptual ones. This co-existence of numerous opposing narratives is something one easily finds in India even today where most people have no qualms in visiting the local hospital, the village priest, and the local shaman at the same time.

The new Lunacy Acts by the colonial powers were released in 1858, a year after the sepoy revolt of 1857. However, this interest in lunacy wasn't new. Mahmood Khilji (1436–1469) had already established a "mental hospital" in the state of Madhya Pradesh (Somasundaram, 1987), and Muslim rulers across the world had been establishing hospitals for as early as 707 AD (founded by Walid. B Abdal Malik). There were fixed and mobile hospitals and it was common to keep the mad locked up and under supervision. Ruler Firoz Shah (1351–1388) added many such hospitals to Delhi while others had already been established by his predecessors. He called for treatment of the mad through medicine and a special diet prescribed especially by him (Siddiqi, 1959). Though these early efforts existed, it was under the East India Company in the mid-eighteenth century that the institutionalization of the mad gained unprecedented traction, and the first recorded evidence of one such institution was in 1787 in Calcutta. In 1817 another was opened in Calcutta (now Kolkata) but only for Europeans, and exists to this date as the Institute of Psychiatry. In stark contrast to other asylums, this one was reported as pleasing, clean, and cheerful, and known for mild treatment of the patient population. The East India Company had established more lunatic asylums by the early nineteenth century for local criminals and the vagrant population, but unlike the European counterparts, there was overcrowding and a high percentage of deaths among inmates in most of them (Basu, 2004).

The revolt of 1857 marked a major break as power was transferred from the East India Company to the Queen in 1858, which led to increasing legal management of the insane. The Queen's proclamation brought with it the Lunacy Acts of 1858. While the laws proclaimed ethical treatment of the mad and suggested use of restraints only in extreme cases, they also legalized the process further by giving magistrates control over detaining anyone who had been examined by a medical practitioner. Basu (2004) states how superintendents of the asylums were concerned about illegally detaining those not insane, and cast doubts on the ability of British magistrates to determine lunacy. This was the beginning of systemized record-keeping that reveals a history of overcrowded asylums and over-diagnosis of mania among the population. Moral treatment was prevalent and involved constant observation, keeping patients busy through gardening, exercises, and an emphasis on cleanliness. Soon, this translated to profiteering from goods produced through cheap labor, and in an 1862 report, superintendent Arthur Payne wrote about other supposed benefits of labor-intensive activities, like how it was beneficial in keeping mortality rates low among inmates while at the same time *keeping profits high* (Basu, 2004). T. Hastings (1856), in a review, mused over natives' kind treatment of the insane, which to him seemed incongruous with their otherwise unruly behavior: "Cruel as the natives of India naturally are both to man and to beast, cruelty to lunatics is not one of their characteristics …".

Anouska Bhattacharya (2013) problematizes the simple demonization of the Western import of psychiatry into the Indian milieu, and asks us to pay attention to the nuances of how two diverse sets of *knowledges* came together. She presents a picture of colonial asylums in India as a heterogeneous space that can't simply be categorized as the archetype of colonial power – the British officers in charge were constantly working with local staff members and other native regular member of the asylums like "tea sellers, local visitors, janitors, cooks, and holy men". These local actors, while non-participative in the *scientific* practices, were still just as important as the doctors in therapeutic practices. This type of space, where the expert is everyone and no one at the same time, and where numerous actors play various roles in order to cure the insane, still exists.

Bhattacharya (2013) emphasizes the examination of everyday practices of prison management and insists that the early colonial asylums were not derivative of other state institutions like hospitals and prisons. Instead, "native minds and bodies were complicit in the production of colonial knowledge" (p. 30) through their management and involvement in daily asylum life. The beginning of the twentieth century saw a more rigid consolidation of the Western psychiatric doctrine that had been quietly initiated earlier in the form of the asylum-wide survey in 1868 and an increase in university education leading to the professionalization of psychiatry in India. Bhattacharya (2013) traces how between the 1858 acts and increasing legislation over the next few decades, the colonial asylum changed from a place of complex discourses to a homogenous space. Soon a complex hybrid space with exponentially more nuanced power dynamics than their European counterparts turned into a top-down symbol of colonial power; an example is the consolidation through lunacy laws in 1912.

The asylum was a space where the boundaries between the colonizer and the colonized became blurred, as it wasn't merely tolerated by the locals but was also an important part of their economy. India had a long history with the involvement of its rulers in matters of public health, which is why neither the Lunacy Acts nor asylums were met with much resistance. Three hundred years of Mughal rule before British colonizers had introduced the nation to some of the first hospitals called *bimaristans* (place for the sick). These were state-run and sought to look for cures of insanity and not just confinement of the insane and the vagrant. From the presence of ancient Sanskrit texts like *Arthashastra*, which expounded on the importance of protection of weaker sections of society like prisoners, laborers, minors, aged, ascetics, the sick, the drunk, the hungry, women, and most importantly, the insane, to the existence of Hindu laws like *The Mitakshara* and *Dayabhanga* that laid out the rules of inheritance in the case of insanity in families, the involvement of the ruling class in managing the welfare of the insane was already present in the collective psyche and in Indian history.

Indigenous approaches in India

Currently, several indigenous approaches to healing exist alongside the psychiatric discourse in India. These approaches range from local systemized medicine such as Ayurveda, to faith-healing sites found all across the country. People who take recourse to Ayurveda or local shamans and shrines suffer from a variety of problems – life problems (financial, family), general disappointments, physical ailments, and mental disorders. All these are clubbed under the rubric of *sankat*, which can be translated as problems or troubles.

These methods of healing are quite popular and thrive amidst the prevalence of a medical approach to mental disorders. At the same time, the last few decades have witnessed an attack on the reputation of faith-healing approaches (sometimes not without good reason), which are now seen as unscientific, and demoted to be the recourse of those who don't know better – the uneducated, the lower caste, the poor, etc. Davar and Lohokare (2009) emphasize that both state and non-state agencies are conducting a witch hunt against indigenous practices in the name of reform. Despite these attacks, these sites remain popular and populated. In many cases, people take action on both fronts – they visit doctors and local healers, and many doctors and healers are known to encourage these second opinions. Some of the advantages of these methods over mainstream psychiatric treatments are that they are more accessible, affordable, and take place in a familiar and comforting environment in the presence of family and loved ones. For Ranganathan (2015): "Such a healing process that addresses sociomoral and spiritual concerns in addition to physical and psychological problems is more appealing for those in distress" (p. 185). The tertiary benefits of public spontaneous possessions and temple stays can range from increased family cooperation to an enhanced sense of community and refuge with others encountering similar distress (Ranganathan, 2015). Nabokov (2000), cited in Ranganathan, 2014, notes that this experience of a "distress community" and shared troubles is essential even for healers for whom initiation can be a painful process.

Ranganathan, in her research, observed the Mahanubhav temples in the state of Maharashtra and found that it is mostly the mundane, everyday tasks of temple living that are considered highly beneficial – a finding supported by Bellamy (as cited in Ranganathan, 2015) whose work with Muslim saint shrines in India also suggested that it was everyday living, "the unstructured and ambiguous nature of healing in this shrine that is its most effectual element". Unlike many other temple healing places, Mahanubhav is unique for its lack of rituals performed by priests or healers; instead, it is staying at the temples itself along with taking part in work and prayers that is considered therapeutic. Patients are not passive receivers of the healing process, but active participants in their own cure. In the Mahanubhav temples, Ranganathan found that healing was talked about by temple-goers as something that "automatically" happens by just staying in the temples, being a part of the trance experience, and a member of the Mahanubhav community for a certain period of time. Importantly, the experience of trance and its beneficial effects can only take place in the temple or in presence of the shrine – it cannot be transported outside the premises.

Raguram, Venkateswaran, Ramakrishna, and Weiss (2002) used objective measures of mental health, the Brief Psychiatric Scale which assesses 18 symptoms on a seven-point scale, with people before and after their stay at the Muthusamy temple in the state of Tamil Nadu. People who visited this temple were known to suffer from serious psychiatric illnesses, mostly psychosis. Out of the 31 temple-goers they tested, 23 were diagnosed with paranoid schizophrenia, and six others with delusional disorders. They found that scores on the psychopathology scale dropped significantly at the end of their stay at the temple: "A reduction of nearly 20 percent in Brief Psychiatric Rating Scale scores represents a level of clinical improvement that matches and is achieved by many psychotropic agents, including the newer atypical agents" (Raguram et al., 200, p. 39). Inputs from the subjects and their family or caregivers indicated relief from symptoms and improvement in health. The average stay of subjects was merely five weeks and was free of cost; most sufferers were accompanied by their family members. The researchers attribute this improvement partially to the cultural power of the temple that is known for its healing properties in reducing psychotic distress and symptoms. More importantly and similar to Ranganathan, they point to the role of simple daily activities like cleaning, watering plants at the temple, and some light prayers – not elaborate rituals. This is congruent with local beliefs which focus on curative properties of the temple as a space that is inherently healing.

These centuries-old descriptions and systems of knowledge still have cultural relevance, and with some modifications, even now constitute a popular indigenous theory of madness that survives, nay thrives, alongside recent psychiatric interventions. In the following pages I have refrained from using words like "psychosis", "hallucinations" and "trauma" as they inhabit the discursive realm of medico-psychological lexicon, and inhibit my attempts to *make strange* that narrative. I now outline the indigenous conceptualization around psychotic experience, "the what" before I move into revealing the implicit conditions that make "the how".

Hearing voices and seeing things: a rural North Indian perspective

The nature of affliction

Dramatic behavior, mood instability, co-dependence, etc. – one way to study a culture is to study what it considers to be a problem, and decides to shun, or maybe to resolve. The traits listed above and a thousand others find their place in psychological terminology of what is considered healthy and what is not. In attempting to understand what is considered to be a behavior, emotion, experience, or an event of concern – in other words, what is believed to be problematic or pathological to the people of Uttarakhand, I made several attempts to devise clear classifications, and failed. What makes the people of Uttarakhand (and mostly all of the Indian sub-continent) unique is that their conceptualization of problematic or pathological behaviors and events is utterly non-categorized and unsegregated. Financial troubles, health problems, spiritual concerns, mental issues, life-changing events, and deviant behaviors have no divisions − they all constitute what I would call *afflictions*. This uncategorized gamut of issues and concerns is vastly different from what we are normally used to − sharp divisions between life problems, psychological and mental health concerns, physical pathologies, etc. Even our explanatory frameworks have historically fought over whether to focus on interiority, pure behavior, or biology. I will temporarily divide these concerns into those of deviant behavior (breaking social norms), physical health, emotional distress, and life problems. The people I spoke to did not make these divisions and they are merely for our benefit. One must remember that the primary question posed to the people was "Have you, or anyone you know, ever seen or heard things that others don't or that are not there?"

Behaviors one would classify as emotional and mental troubles are estimated to be problematic. People mentioned mental and physical agitation, incessant rants (verbosity), overly gregarious attitudes, and irritability, especially towards family members, to be of concern. The opposite is also thought to be troublesome − a seemingly depressed state of mind that could on occasion present as introversion and apathy, or what we might call negative symptoms of schizophrenia when accompanied by hallucinatory phenomena.

Most importantly, some hallucinatory phenomena, that is, the experience of hearing and seeing things not seen or heard by others, is categorized under the rubric of afflictions. I remember talking to a young man as he sat with few of his neighbors in a tea and ramen shop balanced precariously next to a cliff. He cautiously told me that he heard clear footsteps behind him while walking through the mountains and when he turned, there was never anyone there. A middle-aged woman casually told me how she would, with glaring clarity, hear the sound of footsteps and anklets behind her; it should be noted that this particular form of *hearing sounds* where a person hears footsteps and jangling anklets behind him, especially in the night, is quite common and has made its way into popular Indian movies about the paranormal. Most intriguing to me was the same woman explaining how her mother regularly heard and saw the music and celebrations of wedding processions, *baraat*, while being fully aware that no one else could. Wedding processions, or *baraat*, are a common phenomenon across India where the groom's family and friends walk up to the bride's house with much fanfare, dance, and music – a loud and fun affair. The woman's mother, interestingly, instead of feeling scared or disconcerted, would want to join the non-existent celebration:

> My mother can actually see it clearly. Like she would be coming home in the night, it would get a little dark, and she would be coming and she can see it clearly in front of her, she can see the ghosts *(bhoot)* ... right in front of her. Like when a wedding procession comes to someone's house *(baraat)* ... there's a lot of music and band, those are the kind of sounds and voices that she hears. And her heart is into it, she feels like ... like she sees people dancing and she says that she also feels like dancing with them. Nobody else can see anything. My maternal grandparents, my uncle and aunt. All of them had gone to the fields. So she told them that there is a band playing down there ... and of course they asked her where is it playing, what is playing?

A week later I interviewed another man, the owner of a hole-in-the wall grocery store/omelet shop who presented another eerie anecdote of *seeing things*. This man is my personal hero since I watched him, without hesitation, jump into a pit to save a crying stray dog while his customers waited and his omelets burned. He spoke at length about his sister. His sister, late one evening, after visiting a local fair, encountered what he called an apparition. In this case the reaction, unlike that of the mother who danced to the tunes of ghosts, was that of fright:

> So when they went there, she went outside to go to the bathroom (in the field). While she went outside, her friend was still inside but ... she saw ... her friend outside. She shouted her friend's name and said "what are you doing outside, go inside". The face was the same as her friend's, same face ... Now when she shouted, her friend who was inside came out ... She must have shouted her name right? So her friend came out and said "I am inside, who are you talking/shouting to?" My sister replied "you were just sitting there, how did you come from inside?" The friend told her "No no, I wasn't sitting there, I was inside, why what did you see?" So my sister, she caught a fright, got really scared.

On the same day as this interview, the guesthouse manager of the place I was staying at delivered a powerful personal anecdote of what we would consider a vivid tactile and visual hallucination. On a stormy night during his pilgrimage to Kailash Mansarovar he was walking up the staircase towards his room with his friend. The bone-chilling anecdote is best read in his own voice:

> So halfway up the staircase (sighs) … see, if a person, his foot trips on one side he would normally just fall down straight, right? Straight, direct down. But suddenly I felt as if somebody had held me and thrown me with great force on one side … *patakna* (to throw someone on the ground) is a different thing, right? Now imagine if I am walking up the stairs step by step, and my foot just twists on one side, so I will just directly fall like this right? Or will I be thrown off with force? So if this is the stair, I was thrown right there (points far away) …. What happened after that was, after I fell on my face … and there was this … (sighs) so big, I haven't in my life seen … I have never seen anything like this … a bright light is what I saw on the ground. Where I had fallen on the ground, I was hurt very badly. There was a spark like there was an explosion on the ground, like after a bomb explodes there are sparks on the ground … How do you I even explain it? But the other guy with me didn't see anything.

These instances and anecdotes point to how the phenomena otherwise categorized as hallucinatory are also considered to be alarming in our population, but they do not necessitate distress, or always warrant intervention. It is essential to recall that people don't always speak of these issues as mental concerns, but some do by emphasizing the psychological response to these experiences. I have categorized them under mental issues here for our ease; for that matter, most of our vocabulary condenses their experience in psychological rhetoric, for example the use of "introversion" to refer to people who stopped being social, spoke little, and started staying indoors. But words create things, and if I said introversion or hallucination, it would conjure a different psychological being in the minds of a reader than would "being at home a lot" and "hearing a *baraat*". Importantly, there are instances where the word "madness" or "mental problem" is used to refer to a range of phenomena but *seeing things* or *hearing voices* didn't seem to make the cut. Emotional shock due to betrayal leading to repetitive thinking and bizarre behavior is a candidate for behavior believed to be mad.

Along with the behaviors (introversion, agitation), experiences (hearing and seeing things), emotions (compulsions, agitation), and mental states (irritability) that are believed to be afflictions that may or may not need intervention, there are also somatic issues or health concerns. Physical problems which to us might appear to be psychosomatic symptoms range from convulsions, dramatic weight loss, dark circles, bleeding, blindness, "leg lock", lightness/looseness of body, becoming ill, trembling, excessive dryness of throat, losing consciousness, headaches, clamped jaw, loss of appetite, lightness and looseness in body (*dheela pad jaana*), weakness, and death. One of the most interesting physical concerns was presented by the owner of a place I stayed at for three days. Nestled in the mountains and only accessible after a short but arduous trek for someone as out of shape as I am, the owner presented the anecdote about a spirit that walks up and down the mountain on which his small guest house is built. This spirit of a woman doesn't bother anyone except for producing one bizarre symptom in him when he walks a certain path on his property:

> And the thing with me is that if I take that back route my leg stops working ('lock'). Yeah the path next to the last room, next to that, I don't walk there because it creates a problem in my leg; my leg gets locked. So I have been told do not walk around that area, I can walk anywhere else on the whole property, but not there. So I said ok. Everybody else goes through that path, and they never have any problems. But for me it's … It gets locked, and then for the next two or three days I can't walk. Or maybe I'll start walking in the next two minutes.

It should be noted that, to my horror, the said path was next to the room I was renting and it took considerable effort to not express my consternation in that moment.

There was also a set of concerns that I call *life problems* and these truly reflect the versatility, heterogeneity, and unsegregated nature of the afflictions. These concerns, which are bundled together with hearing voices and epileptic seizures, range from financial problems to property disputes. Other examples are: important work getting stymied by random events, sudden and numerous obstacles in work or home life, important goals that seemed accessible begin to fall through – sometimes it is as severe as the death of a baby or infertility in a family member. I should note here that even speaking "bad things" or uttering "wrong words" by the afflicted person constituted creating obstructions. This effect of speech on material reality was taken seriously; it is considered symptomatic of a deeper concern and calls for intervention. Thus, anything from "strange happenings" to life losses, financial and otherwise, and even changes in language, and speech are significant markers of afflictions.

People also pointed to bizarre actions or behavior that deviate from social norms as being symptomatic of deeper issues. We can observe the similarity between this component and the mental health discourse, especially schizophrenia, where bizarre behavior is an important marker of the disorder. The actions included shouting, agitatedly running around, excessive and compulsive talking about a single issue, being violent towards family members, over-religiosity, convulsive dancing (like during trance states), and more. One person talked about a man who was swindled out of his land and because of the shock of *dhoka* or betrayal, went mad. He used words like "mental problem" to describe how this man, naked while carrying a *bori* (a large jute bag) would ask people on the street: "Today I sold this land, I got all this money, do you want? How much money do you want?" Immediately after his sudden death, the family of the man who betrayed him began to encounter financial and health problems. This anecdote lends itself to being an excellent example of deviant behavior, mental issues, emotional shock, and life troubles being spoken about in the same breath, without divisions. Understanding what constitutes afflictions is the first step in interrogating how they came to be so and what forms of knowledge made them possible.

The land and its magic

Uttarakhand is fondly called *devbhoomi*, the land of gods. Small shrines of deities and goddesses are sprinkled across the gorgeous landscape, reminding us that we are indeed always walking among these gods. I found that the people I interacted with had all encountered what we deem to be psychotic phenomena, especially auditory, visual, and tactile hallucinations, combined with bizarre or socially inappropriate behavior. The land in itself is believed to be special or unique, and in response to my query about hearing voices or seeing things that others do not, people would nonchalantly insist that "these things happen here all the time", that they are common, if anomalous.

Many alluded to the land possessing an overwhelming and almost magical quality and that its influence wasn't only confined to the locals but also affected outsiders and non-believers; whether they are from alien countries or adjacent cities, they "automatically" get affected by the land and come into the fold of its magic. Ranganathan (2014) spoke about a similar "automatic" effect of Mahanubhav temples on people who visited there seeking cure. It is important to remember the context of these repeated assertions. Uttarakhand, as stated earlier, is nestled in the Himalayan mountains; it is visually stunning and its colossal mountains, impenetrable forests, and magnificent scenic beauty are awe-inspiring for both locals and outsiders. But people more specifically spoke of an almost tactile quality and that the land "automatically", almost forcefully, induced in people a certain change. I soon realized that land occupies a central place in the discourse around seeing and hearing things that others do not.

The discourse around land is not just restricted to its specialness or its magical and seductive quality which inspires belief. There is, instead, a material attachment and a direct connection to land, especially one's own land (but ownership here has little to do with legality). Returning to *pitr-bhoomi,* which translates to paternal or ancestral land, is considered integral to the cure of different problems, including the experience of *hearing voices.* The very concept of "own land" is different from how we normally understand it; there is a difference between "own land" versus land that is bought/land one owns, implying that a monetary transaction and legal access do not define connection. The owner of a small hotel who lamented that a woman's spirit haunted his property said: "This land isn't mine, I purchased it from someone. Now the person from whom I bought it, what was his problem with that lady, why did the spirit stay here?" This almost physical and material relation to one's land that goes beyond who owns it and where they currently reside was a running thread in what people deemed problematic and how it was resolved. The connection, an undying direct relationship with the land that persists across time, space, and people, and is essential to cure, is independent of where one lives. Breaking connections with one's land can have negative consequences and the resolution of those problems is possible only when one returns to the land.[1] This connection that we observe here has a materiality to it that, as I will soon show, forms the backbone of the underlying discourse around hearing voices and seeing things.

I must note here that the people I met were clear on the superiority of their local explanations and cures when pitted against other forms of treatment, like conventional medical care, and they simultaneously acknowledged that they can discern when a person needs medical attention and will subsequently visit the doctor if that is the case. I tentatively felt this clarification to be a guarded reaction to me and my possible city-dwelling notions about their rural naivety and backwardness. I was repeatedly assured that when conventional medical cure fails them, which happens regularly, they are also perceptive enough to resort to the local solutions of their own people – resolutions they insist not only work but do so instantly.

Of explanations: from vengeful ancestors to whimsical deities

Much like the expression and presentation of these afflictions, the causes they are attributed to are rarely organized and thus change from one narrative to the other. In a land where stories about ghosts, beliefs about spirits, and experiences of deity possession are a common phenomenon, it is easy to assume that the explanations offered by people would explicitly have an external locus of control. After all, possessions and planetary movements compose a major chunk of their causal attributions, which points to an understanding of the world where the people have little control over their lives. A closer inspection would belie such a hurried and superficial conclusion because the people of rural Uttarakhand have a complex and nuanced take on causal explanations of why an individual, family, or community becomes afflicted. I have broadly divided these into five sub-categories: unfulfilled desire, suffering and revenge, broken bonds and connections, *ghabrahat,* and astrology, but there is one common factor that runs through them all which is "interdependence". This implies that the person afflicted might have nothing to do with the cause behind the affliction except that they are somehow related to the people who are directly responsible. Not only can the children of culpable parents suffer but it could be great grandchildren or distant family members who might have to bear the repercussions. Further, the causes of these afflictions can sustain across generations and persist through time and space.

The people I met spoke of unfulfilled desire, or a frustrated wish, as one of the reasons behind several afflictions, especially the desires and wishes of ancestral spirits. One woman beautifully phrases these frustrated desires as "the words that stay in your heart". She further explains why an ancestor's spirit would haunt and create trouble for the whole family:

> If they wanted to eat something and we didn't give it to them, or they wanted to wear something and we didn't give it to them. So then later on ... Even if they don't say anything, even if I haven't said anything to them (implies being callous by denying their wish) ... Later on, they will think "That I felt like wearing this, but they didn't give it to me". Then later on (after their demise) they will come in your dreams, after they come in your dreams then what happens is that (they say) "That I felt like wearing this but they didn't give it to me".

Later she adds:

> But when we get older and our heart desires something ... like my mother-in-law is here and she would want (wish) something but she won't be able to tell us ... because she knows about our problems too that "they have all of these problems of their own and I can't tell them that I want this or that". But her heart still desires this thing (*dil mein hoga hi hoga*) ... that just stays in her heart. So that's what sticks even later on (after her death).

Others noted that frustrated wishes and desires not only apply to ancestors but to deity possessions and ghosts. Deities might ask for sacrifices of things that they desire and ghosts similarly could stick around to resolve a wish they were not able to resolve while alive. The core idea is that if someone dies with an intense unfulfilled wish or desire "in their heart", they can *stick* around and create afflictions across generations.

Much like desire, suffering and distress usually caused by wrongful or untimely death, especially of a violent nature, mistreatment of family members especially the elders, and the experience of severe emotional distress or shock and betrayal, can cause a range of afflictions in a person, their family, or community. People attribute afflictions like hearing the voices of dead family members, health issues, or financial problems, to the fact that the one afflicted or their family/community caused grave suffering to someone at some point in time. Parental neglect and abuse has a special place in the causal narrative, and many commented on the *interdependence* of such experiences by noting how their own neglect of parents and other older relatives will not only negatively affect them but could also have grave repercussions for their children or grandchildren.

Another major cause behind a variety of different afflictions was broken connections and bonds – connections with land, people, rituals, and responsibilities. The people I spoke to believe that afflictions are caused, sometimes partially and on occasion entirely because people terminate connections with their land or ancestors; moreover, unfulfilled duties like incomplete rituals and duties towards family and community also had negative consequences. It is also to be noted that the presentation of an affliction can be on an individual or more than one person, so while one child could start hearing voices, another could fall sick, and the daughter of an uncle could become reclusive and start receiving bad grades in school. Importantly, this is not restricted to the suffering or unfulfilled desires of family members; some even spoke of afflictions caused by the distress of strangers in the village or community.

As observed earlier, the underlying thread among all of these is an *interdependence*; thus, afflictions can occur if one's father breaks the connections to the land or one's uncle doesn't finish a required ritual, or one's ancestors didn't put effort into maintaining and cultivating a clan's relationships. What is of interest to us is the range of phenomena under the rubric of unfulfilled duties. One woman I met clarified that even speaking out words and not acting on them can be problematic, for example, vocally saying that you will visit a temple or take a pilgrimage and not doing so, that is, not following words with actions. Thus, spoken words are a real concern as they seem to have a real effect on the world; in Hindi there is a phrase *"kisi ki hai lagna"* which translates as being struck by someone's ill-meaning intention. It reflects how the relationship between words and things is beyond that of only expression and signification, something that will be of glaring importance as we unravel implicit discourses.

Everyone I spoke with clarified that the subjective experience of fright (*ghabrahat*) is essential to affliction and this belief belies any superficial interpretations about the external locus of control one may have. While initially it may seem that most of the afflictions are caused by external entities (spirits, ghosts, gods, planets, and dead ancestors), leaving the people with very little control, a careful analysis complicates that assumption. Each person mentioned that in order to be attacked by/attached to a ghost, a person has to get scared or catch a fright. They distinguished between people who had heard or seen strange things that others did not but who didn't get scared and came out unscathed; and, on the other hand, those who did catch a fright when they heard the sound of anklets behind them or had some other "hallucinatory" experience would have the entity, usually a ghost, *attach/stick* itself to them, which would then lead to various *symptoms* as stated above. It is, then, essential to note that while the causal attribution at first glance seems to be external – deities, spirits, and ghosts – there is an inherent internal attribution which plays along with the external one, breaking connections, not taking care of elders, *responding with fright*.

One man explained that traveling down a road where someone died in an accident might make one vulnerable to ghosts only if one gets scared. Another narrated an anecdote where he was walking with his friends and saw a woman on an empty road (while others did not) but since he never experienced fright or ruminated over the event, it never attached itself to him. Thus, *seeing and hearing* things by itself does not necessitate distress and concern – the outcome depends on the person's reaction to the experience as noted in the positive response of one woman who liked to dance and sing with non-existent singing voices only she heard. Another important characteristic of this experience is closely related to what we have already observed about the land – participants spoke of ghosts as attached to certain landscapes like bodies of water (rivers) and small valleys leading up to the rivulets (*ghats*), so much so that on occasion they referred to the entities as the "ghost of the river". It is believed that people walking past these landscapes were especially vulnerable to such experiences.

Lastly, I should note that the people also believed that weakness in Hindu astrological signs made one vulnerable and susceptible to the phenomena of seeing things and hearing voices. Before I discuss this further, it is essential to note that, for Indians, the knowledge of planetary movements is not only different in content than that encountered in the West (for example, different calendars) but it is also deeply intertwined with their lives (and not casual entertainment), so much so that individually created birth charts and signs decide a child's name, who he/she can and cannot get married to, when they can get married, what health problems they will encounter, and even what career path suits them. People spoke about "planetary weakness" in certain times as being responsible for experiencing perceptions without sensations.

Overall, the people I met presented a range of explanations for experiences we would otherwise constitute as symptomatic of psychological disorders; these were planetary weakness, being a cause of suffering to others, responding with fright, dying with an unfulfilled desire or unresolved duty/responsibility, and breaking connections with land, family, and community. The most important observation remains that the cause might have nothing to do with the individual but s/he may have to bear the repercussion of the actions of others – across time and location.

Resolutions

The ways most people resolve these afflictions are just as complex and contradictory as their explanatory frameworks. Most people insisted that the first step towards resolution of afflictions is their diagnosis, or figuring out what has caused it and what type of entity they are dealing with. Ghosts tended to be more mischievous while deities were relatively peaceful, and ancestors could go either way; I am guessing annoying relatives always stay annoying, even after death. While there are numerous rituals and methods employed to deal with these problems, I will only focus on the commonalities between them. People spoke of figuring out the cause of the affliction to be imperative to its resolution. Some talked about dreams as diagnostic, for example one spoke of ancestors appearing in dreams to convey why they are restless and what their wishes are. Others talked about the method of "reading rice" to find out what the nature of the said affliction was and why the entity had appeared in their lives. This diagnostic custom of "reading rice" was conducted during a *jaagar*, which is a collective ritual conducted for a variety of reasons – familial and financial problems, curing possessions, health problems, seeing things others do not, etc. It reveals whether someone betrayed a neighbor or ignored familial rituals after leaving the village. The *jaagar* is where family, extended family, community, and village are all invited. The ritual involves music (mostly percussion instruments like steel utensils otherwise used to cook and serve food), dances, and induced and spontaneous trance states.

The two other methods of diagnosis are simultaneously methods of resolution – *vibuti* or sacred ash and the use of narratives or *bolna*. *Vibuti* is the ash made by the person who is taken over by a deity or a god; it could also be a product of the ritual fire. Each participant spoke of it as an immediate and effective form of cure for certain forms of afflictions like physical and mental agitation, seeing and hearing things, incoherent speech, and bizarre behavior. *Vibuti* is applied in a small quantity (a pinch) on the body of the afflicted individual during the *jaagar* and it seems to provide both knowledge about what has gone wrong and a cure for it. One young man explained: "Yeah, to the person who is screaming and shouting you just put one little *vibuti* on them and they get fine immediately. You should actually take a look at it – it's amazing." Another talked about how, after the failure of city doctors, *vibuti* helped diagnose and cure why the elder son of a local family was gravely sick.

Apart from *vibuti*, narratives or *bolna* (literal: to converse, talk) seem to play an important role in diagnosis and resolution. By narratives I mean stories that are verbalized during the *jaagar* by the afflicted person – it could relate to the cause of the affliction, the identity of the entity, or the requirements for resolution. The ghost must talk! The root of the affliction, why it began, what happened, and who had wronged whom, are all narrated, usually by the afflicted person in a trance state during the *jaagar*. The importance of a narrative relates to the importance of the verbal act – language, spoken language. As mentioned earlier, verbalized stories about the nature, identity, and cause of the entity are important for treatment and diagnosis. But the importance of spoken word goes beyond that – spoken word whether it's the curse of an older ignored ancestor or the unfulfilled vocalized promise of a pilgrim, can lead to real-life consequences. At times the afflicted person speaks in an unknown language during the *jaagar* and is sometimes even cured by the strange words. Similarly, the words of a mantra, verbalized or non-verbalized, are considered a potent protector against the "the traps of air and water", in other words, ghosts, and other entities.

Another important factor in resolution is the presence of family, extended family, community, and even the whole village. It was time and again pointed out that, without the presence of other people, a resolution was not possible. Since afflictions are interdependent in nature in that they can afflict your great grandchildren even if the fault was yours, it makes sense that the resolution should also be based in a similar dependence on others. The second person I interviewed explained:

> Through whom it has happened and to whom it has happened, and his own family, and someone else's family. You will have them also, that family. These things happen in the way, these things happen together because if they only tried to do it on their own, they will also get infected by it, if they do it alone, because it's the same family ... Here people actually come together. Everybody has to come. Otherwise even to them something keeps happening, going wrong ... Everybody has to be together (for resolution).

Another beleaguered man I spoke to reiterated the importance of inviting the village to a *jaagar* and then bemoaned that his extended family won't come together for a *puja* (ritual) and that their general non-involvement has caused him financial ruin. He further added that the bond of the family cannot break even if people are far away and have not met each other for generations.

We must make a note here to not wrap this in our own second-order judgments and understand this bond as emotional. At no point did anyone refer to the bond or connection as something akin to psychological support and it is easy to force that interpretation on this narrative – the idea that coming together is essential because it lends psychological and emotional support to the troubled individual and family. Many writers have often focused on the emotional effects of refuge, community, and cooperation behind family involvement and posit that these ways of healing have socio-moral components that are more appealing to our participants than medical treatment. I would instead assert that the socio-economic component (like lower costs), while essential, is only partially the reason for this prescription to maintain connections to land and people. A descriptive analysis shows that people are speaking of literal connections with others – connections that span across generations and geographical locales. Nowhere did anyone allude to family being important for mental support or emotional need – one individual actually talked about deep animosity between his father's brothers, so much so that last time he tried to gather them together for a ritual "the swords came out"; despite that, he needs their presence for the ritual and for the successful resolution of his financial and property problems.

It is essential to re-establish bonds with not only family and community, but also with the physical landscape. Rituals for resolution can only be conducted on the person's *pitr-bhoomi* (paternal/ancestral land). Again, we must not understand this in terms of safe spaces or the familiarity of home; the participants are clear that it does not matter how many generations you have been away, the return is essential because the connection is physical. Ranganathan (2015) had observed a similar pattern while studying healing at the Mahanubhav temple: staying at the temples was inherently curative and the effects of the physical space could not transfer outside it. Thus, one of the most important aspects of resolution apart from the technologies of trance and *vibuti* is the rebuilding of severed connections with family, community, and land.

The last important component of resolution is the much-researched trance state. The process of trance has been thoroughly investigated in psychological and anthropological literature and usually associated with a dissociative state. During a *jaagar*, the individuals in whom deities present themselves usually attain a trance state and dance to different percussion instruments like drums; the dance has a peculiar quality to it and sometimes can be accompanied by trembling of the body. These experts or curers then use *vibuti* to either alleviate the trance and suffering of the afflicted or to diagnose it. The afflicted and the curer have similar behavioral presentations – trance state, dancing, speaking in tongues, and sometimes self-harm (putting burning coals on their tongue) that they seem impervious to in that moment. The trance state of the afflicted, with some help from the expert, is inherently curative, especially after *vibuti* is applied on their body. I met one *dangaria* ('dancer–curer' in whom the deity presents itself) whose day job was running a small grocery store and who, when required, helped his neighbors and others through trance and *vibuti*. While reluctant to describe the experiential process of deity possession, as it is considered improper to openly speak about it, he did mention convulsions/shaking and lack of control over his own body. He described that memory remains more or less intact, but one's "natural behavior" alters completely. He further added that initially these states were painful and difficult to deal with due to the lack of control and convulsions, but with time a person gets used to it and the experience doesn't bother him/her with the same intensity.

But what about trauma?

At this point, there is a glaring absence of any mention of event trauma in the different narratives. This was slightly disconcerting because I was hoping to unravel some relation between hearing voices and traumatic life events in light of some excellent research that has recently come to the fore (e.g. Romme & Escher, 2012). It turns out that the absence is the relation. The conversation about trauma was met with confused looks and always ended with dismissive shrugs. I was painfully aware of the power of suggestion and thus touched upon the topic of event trauma timidly; I referred to it as some very painful or difficult life circumstance or *sadma* (shock). From there it took two directions – either people thought about it in terms of some recent and ongoing major stressor or painful event that could have caused an affliction, or, when I gently pushed a developmental narrative, some were forced to think about significant losses over a person's lifetime, especially in childhood. Both directions took a similar turn where people insisted that painful life events or losses had nothing to do with these afflictions. The first person I interviewed, a young man himself experiencing *ghabrahat* (fright) as he heard footsteps behind him that no one else did, was utterly flippant towards my question about big losses or stressors in life; he said: "No, nothing like that. I have been pretty lucky, had a good life". Another clarified: "In the times of happiness and in the times of difficulties, it happens anytime. There is no particular time for it" when asked about the timing of these difficulties around traumatic events. Still others reiterated this assertion by saying there is no time or circumstance that can trigger these afflictions, it can happen "any time".

It should be noted that there was one anecdote about the man who was cheated out of his land and "went mad" that comes closest to how we understand trauma and shock. There are two subtle differences here in the indigenous and our psychological understanding. First, the person who narrated this anecdote did not include hearing voices and seeing things in his description of madness; instead, the focus was on bizarre behavior. Second, instead of focusing on the man's suffering while he was alive, the person paid attention to the effect of his suffering on the culprit's family after his death – pain and suffering could be of consequence, just not necessarily personal suffering. All participants were dismissive of life stressors, big losses, and painful circumstances, recent or older, as having anything to do with these afflictions, at least in the ways we understand. But as I will now explain, negative affect does have a part to play, just not how we would expect it to operate.

The "how": beyond meaning

Foucault, who for long insisted that he was a historian of thought, was essentially interested in the "history of the present", where he used history as a way to diagnose the present, that is, to introduce strangeness into our current ways of being, despite their apparent sensibleness to us (Kendall & Wickham, 1998). He pointed to epistemic discontinuities in that he was able to ascertain historical breaks in underlying ways of thinking to diagnose what current ways of thought sustain certain discourses (sexuality, punishment, madness). The following sections of this chapter have a similar but vastly narrower scope.

Subjects are constituted by more than words and any investigation into their structure must also attend to visibilities (like the process of *jaagar*, the ritual of sacrifice, of giving material goods to the priest, the physical landscape, and the architecture and built environment of the Mehandipur Balaji temple as an institution) to unearth the implicit styles of thinking that animate the discourse around madness. I did not look for causes behind a phenomenon nor for any deeper meaning. The overarching themes described previously are all contingencies. So while there could be a causal relation between the offered explanations and their subsequent resolution, there could just as likely be none; there could also be multiple relations. As an example, let's consider the ritual of giving *daan* (small material gifts) to assuage an unhappy ancestor; some of these gifts are immersed in the local rivers while others are given to the priest after rituals. An obvious causal relation is that, since unfulfilled wishes of ancestors are believed to be of concern, fulfilling those wishes through sacrifice and giving them what they desired would lead to resolution. On the other hand, it might be that the ritual of sacrifice and giving *daan* was created by upper-caste priests to ensure their own economic sustenance and specialized status. Lastly, the two might not have any causal connection at all. This does not mean Foucault was implying that anything could have happened and it is all accidental; instead it puts forth a view of the world that is non-linear and makes our current social arrangements seem odd. Further, observing contingencies instead of causes allows us to divest second-order judgments that rest in our previous knowledge and are always enthusiastic to make their presence known. It is with these cautions that I will now expose the implicit style of thinking that animates the meaning-making framework that speaks about deities, djinns, and evil intentions.

A stickiness of affect and word

A close inspection of the constitution of an affliction and the range of explanations brings to light certain forms of thinking that make the stories about ancestral revenge, ghost experiences, spirit possessions, and the gamut of mental, physical, financial, and behavioral phenomena possible and reasonable. These repeated statements are sustained by certain rules, in this case, the rule that intense emotions have a *stickiness* about them – they stick/attach to places (landscapes like rivers), to people (especially those catch a fright) – and they are unrelenting through time and space. This is subtly reflected in the linguistics of their narrative – a ghost or a spirit *lagti hai* which translates to sticks/attaches/applies, most of the times, *on* the body and not inside, as in the case of possession. Consider the statement by a woman talking about the elderly of the family who haven't been taken care of; she said that "their tears stick/attach to you", which points to a physicality of affect but not through indirect psychosomatic presentations which also connect affect and soma. The mind features nowhere here; there is instead a real one-on-one relation between affect and its physical consequences. When a man talked about the girl violently murdered and her body cut in half and thrown away in the mountains, he stated that generations later this ghost stuck itself (*lag gaya*) to another girl who was passing through, almost as if by touch. Another man presented the anecdote of a young woman murdered by her sister-in-law; she then haunted her sister-in-law and others in the community, and the culprit had to pay by losing her fertility and her beauty.

These narratives imply that intense emotions and intentions, sometimes created by extreme events, have a material presence, a life of their own – an ability to stick to landscapes like rivers and from there become attached to unsuspecting people. Places can have an overwhelming presence but it is this underlying way of thinking about the direct association between intensity and space that reveals that people are not referring to serene beauty or talking in metaphors. The recurring statement that Uttarakhand is a special place and can initiate faith in the non-believer suddenly takes a different tone – it is not the landscape's influence on their mind but instead a more direct and material connection. The whole narrative is sustained by a tactile principle. This understanding is built around the implicit assumption that intense affect has the ability to leave a physical stamp on places – like a stickiness that left behind its intensity, or a force that can throw people off staircases. Violence and suffering have a special place here; the suffering of an elderly person in the family who wasn't fed or was abused (*satana*) can *stick* around and trouble generations – it doesn't matter whether they reside in the same village or leave for another country. Violent death or attacks that could have caused intense suffering and negative affect can similarly stain places and landscapes.

At the same time, violence and suffering are not the only intense emotions that carry such animal force – unfulfilled desire, which can sometimes appear as betrayal, also has a similar physical life. I have already written about the woman who said that the elderly can keep a small wishes or a big desire *in their heart* only for it to sustain through ages and reveal itself to the great grandchild of the person in his/her dreams. She further stated that if her mother-in-law couldn't express a desire, knowing her children's financial trouble, the "speech" (*baat*) or desire would be wedged in her and later return to inflict demands on her children. Not only is unfulfilled desire an unstoppable force that crashes through time, but it can attach itself to different people, in this case, in the same or extended family. There was also the anecdote about the man whose last wish, which eventually drove him mad, was to get his land back: a desire whose materiality sustained itself despite his death. Thus, the power of the landscape lies in implicit acceptance that physical spaces can contain or hold on to intense affect or that intense affect can attach itself to physical spaces.

This is not only true for landscapes but also for the discourse around black magic and how it is performed and transferred. One individual, when referring to a neighbor's child inflicted by black magic, said that someone gave the child "food or water" that had the magic *attached/stuck to* it. This implies an unspoken acceptance of materiality of intention that can attach itself to a physical object and carry its effects through that physical object; in this case, food and water. Similarly, *vibuti* as a method of curing some forms of afflictions is the ash that comes out of the ritual fire and a pinch of it is applied *on* the body and not ingested like medicine – again pointing to a transmission of cure through touch-based physical channels. *Mere bachon par lag jayega* or "it will stick to my children" is a real concern for many mothers. This loose translation does not do justice to the way one woman phrased this concern; the literal translation would be more akin to: "Upon/On my children it will get applied". This small linguistic detail speaks to the tactile principle underlying these intense affects and almost always gets lost in translation when people research these experiences.

Apart from desire, revenge, and suffering, another intense affect that was important was fright or fear. People even alluded to it as having a physical life of its own in the form of a force that is left behind by violent accidents. The stickiness of fright was spoken of by many as they explained the importance of subjective experience. It is essential to remember here that different discourses illuminate different ways of looking at the same phenomena. Thus, while the discourse of psychology would understand the relation between intense emotions and problematic phenomena as psychosomatic or maybe trauma-driven, the local discourse instead brings into focus what we would call a paranormal interpretation driven by ideas of mutilation and murder of people who left a "mark" on a place, or of deceased individuals with unfulfilled desires that stain landscapes. There is a substantial difference between the two discourses which highlights the different rules of thought that animate them. The psychological discourse is restricted by these rules and can only study the relation between intense emotions and somatic concerns, whereas the underlying conditions of the indigenous discourse allow them to include financial troubles, tactile hallucinations, general life problems, infertility, loss of property, etc.

This very material and physical stickiness of intense emotions that can have real effects on things, for example, to cause someone to unexpectedly bleed profusely, have their children fall sick, etc., also exists for and in words to some extent. We see an underlying belief about a direct effect of words on things. People insisted on the negative consequences of saying things out loud and not following them with action, for example, saying that you would go on a pilgrimage and not doing so, or they talked of the protection awarded by the words of a mantra. The words carried out into the world have an effect, with physical repercussions. It is as if spoken words alter the fabric of their physical surroundings. The spoken word is also important for resolution, as people remarked on how the afflicted individual verbalizes the cause and nature of the entity that is attached to them. Of interest to us is the glaring absence of mind in these forms of thought. Earlier in Charaka's work we had noted the absence of the mind–body divide in Ayurvedic systems of thought and medicine, where the symptoms of kapha-induced, pitta-induced, and vatta-induced madness ranged from nasal and salivary discharge to introversion. We observe a similar absence of the divide here. Concepts of wish fulfillment and symptoms like "leg lock" lend themselves effortlessly to the psychological discourse and the influence of mind on body. But people here do not speak of any kind of interference or channeling through the mind. Whether it is the requirement of having their family and community present during a ritual, the need to return to *pitr-bhoomi*, or the belief about a relation between intense affect and its physical ramifications – their understanding has a materiality to it and implies a direct connection to the physical world that is unfettered by the mind and oblivious to interiority. This lack of focus on interiority will become more evident as I discuss the next implicit belief. In conclusion, the first style of thought that runs through various indigenous assertions, statements, and beliefs is the idea that intense affect has a material stickiness that gets attached to things, land, and people, and also leads to direct alterations in the physical world.

Radical enmeshment

The other pattern of thought which supports much of the local discourse is what I earlier tentatively referred to as interdependence; a better phrase would be radical enmeshment. It should be noted that enmeshment itself, like interdependence, is a troublesome term, as it implies the presence of separate objects that merge together. I would recall the words of one interviewee which describe this style of thought succinctly: "through whom it has happened and to whom it has happened, and his own family, and someone else's family" everyone is involved in the explanation, presentation, and resolution of an affliction. As we observed earlier, these afflictions do not have any divisions that categorize them as physical, mental, social, or financial in nature. Thus, for a person who hallucinates a wedding procession or hears nonexistent footsteps behind them, or even experiences being forcefully thrown off a set of stairs – the causal explanation offered incriminates their close relationships and other people in their community. These people could be responsible for the suffering of a dying individual or their violent demise, or their elders could have, generations ago, broken their connection with the land by leaving, eventually leading to hearing the voice of their dead mother. Thus, an individual's personal actions are not the only ones of consequence – it does not matter if s/he has treated their parents with care and catered to their needs in old age; in case anyone in their family or extended family, dead or alive, failed to do the same, they could be inflicted with the spirit of a dead ancestor they have never even met. Lives and stories are not just intertwined, they are inseparable in the first place. Actions and intentions of different people and even inanimate things are not just related, they are radically interwoven – built through each other.

This same enmeshment applies to resolutions where the presence of *pitrbhoomi*, family, and the whole village is imperative to a cure. While this may seem unfair and harsh, we observe here a way of understanding the world where we are consistently and perpetually defined or rather structured by other people AND things – not only mentally or socially, but rather in very physical ways – a materiality I pointed to in the last implicit belief. Others' actions affect your fertility, their intentions can alter your finances. The individual, self-contained, as a unit of society, whose interiority matters and whose choices are important – barely exists. This should not be interpreted to mean, as many wrongly do, that the society lives in collectivist bliss. Rather, to be constituted by others (*including* inanimate objects) and to constitute others, this way of being is wrought with tensions – jealousy, revenge, anger, betrayals. No ritual is complete without the presence of others (extended family and community) and no explanation valid without their involvement. The grocery-store owner reminded me that everyone in the village could be punished for a crime even in the most mundane and unparanormal of ways. In talking about the young girl who murdered her sister-in-law, he stated that the family "showed it as a suicide. Because if someone brings a police case, the whole village will get punished". Animating the discourse of spirits, ghosts, and angry ancestors is the underlying idea that everyone is connected, or rather *made up* structurally and functionally, of everyone else. Personal responsibility, individual concerns, and private matters do not exist in the same way we in the Western industrialized world understand them to. For that matter, the absence of the notion of privacy and individual space can be observed in the consternation expressed by one man as he talked about a young girl who would lock her room from inside; this behavior was presented as deviant and disconcerting – a symptom of an affliction.

This underlying style of thought permeates all narratives – the fact that we are constituted by and constitute other people, other things, landscapes, objects, and even heavenly bodies – in a very material way. As observed earlier, Hindu astrological birth charts have a much larger influence on a person's life than the way we usually understand horoscopes. It is this style of thought that makes resolution through time and space, across generations and dead ancestors possible, as radical enmeshment requires the physical presence of everyone to assuage a disgruntled ancestor ("We are four families and till they come together, till all the members of the family also come together the *puja* won't be successful"). It is this style of thought that allows for these explanations because it is due to radical enmeshment that your paternal aunt's actions or intentions can lead to your suffering. One individual I spoke to said:

> What I mean is that imagine that I am here but my family members are outside the town. They'll also get sick they will also get affected. Yeah it is joint. This is how it happens, that I am here and there are there but something bad will happen to them also.

It is also what allows certain events, behaviors, and phenomena to be problematic and sometimes pathological, because radical enmeshment means that breaking real connections to animate and inanimate objects will have real consequences ("So they got this goat and sacrificed it in the temple *on their own*. What happened then was, that his eyes started giving [him] trouble. He went blind, he still is blind.") And this implicit strain of thinking is what sustains the discourse that Uttarakhand is a special place and that *pitr-bhoomi* is of utmost importance because people's physical bond to it cannot be broken, as they are structured via each other

> Their home is here but they stay there but they had to come all the way from there to here to fix these things .... They have to come back. Yeah they have to, they have to come to their paternal/ancestral home.

The people I met, and this includes me to an extent, do not conceive of themselves as self-contained individuals or simply interdependent on each other, as much of cultural psychology insists; instead their fate depends on the actions, words, and even unfulfilled intentions of others – across time and geographical location. This formation of the subject through radical enmeshment can shed light on the misguided questions many Indians are asked about arranged marriages: "why don't you, as opposed to your family, choose your spouse?" There isn't, or for long hasn't been a style of thought that allowed the differentiation between one's own and one's family's choice. The demands of a society are not simply seen as demands or experienced as impinging on our choices and freedoms – radical enmeshment dissolves any such differences for most people. If I asked my mother or one of my interviewees how they could allow their family to choose their spouse, they would and should probably ask me how could I not. Similarly, the idea that your family can choose your career may seem deeply oppressive to an outsider but it is just *natural* when you are structurally constituted by your family, villagers, dead ancestors, rivers, mountains, and more; it is so much more than a superficial Other-orientation.

It is this radical enmeshment that restricts ideas around identity and self – questions of "who am I?", "what do I want to be?", "what is my true self?" Our subjects are open/vulnerable to rocks, rivers, stranger's ghosts, and dead ancestor's ill-intentions – a physical connection with quantifiable consequences. The pattern of thought that displays that their connection to land is material and sustains itself across generations is seen in the way they talked about "our/own land" versus "bought land". Since their subjectivity is intrinsically tied to their *pitr-bhoomi*, exchanging money and legal documents cannot create a direct physical relationship. Just like the ghost of an amputated limb persists long after and leads to pain and discomfort, breaking the connection to land is physically traumatic, with repercussions similar to that of a real amputation.

The physicality, or the material nature, of these connections is important to note – *vibuti* is applied on the body; the dance is shaking of the body, self-harm that sometimes accompanies trance during *jaagar* is prominently physical; one man spoke of his relation to the land as: "he is attached to the dirt of this place". We can observe a similar materiality in the linguistics around these phenomena. What we normally call possession – a word casually thrown about by many Indian and Western authors, including me, suggests that there is an individual to possess. On the other hand, the Hindi word used consistently by locals suggests a certain "attaching" or almost sticking, even mounting (*chadna*) – *lagna* which is a word that can be used to describe a stain on a dress. The spirit that ruins your finances or the ghost that causes your leg to "lock" doesn't "enter" or "possess" you – they stick or attach themselves – now to you and later to someone or something else. As for the narrative around their connections to land and people, nothing in what they said implies an emotional support or mental dependence – rather, everyone spoke at the level of a real and physical connection, which if broken would lead to unforeseen negative consequences.

It is important here to note the difference between materiality and physiology. While the indigenous explanations are material, in that there is a force and physicality involved in the contagion of deviant behavior, the discipline of psychology offers explanations that are physiological, and it is easy to confuse the two. Materiality implies a physical contact of things we consider mental: intensions, emotions, etc. in turn maintaining the exteriority of these phenomena; physiology internalizes and individualizes them as occurring and existing inside a person – not contagious through contact, but produced through the organic and the genetic. While materiality abhors linear causality, physiology seeks causes in the molecular and the developmental. While materiality marks the deviant as problematic, it also seeks to include him/her in the general; all spaces that specialize in the deviant are also littered with the normal – Balaji, *jaagars*, etc. The deviant is deviant transiently, and attempts at helping him/her are geared towards their inclusion with the rest. People who take their relatives to Balaji and other healing temples stay with them for days; *jaagars* happen with the whole family and community around. As opposed to that, physiology encourages exclusion and demarcation of special spaces reserved for the deviant, for example, older madhouses and newer hospitals. Even though the recent explosion in words around the experience of mental illness has created more sophisticated communities, they still maintain exclusion – support groups for patients, separate groups for family, online forums for patients and separate ones for caretakers, charities, and movements, which ironically create isolated communities. As the language around these concepts changes (e.g. neuro-atypical, hearing voices, etc.) the reality of the experience shifts, but despite that the level of explanation remains organic or psychological at its core – these are spaces for people who are wired differently or have a different genetic presentation, or a traumatized past.

Visibilities and institutions: inside the haunted temple of Balaji

I revealed two distinct implicit styles of thought that sustain the narratives around the experience of *seeing and hearing things*, as seen in the statements about spirits, ghosts, angry dead ancestors, and more. But as Kendall and Wickham (1998) state, discourses are not merely linguistic and a Foucauldian archaeological analysis requires us to take into account certain visibilities. For example, in Foucault's description of the disciplinary system, the prison was a visibility and so was the written codification that accompanied centralization. In my work, everything from the percussion instruments to *vibuti* are forms of visibilities that makes certain discourses and subject positions possible and are also in turn determined by them. The two important visibilities I will elaborate here are the process of trance during the ritual of *jaagar* and the temple of Balaji known for spontaneous possession/psychosis/hysteria (depending on who you ask).

Jaagar as a visibility

The *jaagar* as described earlier is a collective gathering which involves the family, community, and the village at large; it includes certain ceremonies, regular trance states, and ritualized dancing by people who are either captured by deities or non-deity entities. The former help the latter reach some form of resolution using trance states, verbalized narratives, and *vibuti*. There are certain visible aspects of this gathering which together reinforce the understandings offered by the interviewees. First, the narration feature of the trance phenomena sustains the discourse that insists that certain afflictions are caused by unfulfilled desires, rightful anger, or betrayal. Narration requires a person to verbalize why a certain entity is present, who s/he is, and what they need in order to be pacified. This verbal practice justifies the explanations offered and at the same time the explanations offered justify this verbalization.

Second, the physical ceremony of *daan*, or offerings to the priest, and also the ritual of animal sacrifice, similarly reinforce the idea that unfulfilled desire as an intense affect leaves marks that survive across generations, and need to be satisfied through *daan* and sacrifice. Third, the fact that *jaagar* can only be held either at their own home (ancestral home) or at the local shrine of their ancestral deities furthers beliefs around the importance of maintaining material connections and physical bonds to the land. One old man explained:

> A man can go anywhere from here, America or Delhi, wherever in any country, but they have their paternal land here, the soil of this place ... he is attached to the dirt of this place (*mitti*). So wherever he goes he has to come back to take care of the affliction (*kasht*). Let me tell you something, there was a *jaagar* just day before at Ramnagar. The house was broken, turned into a ruin (*khandar*) ... So they (clan's deities) said, don't organize it inside the house, do this thing – take the stones of the garden ... just clean it and purify that area and light a lamp there, in our name, and organize a *jaagar* there.

This whole anecdote shows how the physical ritual/visibility of *jaagar* conducted on the *pitr-bhoomi* reinforces the implicit and explicit beliefs about material connections to the "dirt" and these connections last even after real homes have turned to dust. We observed a similar implication in their assertions differentiating their own land against bought land.

The haunted temple of Balaji

The second form of visibility that I decided to investigate was the famous temple of Mehandipur Balaji which I visited less than a week after returning from Uttarakhand. The temple of Balaji which is a four-hour drive away from Delhi falls in the state of Rajasthan and is always included in the lists of most haunted places in the country. While Uttarakhand and Rajasthan couldn't be further apart in the appearance of their landscapes, for the former is made of lush mountains while the latter is a vast desert, both have exceedingly large Hindu majority populations and people from across the nation regularly come to Balaji seeking treatment. The temple is primarily known for spontaneous possessions or, if you ask the many psychologists who have studied it, it is a site rich with spontaneous mass hysteria. It is the temple where people from around the country come to heal possessions and other illnesses that seem to be caused by nefarious deities, vengeful spirits, and petty ghosts. Furthermore, and most importantly, it is also the place where those diagnosed with schizophrenia or acute psychotic disorder in the cities come to cure themselves or their family members; sometimes they are still on psychiatric drugs while they seek cure. Science and magic do not contradict each other here.

Before you ever set foot in the temple or Dausa, the small district where it is located, or even begin the journey from home, the reputation

Deities and desire **119**

of Balaji will reach you. I know of universities that organized trips there only to stop after a young female student had a breakdown in the temple. I had personally wanted to visit Balaji for about a decade but found no one willing to accompany me. This time, a few drinks emboldened a close friend to promise me that she and I would leave early next morning. As this took place right after my Uttarakhand visit, my head was already swimming with stories of haunted rivers and murderous sisters-in-law, and as a result the night before the trip was marked by sleeplessness interspersed with terrifying nightmares.

As I and two other friends entered the Dausa district, small shops crowding both sides of the road, selling everything from shoes to ritual offerings, gave it the appearance of a generic lower-socio-economic commercial area; that changed radically as we got closer to the temple. Figure 4.2 shows the entry to this area, after which one encounters small shops littered on either sides of the road. My first glimpse of something odd was noticing a woman crying and laughing (at the same time) at the top of her voice in the small shrine opposite the main temple. In my very middle-class upbringing I had never seen a woman convey her joy, sorrow, or pain that openly, loudly, boundlessly, and viscerally. The temple of Balaji itself is a dark and oppressive place, unlike many other popular temples that are adorned in resplendent colors. In order to enter we were required to get in queues with hundreds of people, queues that are caged from both sides to stop people from cutting in, but it feels more like they are there to stop us from getting out – it's a claustrophobe's worst

FIGURE 4.2 Area a mile away from the temple

nightmare. But then this is India and if you mention feeling suffocated in small spaces or crowds to other people, they will give you a perplexed look and tell you, like my mother once did when I told her I was claustrophobic, to stop making up things. I held my friend's hand in order to not lose her or myself. My abnormally tall self could glance above the heads of everyone and the air in my face stopped me from fainting.

Once you make your way through the cages, which can take hours in suffocating heat but luckily took us around 25 minutes, you reach the shrine of Balaji which is another name for the god Hanuman. Hanuman is revered as he is considered the remover of obstacles and specializes in crises caused by ghosts and spirits. The shrines are small and dark, and as we were passing them we noticed another young woman on our right fall on the ground, shake convulsively, and laugh-cry at something in front of her only she could see. People were constantly chanting different songs and mantras but sometimes their voices would come together in unison to recite the same verses; as nervous observers and non-believers we felt that we stuck out. Apart from our delicate selves, no one else seemed to feel the discomfort, the heat, or was bothered by the crowd. We moved from the cavernous queues to a nondescript sheltered area where people were just casually sitting around, and a big ritual oil fire burned in one corner. People regularly approached the fire to throw offerings or ritual items that must be destroyed. Sitting on the floor I noted one older woman with an imposing presence and open, unkempt hair burst into booming laughter at something that was visible only to her, and others around her followed suit; I could not figure out if they saw what she saw whether her mad laughter was just that contagious. No one who has visited a mental institution can deny the similarity in appearance of these two places. It is on the other side of this building that I caught a glimpse of a big hall with narrow divisions like in airport security, with iron chains tied to the steel poles, and few people seemed to be tied here. Some of them were poised oddly, which was very reminiscent of a catatonic stupor while others were agitated and screaming loudly; some seemed distraught while others appeared quite pleased. All had their families either around them or somewhere on the premises. Balaji, if nothing else, is a gorgeous spectacle of distress, misery, joy, and laughter – all at the same time.

It is easy to interpret spaces like Balaji and other such temples as pockets of subversion, spaces where behaviors that are otherwise deemed socially and culturally inappropriate are allowed (loud women ripping their clothes off), but that is not my concern. For to me Balaji is an important visibility, an institution that sustains the discourse I heard from the people of rural Uttarakhand. People who come here, like the people I had already spoken to, had afflictions that could range from financial troubles and health issues to symptoms that earned them a diagnosis of schizophrenia. But instead of creating mentally ill subjects ("the sick") these institutions and discourses create "the afflicted". Considering the fact that spontaneous mass hysteria/possession is common here, in that otherwise normal people come here and begin to show symptoms, the place in some ways literally creates these subjects.

Much like Uttarakhand, Balaji has an aura and an overwhelming quality about it – stories about this place spread far and wide. The presence of these "mad women" who have shed all propriety – their cries, their screams, and laughter, their curses, and naked bodies, and their self-inflicted wounds – reinforce and constitute what Balaji has come to be as an institution. Just like the prison architecture pinned the prisoner under the glare of self-discipline and the tea parties in Pinel's asylums initiated bourgeois guilt in its inmates, so does Balaji, with its dark cavernous spaces that force bodies together, the heat of the desert, the chains, burning fires, and oil stains on the walls sustain the expectancy of "mad behavior", create the subject position of the mad/possessed person, and reinforce the behaviors that come with it. This is furthered by the stories about Balaji – about its power, its hauntings, and its mystery; the stories, the visible architecture, the material rituals, and the subject positions co-constitute each other.

To exemplify, the oil fire lit for the purpose giving offerings to deities, spirits, and gods is a visibility that furthers the discourse around unfulfilled wishes and the material nature of needs that span across time. Since affect and intention have a materiality that sticks, their destruction has to be equally intense and physical – in fire. Thus, the destruction of certain ritual items in the oil fire lends itself to the idea that intention and intense affect has a stickiness that can attach itself to things and thus needs to be destroyed (black magic).The pressing of bodies against each other and the bizarre transmissible nature of symptoms (inexplicable laughter, shaking of the body that starts with one person and moves to surrounding strangers) – this physicality of the experience strengthens the discourse of material connectivity between people and things – a contagion of sorts. The repeated stories about spontaneous hauntings and spirit attachments at Balaji reinforce the discourse that these afflictions are caused by different entities and some, not all, people have an inherent vulnerability caused by numerous factors.

These bizarre and paranormal stories of hauntings and possessions that seem so alien to us are contextualized very differently at Balaji and amongst my interviewees. Kakkar (1982), in *Shamans and Mystics and Doctors*, presents a delightful anecdote about Balaji where he encountered a group of women sitting with a Pandit ji, a Hindu man who had been possessed by a Muslim ghost and thus wanted to eat meat. The women mocked the man and the spirit, telling him that until he is on Pandit ji, he will never get to eat kebabs; Pandit ji's wife then goes on to scold the spirit for his rudeness. Not only does this anecdote animate the idea around unfulfilled desires that may persist after death (like an appetite for Mughlai food which one cannot blame the spirit for) but also presents to us a context where these phenomena don't carry the same grave seriousness as they do for us in the West. One might say that many take these experiences literally but not as seriously. People I spoke to stated how distress was only occasional with these spirit or ghost attachments and that a person remains "normal" until the *jaagar*; moreover, people continue to be functional and hold jobs even when they are regularly experiencing auditory and visual hallucinations. Their existence is not paranormal because it informs a characteristic style of thought – the force of intense affect and the existence of radical enmeshment – making them just as normal an experience as working in the field.

The temple, as opposed to a sterile hospital, is filthy – from ritual flowers to food offerings, oil stains to plastic bags – everything is littered inside and around. The sterility of the hospital is tethered to the medical discourse of the disease model; maybe it even harks back to Foucault's assertions about bourgeois morality, which we know worships cleanliness and organized living. The sterility creates the schizophrenic and his many historical permutations, from the vanishing catatonic or the obsolete hebephrenic. On the other hand, in a space like Balaji, it is not germs that must be conquered but material affect and intention that must be destroyed (ritual fires); psychosis might be present but the psychotic sure isn't. The afflicted, as opposed to being treated like they are unwell and thus fragile, are instead dealt with like you would deal with a particularly mischievous child. Behind the main temple, I saw one of the priests shouting at a young woman, asking the spirit to detach – he threatened her, even hit her gently, demanded that she leave, and then pleaded to her – the same sequence most Indian parents would use with their child. These visibilities, from the temple architecture in Balaji to the hand sanitizers in hospitals, create people much like words can and it would be helpful to observe the kinds of people they create if we are to understand the subjectivity that underlies subject positions.

Subject positions: the delinquent, the criminal, and the afflicted

From a careful analysis of the statements and visibilities in Uttarakhand and at the Balaji temple, one can notice a few emerging subject positions. A question that was helpful to excavate these positions was: who is the object of these discourses and their investigation, diagnosis, and cure? The answer is *the afflicted*. In the same way that Foucault exposed how the disciplinary forces and the psychological discourses and institutions respectively pinned down the delinquent and the mentally ill, it is evident here that the point of convergence of these indigenous discourses and practices is the afflicted subject. This is the person (or family, persons) who might have seen apparitions or heard non-existent voices, who might have caught a fright, who could be suffering with constant fatigue and ill health, or might be encountering troubles with the family business. The afflicted is where all of these concerns meet; it is where cure is applied and symptoms are expressed – s/he/they are the object of local knowledge. This subject position in return reinforces the discourse and the institutions surrounding it (for example, the afflicted who are *created in* Balaji) and it also limits them at the same time.

There are even a few sub-positions that operate under "the afflicted", the first being that of the "bad child" or "bad/irresponsible family". This is the person (or family) who failed to take care of their elders and fulfil their desires and wishes. This subject was present in each conversation I had; further, this "bad child/family" could also be defined by their irresponsible actions towards their community, family, and land, as they failed to maintain bonds and broke off connections. The methods of resolution like *daan* and sacrifice bolster this sub-subject position by allowing for the pacification and fulfillment of the wishes the bad child/family were not able to. The practice of a narrative (having the entity talk about why it is present) during trance further consolidates these positions; it reinforces the implicit idea that the bad child/family caused the affliction, that there is a reason for the affliction that must be narrated to be resolved. Thus, the practice, the discourse, and the subject position sustain each other in an elegant loop.

The other sub-position under that of the afflicted is that of the "fright-prone person". This type of individual was unique in that s/he catches a fright while hearing voices or seeing things, while others do not. This characteristic, which is not always shared by others, creates a type of individual *jo ghabra jaata hai* ("the one who gets scared"). I should point out that the underlying discourse around ghosts and spirits (or hallucinations), which is that intense affect sticks to certain places, is bolstered by this type of individual whose personal characteristic of catching fright explains why not everyone who walks through certain woods or crosses a haunted river encounters similar experiences. This individual has an inherent quality of catching fright and ruminating over that fear, which is a weakness and a vulnerability. This quality protects the indigenous explanations from critique, where a disbelieving neighbor cannot say "I was there yesterday but saw no such thing". The marked characteristics of this subject are an initial vulnerability and subsequent rumination, and they help to ground institutions like local temples, and practices like *jaagar* where the fright can be removed.

An intriguing local tale about the birth of the Balaji temple reveals how this subject has a place in history and legend. Myths and stories surrounding any Indian tale are always myriad; there are popular versions and then regional ones. While walking through the caged entryway towards the temple, I met a man who regaled us with this regional version of the beginnings of the temple: centuries ago, the king of Mehandipur died but he decided to *stick* around and scare people in the region. After years of doing this, one day a young boy (Hanuman or Balaji himself in a boy's form) was passing along the path, and the king's spirit attempted to scare him but was unable to because Balaji *recognized him for who he was*, and didn't experience fear. The king's ghost, impressed, revealed himself to the boy and later the temple of Balaji opened its doors as a place where those afflicted by spirits and ghosts could come and seek help. Thus, the one who catches a fright (and in this story he does not because he is a god) is the subject that has a place in the initiation tale of Balaji. This subject is the one at whom a cure is directed (*jaagar, vibuti*) and from whom explanations about the nature and causes of the presence of an entity are sought (narrative). As always, this subject position in turn enhances the strength of these discourses and institutions (like Balaji).

There is another subject position that a few people in Uttarakhand spoke about but it appears more frequently in the discourse and academic research around Balaji – that of the "mad woman". The mad woman regularly made her way in my conversations and she is especially visible in Balaji where spontaneous hysteria has been noted in women at a higher rate. The markers of the "mad woman" as seen in Balaji and in the interviews are similar: open, unkempt hair, "un-womanlike" behavior – dancing suggestively, screaming, using explicit language, expressing sexual desire, etc. Whether it is spontaneous possession, a deity attachment, a mass-hysterical episode, or even an acute psychotic break, the place that is Balaji, with the stories and mysteries that surround it, has been documented to have a special effect on girls: an excellent example of how an institution creates a subject who is characterized to be constitutionally susceptible. In the mountains and in the cities, the mad woman is a scandalous character, threatening to bring dishonor to families and communities; but in Balaji and during *jaagar* her behavior is normalized, contained, and, most importantly, created.

Another important subject position, apart from the afflicted, is that of the *dangaria* (dancer–curer). As one person vehemently stated, during the *jaagar*, both the afflicted and the *dangaria* dance, but the latter has "permission" and the former doesn't. The curer is more of an expert than a specialist; he does not practice his "trade" but usually has other common jobs and on occasion is asked for help by his villagers and townsfolk. The affliction, as we previously noted, is not divided into specialized categories of mental, physical, etc., and a specialist isn't required for its resolution. The *dangarias* as opposed to the specialists (doctors, psychiatrists) we encounter in our trade, look and behave in a manner similar to that of the afflicted – both indulge in the peculiar dance of a *jaagar*, both speak of not having clear memory and control over their bodies, both experience trance states. They not only look similar, as no uniforms are involved, they also speak the same language since they are steeped in the same discourse, and they have the same beliefs about the reason and the nature of the affliction. Thus, while a schizophrenic might think that the government has implanted a chip in his head, his doctor does not prescribe to a similar theory. On the other hand, the *dangaria* and the afflicted/s have similar explanatory frameworks, whether it is the attack of a random spirit or the curse of an ancestor.

There are not many elaborate ways through which a clear distinction is created between "the afflicted" and "the curer" but there are a few that matter: the *dangaria* experiences deity possession instead of spirit or ghost attachments. Also, certain visibilities like specialized seating for the *dangaria* in the architectural set-up of a *jaagar* help to consolidate their status and differentiate them from the afflicted. This position of the *dangaria* is peculiar because it entails a certain helplessness and expertise at the same time. Everyone noted that he/she experiences a lack of control over their bodies and, on occasion, a dimming of memory. There could also be convulsions and shaking that might appear comical to others but propriety demands that people do not comment on them. The *dangaria*, with the help of other senior dancer-curers and family and community members, has to learn to develop skills and balance in his life in order to be successful in helping others. There is a well-defined learning curve and the person, in some ways, has to get used to the deity attacks so s/he is not overwhelmed by distress. The *dangarias* are from the general population; there are times when formal priests with specialized knowledge are called, but *dangarias* do not have any formal erudition or education. This characteristic bolsters the narrative about the superiority of local knowledge and local land – you don't have to have city education, you just need to be a local who is chosen by the local deities, many times the clan's personal deity or Uttarakhand's favorite god, Golu Devta. Another interesting characteristic of this subject is that, unlike spirit or ghost attachments, which have legitimate causes behind them, deity possessions are random. No one needs to be murdered or an elder to be abandoned for one to be possessed by a deity – this form of affliction is both an affliction and it is not; people often insisted that they did not try to get rid of a deity or a goddess, as their presence is a privilege, not a problem.

Conclusion

I had assumed that in my research I would find psychotic subjects who were not insane. I think I instead found madness but no psychosis, keeping in mind that the parameters of what constitutes madness and how it is explained are different. So, to answer the question I had raised earlier: what conditions – discursive, socio-cultural, epistemological, and hermeneutic, make the experience of what we term psychosis possible for our participants – I have arrived at some partial answers. The discursive conditions are the two underlying styles of thought: first, that people are constituted (in a very material way) by other people, lands, things, words, and intentions; and second, that intense affect like unfulfilled desire and acute suffering physically sticks to places and people across time and space. The socio-cultural component which will be elaborated on in the next chapter is the absence of a nuclear-family dynamic. The epistemological components are: first, instead of focusing on man's interiority as an object of knowledge, the focus is on his extensive external connections to all things; and second, the idea that local knowledge is special, superior, and secretive. This type of knowledge is clearly demarcated from other forms. The hermeneutic component is the way meaning is created out of these experiences, which is through beliefs about dead and disgruntled ancestors, spirits, and ghost attachments, deity possessions, and broken connections to land, people, and things. These meanings define their response to the experience of seeing and hearing things and explain the absence of distress for the most part. The question we are faced with now, and which will be answered in the next chapter, is how are these implicit discourses, subject positions, and visibilities informed by a type of subjectivity that is born in chaos and raised in contradictions, and as a result renders psychology and all its trappings useless?

Note

1 I understand that this can be interpreted as the therapeutic effect of returning home to a familiar community, but I intend to stay faithful to descriptions and shun interpretive psychological frameworks. The reader might at times experience frustration at my surface-level descriptions. He/she might recognize patterns that perfectly align themselves with psychological theories and might be seduced into making second-order judgments. I would request a bracketing of those judgments because second-order judgments, as Kendall and Wickham (1998) assert, blind us from excavating implicit discourses. That said, I will on occasion surely indulge in some restrained interpretive work but more as a warning to ensure that neither I nor the reader fall into that trap, and also to convey that this attachment to appearances is deliberate and not a function of academic ennui (or so I would like to believe).

5

THE SLIP AND THE SANE

An analysis of subjectivity

It is widely believed among the educated people of India that Ekta Kapoor ruined Indian television. In the year 2000, Kapoor released a television show called *Kyonki Saas Bhi Kabhi Bahu Thi* which epitomized the values and traditions of a large joint Indian family. What followed and still follows 20 years later, are more soap operas that can only be defined as "sanskars on steroids" (hyper-traditionalism). In Kapoor's defense, stories about large families and threats to their values and existence had been a common narrative in Hindi movies for decades. She was phenomenally successful because she knowingly or unknowingly tapped into post-liberalization collective uncertainty and skillfully garnished this narrative with beautiful clothes and lavish houses.

The Indian family's psyche, and by extension the community's psyche, could easily be shaken with the word "batwara" or division, which referred to separation of large joint families into smaller units with separate finances, and to the consternation of feeble-hearted mothers-in-law, separate kitchens (*iss ghar mein doosra chulha nahi jalega*). On television, "batwara" was usually initiated or fueled by the desire of a woman, the glamorous vamp who was the antagonist to the beautiful (read fair-skinned) but conservative daughter or daughter-in-law. On occasion, this blasphemous suggestion could be made by the spoilt son or a greedy relative. In the previous chapter, I showed how the local people of Uttarakhand considered the breaking of bonds to have dire consequences in the lives of everyone involved. The omnipresent trope of "batwara" on television reflects this preoccupation but on a national level. You see, misogynistic tropes aside, the interruption of personal desire in an interpersonal landscape is a threat that has kept terrible television afloat for two decades. While the last chapter occupied itself with the danger of disconnection, in this chapter, as I unravel the structure of Indian subjectivity, it is not danger but desire that will lead the way.

The madman is proficient in laying bare the strangeness of the other; he reveals this other in all its absurdity – impossible to ignore, unbearable to contain. These words initiated the expedition into the nature of madness and how it reveals the structure of subjectivity. We traveled through the bucolic, mountainous regions of northern India, and the intense and tragic expanses of Western thought. In this chapter I do not aim to bring coherence to the dialogue between the East and the West, whatever that looks like; instead, I focus on a type of subjectivity that precludes schizophrenia as a disorder, and through that bring into focus certain points of convergence between the modern schizophrenic and the rural North Indian subject.

The reader will notice that in Chapters 5 and 6 I speak of rural India, rather than *North* rural India. I make this shift because I believe that my theoretical findings regarding structure of subjectivity are true across the country, and to some extent across the Indian subcontinent. It applies to most *Desis*, as we like to call ourselves. My use of the girl-child's case study in Chapter 6 validates this assertion as the double-bind of female feticide and goddess worship are not just contradictions that plague the North.

Madness – how it is experienced, constructed, and mitigated is the thread that connects two diverse cultures and their corresponding subjects. But while these cultures are different, they are no longer isolated because liberalized borders bring with them globalized knowledge like psychiatry, with its claims of universal applicability. By unearthing the structure of the *type of subjectivity* that is on the receiving end of this knowledge, I will later inspect whether these claims of universality hold true. You see, the different subject positions, implicit thinking styles, and visibilities between the two cultures are not sufficient evidence that psychology's prescriptions of health and happiness are irrelevant here; for that we need to observe a deeper and a more structural difference between these groups of people, a difference that not only reflects, but also explains why one group looks towards deities and the other towards dopamine for answers. To this end, Deleuze and Guattari's (1983) work *Anti-Oedipus: Capitalism and Schizophrenia* offers a unique perspective on Western subjectivity and schizophrenia. Let me make clear that I am not assuming that *Anti-Oedipus* perfectly explains the operation of desire and the nature of social formations in India. It is their conceptualization of the "nomadic subject" that is of unique significance, as it comes closest to how I posit "slippery subjectivity".

Before I expound on this peculiar form of subjectivity, I must make transparent my own position and location in this project. While I am absolutely the girl-child I write about in the next chapter and thus to an extent this subject that thrives in multi-positionality, I am not the type of postcolonial subject that will appear in the next few pages. The liberalization of borders in the early 1990s, access to a modern English-medium education, and a cosmopolitan upbringing has not allowed me to be created in the image of my elders. Me and others like me were birthed by one culture and adopted by another; our voices are big and our ideas are popular for we are educated, Hindu, upper caste, and upper class, but we are not the majority. We might occupy the bulk of space in academic literature, both as participants and researchers, but the large cultural shadow that we cast is artificially engorged by our privilege. This project has little to do with me and others stuck in this epistemic *bardo*. It is instead about those who created us but failed to do so in their image; about a culture that structured us but was stalled by interruptions and wrought by conflict of thought. Essentially it is about a dying breed of people, and we are weary witnesses to the demise of a certain way of being and thinking. The honor and the tragedy lie in being able to inspect this looming discontinuity in the style of thinking (and not thinking). This is not my story, and as for the population I write about (the interviewees, my familial-community), they could not care less.

The nomadic and the afflicted: parallels in desiring-production

The most intriguing and significant characteristic of the rural Indian subject turned out to be its slipperiness. Slipperiness is the feature that ties together the discourses, visibilities, and subject positions we explored in the last chapter; it refers to the fact that the inner structure of this type of subject is shifting. It is mobile and slippery and thus can sustain the enmeshment that psychology cannot begin to understand, and might erroneously define as interdependence (cultural psychology), pathological co-dependence (clinical psychology), or even need for relatedness (psychodynamic theories) as it lacks the language of materiality.

It is not just the comfort with oppositional dyads that precludes the production of a fixed subjectivity; instead it is the creation of multiple positions that sustain non-rational ambiguity. The fact that the subject position of "the afflicted" does not have to signify one person but can point to a family, and can shift from one person to the other, belies any ideas one might have about the singular fixed subject. Up until now I have been consistently attempting to avoid second-order theories, so it is with great caution that

I will utilize ideas introduced by Deleuze and Guattari because the absence of mentalization that is a mark of Deleuze and Guattari's *Anti-Oedipus* makes it tentatively suitable to translate some ideas. Something similar to this slippery, unfixed type of subjectivity has been explored by them in their description of the nomadic subject, and desire and its operations play a central role in their theories. It is essentially this drive and connectivity of desire that resonates with some of the ideas presented by people in Uttarakhand. Desiring-production has a force and physicality to it; as they so lyrically explain:

> It is at work everywhere, functioning smoothly at times, at other times in fits and starts. It breathes, it heats, it eats. It shits and fucks. What a mistake to have ever said the id. Everywhere it is machines – *real ones, not figurative ones* [emphasis mine]: machines driving other machines, machines being driven by other machines, with all the necessary couplings and connections.
> *(Deleuze & Guattari, 1983, p. 1)*

Desire *does* things, it seeks or targets partial objects to connect and does not need to be sublimated (unlike the libido) to enter the social – it therefore already there in the political and historical; its flow is fast, prolific, and linear. This materialism resonated in the implicit style of thinking of the people I interviewed. Both types of understanding side-step meaning and mind. Whether it was a material bond with their land, the stickiness of intense affect, the physical connections with family and community, or the burning post-death *desire* for special desserts – much like the operations of desiring-production, our participants spoke of direct physical extensive connections, not figurative or metaphorical ones. Moreover, just as locals asserted that intense affect and unfulfilled desire can stick to land, objects, and other people, desiring-production is not only restricted to people but this connectivity encompasses nature and inanimate objects:

> Second, we make no distinction between man and nature: the human essence of nature and the natural essence of man become one within nature in the form of production or industry, just as they do within the life of man as a species.
> *(Deleuze & Guattari, 1983, p. 4)*

Deleuze and Guattari's insistence on making the partial, the machine-ic, and the inanimate, targets of material desiring-production tentatively allows me to seek these parallels between their writings and our narratives.

These parallels seduce us into anticipating universalized forms of desiring-production but such hurried conclusions would be naive. Deleuze and Guattari (1983) performed an extensive exploration of subjectivity and its partial dependence on social formations. They posited that the oedipalized fixed subject is a peculiar function of the capitalistic, nuclear family; in other words, an oedipalized form of desire that takes over the "body-without-organs" is neither a universal nor an ahistorical phenomenon and is grounded in the institution of the nuclear family. This representation/repression of desire is both intense and effective because the points of identification are confined to mommy-daddy-me. The intensity and sealed boundaries of this matrix traps desire in one fixed configuration producing different formations of fixed subjects ("neurotic", "pervert"), and are thus an example of what Deleuze and Guattari termed *illegitimate use of the conjunctive synthesis* (Buchanan, 2008).

The question we are faced with is: as opposed to these fixed subjectivities, what allows for the emergence of the post-colonial rural Indian subject so at home in chaos, contradictions, and ambiguity that it is difficult to pin it down into rigid positions? The answer lies in the nature of social formations in India, which constitute and are constituted by the familial-community matrix. Family in India is not an isolated institution and its boundaries are porous, and, some may say, non-existent – production and reproduction are not separated. The complexity of relationships that a child encounters in a non-nuclear Indian family, colloquially known as "joint families", have been explored in depth in sociological, anthropological, and psychological literature. As Banerjee (1944) states, "The joint Hindu family consisting of a large number of individuals of both sexes of varying ages in different types of relationship, are afforded opportunities of socialization of instincts ..." (p. 184). While Banerjee restricts his investigations to the Hindu household, the same holds true for the familial organization of other religions. I distinctly remember a friend of mine tell me that until she was 5, she called all the women in her family "ma" (mom) because, in a way, they were all her mother (aunts, elder cousins, sisters, grandmothers). As a result, the singular authority of parents is enfeebled by the presence of elders in the family, aunts in the neighborhood, and others in the community. This difference in the family matrix and its corresponding effects are an important factor that distinguishes the Western, Freudian subject from the Indian, rural one. For example, it is the norm that parents, children, aunts, grandparents, and cousins share beds or other sleeping spaces – bodies thrown about, one upon the other, resist the privatization of desire and personalization of soma. In the absence of this triangulation (mommy-daddy-me), the fixed subject whose desire is captured in a reified configuration and who is asked to make an impossible choice (mommy or daddy, imaginary or symbolic), is nowhere to be found. Deleuze and Guattari's skepticism regarding the ahistorical and universal applicability of the Oedipus resonates in the work of Bhugra and Bhui (2002), who state that the "Oedipal complex is not built into the collective mind but is found only under specific historical circumstances, such as societies with patriarchal authorization structures and competition for wealth that stimulate rivalry and hostility" (p. 84). As opposed to the nuclear family's "illegitimate" use of the synthesis of conjunction that produces fixed subjects who mistakenly believe themselves to be the agents of their desires and choices, a "legitimate" one is supposed to create nomadic subjects that are not restricted to binary positions (Deleuze & Guattari, 1983). Nomadic subjectivity welcomes multiple and contradictory narratives. Does the rural Indian familial matrix use the synthesis of conjunction "legitimately"? I highly doubt that because the rural Indian social complex has many different ways in which it traps desire and creates subjects (the caste system being the most obvious one). It does however have few similarities with the "legitimate" form of conjunctive synthesis, for example the absence of illusion of sovereign subjectivity. It should be made clear here, given the terms "legitimate" and "illegitimate", that I am in no way implying that the Indian social formation is superior – these theorizations are simply an observation of difference. While the capitalist nuclear familial matrix allows desire only to seek an intense relationship where the prohibited object and the agent of prohibition are its targets, the Indian family-community matrix has extensive relationships and desires and instead of being pushed inwards it is thrown outwards, connecting with numerous partial objects the subject encounters every moment since its birth.

In the people I interviewed and the ones I have lived my life with, I have found to be missing the assumption of sovereignty or the classic misrecognition that one is the agent of one's desires and choices instead of, to use Deleuze and Guattari's words, being a product of the flows of desiring-production and anti-production. These people, my people, consider themselves to be constituted in very direct and material ways, by other people, things, and landscapes. Planetary movements may decide where one works, and family and communities decide who to marry; the people of rural northern India are aware of being founded by others' choices instead of their choices being the sole product of isolated individual desires. Notions like "you can be whoever you want to be", "know who you are", "follow your true self", "find what you love and go for it", "follow your dreams" are more or less non-existent. As far as we know, no one is less or more happy because of it. The personalization of desire is the effect of a social formation, not its foundation. A preoccupation with interiority and its contents, which as Foucault (1994) showed was a historical emergence in the West, is absent here. This absence of focus on the content of interiority is significant because it is what sustains psychology and makes therapy reasonable. We have here a subject who has no illusions about personal choice, or that he is the agent of his desires and choices, making him somewhat similar to the nomadic subject.

Apart from the differences produced through the "legitimate" and "illegitimate" use of conjunctive synthesis, another difference between the oedipalized and the rural Indian subject can be observed in the operation of the disjunctive synthesis of recording. Deleuze and Guattari (1983) posit that, in a capitalist organization, we are first made to believe that what is prohibited is desired (the incest taboo), restricting our access to only mommy and daddy, and then we are asked to choose between identifying with one of them – an impossible yet inescapable choice. They suggest that this is an "illegitimate" use of disjunctive synthesis and creates restrictive and exclusive alternatives, or in other words it creates and then forces us to choose between artificial binaries (mommy or daddy, imaginary fixation or symbolic resolution). But according to them, these relations do not always require exclusive choices to be made, that is, restrictive, binary choices are a result of one type of synthesis of disjunction in one type of social formation.

I have already noted the absence of forced dualities like mind/body, self/other, male/female in Indian thought; compartmentalized binary positions are mostly absent in our target population. The self/other binary is absent, as reflected in "radical enmeshment" that showed how the question of one's own choices versus those of one's family and society was rendered absurd. The mind/body (mental/physical) binary is absent, as seen in the materiality of affect, that is, a way of thinking where intense affect has physical effects like financial ruin and infertility, and furthermore, in the lack of divisions between mental, social, physical, and financial afflictions. I will also examine in the next chapter, while I elucidate the place of contradictions in psychosis and subjectivity, the non-existence of a clear male/female binary and the ubiquitous presence of bi-gendered, non-gendered, transgendered, and other population categories in India.

Deleuze and Guattari's fluid, nomadic subject is a result of the legitimate use of conjunctive synthesis that is not restrictive; it has multiform possibilities (like the schizophrenic) rather than binary limitations. The "legitimate" disjunctive synthesis is supposed to create undifferentiated subjectivities whose identification with mother and father is temporary, and, much like the schizophrenic, might circulate through other polyvocal substitutes like gods, machines, animals, plants, etc. It shares some of these properties with the post-colonial Indian subject as these essentially fluid and non-exclusive subject positions with transient identifications are not only reflected in the narratives I have already detailed earlier, but also in the myths and stories where people, things, and gods take on multiple appearances, species, genders, and personalities. The *Mohini* avatar of the Vishnu refers to a fascinating myth where the male god Vishnu takes the form of a beautiful enchantress whose ultimate weapon is seduction. One of the popular representations of Shiva dating back to the first century CE is that of *Ardhanarishvara*, which is portrayed as one-half the male god Shiva with the other half his wife Shakti – both are impotent without the other. Another avatar of Vishnu, *Narasimha*, is half-man, half-lion. One of the people I spoke with said that Djinns, which were more common amongst the Muslim population and on the plains (as opposed to the mountains), would change gender and shape, and cause numerous afflictions like hearing non-existent voices in people. The next chapter elaborates further on the absence of binary choices.

Nomadism is a product of fleeting or absolute "deterritorialization" – a breaking of old codes and the formation of new ones on the "body-without-organs" that leads to a different permutation and combination of personalities and identities (Deleuze & Guattari, 1983). Yet again there is this fascinating parallel in how desiring-production's unstable, forceful, enduring, and prolific connectivity with partial objects resonates in the rural Indian discourse about how intense affect, like unfulfilled desire, connects to, or sticks to, partial objects and not necessarily whole persons – "leg lock" caused by the spirit, blindness caused by ancestor's curse, stickiness of affect to parts of rivers, mountains, and objects like food (in black magic). "Intensities" could be an appropriate way to signify this fast-moving, unstable, gregarious, and sticky flow that the locals spoke of and which shares properties with Deleuze and Guattari's formulation of desire. These intensities, instead of targeting whole individual persons, can move from a person's legs to another's eyes, from one's clamped jaw and on to a distant cousin's health – on and on and on …. Just as connective desire is an unstable, volatile, and dynamic material force, so are the intensities sticky (contagious) and unpredictable; they *get attached* to places, people, and things.

It is "radical enmeshment", the implicit style of thought that everyone is physically constituted by everyone/everything else that keeps these intensities manageable and allows this social formation to endure their contagion. Moving from one person's ruined finances to another's ill-health a decade later, the intensities have the freedom of movement and are supported by a social formation that can withstand their unstable and gregarious force. Instead of trapping them in narrow configurations, "radical enmeshment" allows both afflictions and more importantly resolution to happen across time, place, and people (a person can hold a *jaagar* for resolution of the afflictions of great grandparents who are long dead). Finally, much like desiring-production, intensities are mobile, in that they move from one thing to another and another and another:

> An infant's mouth at the breast constitutes such a connection, but so do the relations between an eye and a breast, and eye and a face, an eye and a knee; and between a mouth and a bottle, a mouth and an iron-lung, a mouth and the atmosphere, a mouth and a finger, a finger and a lock of hair ....
>
> *(Holland, 2001, p. 26)*

This contagious flow is echoed in the descriptions of my interviewees when they spoke of the nature of their afflictions and the causes and presentation of them. It is reminiscent of the woman's infectious laugh at the Balaji temple. Her laughter seemed to be in response to something only she could see, and soon either the hallucination or the eerie laughter (or both) had been *passed on* to the strangers around her. It is reflected in spontaneous mass possession/psychosis/hysteria that many healing temples are known for. It is also reflected in the rapid passing through multiple positions of the Indian rural subject (male/female) and in the cultural myths where gods take on multiple genders, personalities, and species. Most importantly, as I will explore in the next chapter, the Indian subject and the schizophrenic maintain an intriguing relationship with contradictions – they don't collapse them, they don't deny them, their non-sedimented subjectivity can tolerate the dissonance without reducing them, which resonates with how Deleuze and Guattari conceptualize the schizophrenic process (not the disease):

> He does not reduce two contraries to an identity of the same; he affirms their distance as that which relates the two as different. He does not confine himself inside contradictions; on the contrary, he opens out and, like a spore case inflated with spores, releases them as so many singularities that he had improperly shut off, some of which he intended to exclude, while retaining others, but which now become points-signs, all affirmed by their new distance.
>
> *(Deleuze & Guattari, 1983, p. 77)*

Thus, India's familial-community matrix results in a different operation of synthesis of desire than its Western oedipalized counterpart, but there is another configuration according to Deleuze and Guattari (1983) where the passive synthesis is legitimate – in the schizophrenic delirium (in the process and not the pathology). The schizophrenic subject, being nomadic, does not limit its identifications to binaries but instead gets absorbed in multiple positionalities – mother, father, machine, alien, god; he moves through them and invokes their affect. In other words, saying one is god is invoking the *feeling* of being god – omnipotence (Deleuze & Guattari, 1983). He might celebrate his sovereignty but is also, unlike the neurotic, acutely aware of not being the agent of his desires and choices ("man" as historically constituted).

In some ways, the Indian subjectivity is inherently schizophrenic (in a Deleuze and Guattarian way) or the schizophrenic subject finds an unlikely home in the social formations, multiplicities, and polyvocal desires of India. In his rigidity and complete absorption into whatever extreme he is caricaturing, the schizophrenic subject is an exaggerated personification of the Western fixed subject. But in his violent oscillations, movement and ability (or inability to stay fixed and stable), the schizophrenic subject is an exaggerated rendition of the slippery Indian subject. The flow of desire produced by the Indian rural familial-community matrix allows it to operate a little closer to what Deleuze and Guattari call its nomadic form.

The slippery subject: effects and comparisons

Despite some fascinating parallels between the theoretical formulations of Deleuze and Guattari (1983) and the discourse of the locals of rural Uttarakhand, I am still unwilling to import an explanatory framework that has little to do with their historical, social, geopolitical, and cultural conditions and context. At this point it is essential to grasp what "slippery subjectivity" is, and yet a static definition eludes me; one might say it is a slippery definition. For Deleuze and Guattari (1983), the nomadic subject is described through the operations of the flows of desiring-production and legitimate passive synthesis. I cannot take recourse to such ontological claims and so, instead of directly defining slippery subjectivity, I would look at the effects of that type of subjectivity, describe its properties, and then compare it with the structure and functions of the stable Western subject.

To look for the effects of slippery subjectivity is to look for its trace, which we can *sense* in the ways it informs and shapes experience. The mobile and multiple positions of "the afflicted" subject – the fact that it can be an individual or a whole family, that it can move from one person to another, from an aunt's infertility to the son's bad grades, is one way we can observe the effects of a slippery type of subjectivity. While "the afflicted" was the most consistent subject position brought forth in the discourse surrounding *seeing things and hearing voices*, the afflicted in themselves were not fixed – as a subject position it was contagious and connective, spanning across generations and geography. The physical contagion of an affliction can also be observed in the fascinating example of a tree wedding. Marriages are partially arranged based on the compatibility of two individuals' birth charts. In cases where a person is under the influence of certain weak planets, negative consequences like death of the spouse are believed to be a threat. The resolution sometimes is to first marry a tree, in turn transferring the effect of the planets onto that tree, and freeing the person to marry someone else. On occasion, one can even be temporarily married off to an animal for similar reasons. While these bizarre stories are always amusing to an international audience who either chuckle in derision or gasp in wonderment at the exotic, there is an implicit discourse that makes the custom and the ceremony sensible for those who follow it – the slipperiness of the subject (the afflicted) whose afflictions/symptoms can be transferred to other things and whose position as that subject is transient and dynamic and can be taken over by a tree or a dog.

The post-colonial rural Indian subject is also strangely comfortable with multi-positionality, otherwise considered as a cause of turmoil in psychological discourse. This can be observed in the multiculturalism which has been embraced post-liberalization. The rapid change that the Indian nation experienced over the past three decades was a bi-product of liberalization (opening trade borders in the early 1990s) and globalization, which together ushered in an enthusiastic era of modernity. Rapid cultural change has been traditionally associated with existential disarray and identity confusion. Sloan (1996) maintains that, irrespective of cultures, countries, or the idiosyncratic nature of personal experience, the essential feature of modernity is the complex struggle with identity formation in a rapidly changing social context. This implies that, in India, an identity crisis should be evident in those who were most vulnerable and directly in the path of the drastic modernization of the 1990s – the adolescents – but research shows us otherwise.

In India, rapid modernity led to the adolescent population developing multicultural identities that held traditional values, customs, and language close to the self but also felt they belonged to and identified with a "worldwide culture" (Rao et al., 2013). Adolescents in India were highly aware of the changes that are a result of globalization and modernity, and had mixed feelings about them. Despite the radical cultural change, instead of succumbing to identity crisis, it seems that individuals grounded themselves in traditional identity orientations and dabbled in global-world orientations at the same time (Rao et al., 2013). We find here again, contrary to Sloan's assertions, an absence of imminent crisis and pathology in the face of dramatic change. This is not to say that globalization and liberalization caused no harm; their devastating effects on tribal communities, cottage industries, rural women's rights, famer suicides, and the environment have been well documented by the likes of Nobel Prize-winning economist Amartya Sen. But as Rao's work shows:

> Adolescents remained strongly identified with traditional Indian collectivist beliefs, values, and practices but also identified and participated in individualistic, "minority world" beliefs, values, and practices as well. Findings revealed that a blending of traditional and minority world identity elements (the identity remix) was a common response to globalization among urban middle-class adolescents in India today.
> *(Rao et al., 2013, p. 9)*

In other words, they maintained multiple positions as subjects of traditional discourse and Western institutions, and averted a crisis usually attributed to the victims of identity confusion and rapid cultural shifts. Moreover, in investigating the level of subjective well-being, no overt crisis of identity or pathology was found (Rao et al., 2013). This lack of pathology points to another *effect of a slippery type of subjectivity* – almost effortless multiple, dynamic, and amorphous identifications that allow them to sustain amidst drastic cultural (and other) changes.

Another indicator of the presence of a slippery type of subjectivity is to inspect its trace through a comparison to fixed or stable subjectivity. To be clear, I am not pitting two forms of subjectivities against each other; instead I am pulling into focus the unique properties of the two to be able to describe the ones that are specific to slippery subjectivity. In Foucault's writings on discourse, power, and institutions surrounding madness, sexuality, and discipline, three central (and fixed/stable) subjects emerge – the mentally ill, the pervert, and the delinquent. All three subject types are almost permanent positions – steady, stable, and consistent for life. These positions do not change, and in some ways, they are the primary identity markers for an individual. For that matter, identification with these positions is immensely encouraged – "I am X and I am an alcoholic" is the first step towards curing the mental illness "alcoholism". You cannot transfer your delinquency to your neighbor and you cannot get cured until you admit that alcoholism is a *life-long* illness. As a modern pervert, your identity and actions are recorded in a centralized database for life, which affects where you can live and work. Whether it is in the presentation of symptoms or for the resolution of a problem, these subject positions are stable and non-contagious.

As opposed to this, the subject positions I investigated in the previous chapter, namely "the afflicted" and "the curer", were partially produced by the discourses of radical enmeshment, sticky affect and desire, and spirit attachments, and bolstered by other visibilities and institutions. But like I stated earlier, these positions are not primary. Everyone I met casually spoke of others or themselves who had experienced what we call psychotic symptoms but that did not make them permanently afflicted. None of these subject positions are central to their daily life – you can be afflicted today and not tomorrow. It has nothing to do with "who you are". For that matter, there is really no comparable individualist concept of who you are; the closest I came to someone describing their identity was an older man who identified himself through his village and the district he came from. This applies to the curer too; as earlier noted, *dangarias* or "dancer-curers" only work as curers when others need them. Otherwise they run shops, manage farm land, work a government job, etc. No one has to identify as the afflicted to be cured, and no one has to permanently and perpetually be the curer to be effective.

While the subject position of the afflicted itself can shift from one person to another and even attach itself to a family and village, the delinquent or the mentally ill cannot. You cannot be diagnosed as schizophrenic today for it to be passed on to your neighbor tomorrow. Even the differentiation between the subject positions of the afflicted and the curer are not stringently demarcated. They look alike, dress alike, have the same knowledge system explaining the affliction and resolution, and behave alike during the trance; both speak of a loss of control and neither have a special education but both are experts in their field. This style of thought and structure of being is reflected in the response to troubling or deviant behavior (which normally constitutes mental illness) like excessive drinking (alcoholism in the West). While India has a fair share of its population who drink their lives into oblivion, the term "alcoholic" is absent in favor of "he drinks a lot" (*who zyada peeta hai*) – a *doing* rather than a *being*. It is not uncommon to see people who used to drink excessively stop drinking because of family pressure, financial concerns, or health issues, and then soon after resume drinking occasionally without falling back into "alcoholism". There is no discourse around alcoholism as a fixed life-long disease. A person is not an alcoholic and does not have to identify himself as one in order to stop drinking (get cured).

A person is not a schizophrenic, instead s/he is currently experiencing transient afflictions, of which bizarre behavior and hallucinations could be a part. A closer inspection of language reveals that the local people spoke in terms of deviant behavior and not the person's identity. They observed that an individual "acted like mad" instead of saying he was a madman. Of course, the psychiatric discourse has made its way into Indian cities and even smaller towns to some extent. But even the inclusion of this new discourse reveals something fascinating about the subject structure and its ease with ambiguity and contradictions. We witness something intriguing in the way people handle this new form of knowledge that asks them to medicate their troubles. Most individuals and families continue to see local shamans, dancer-curers, and healing temples while also seeking medical help. They find nothing incongruous about the two approaches. Further, not only do psychiatrists have to pit their knowledge against local shamans and priests, but also compete against India's own systemized medical knowledge systems. These differences in response to concerns like excessive drinking are deep; this is not a simple matter of identity (alcoholic) but rather subjectivity (slippery versus fixed).

In relation to knowledge

In Chapter 3 I explored how Foucault's (1994) writings examined the problem at the heart of modern philosophy – how to formulate a system of understanding that accounts for "man" both as an object of knowledge and a subject that makes this knowledge possible in the modern era. This exceedingly significant liaison between man and knowledge in the modern era was echoed in the schizophrenic subject, who was suggested to be an extreme and oscillating rendition of the rifts in this relationship. Whether it was the failure of philosophy, the transient victory of the human sciences, or the self-excavating emergence of counter-sciences (that could undermine the concept of "man" and lead to the "death of man"), the relation between man and knowledge is central to Foucault's work on the modern episteme. But this central role that knowledge and self-knowledge play in relation to man is absent for the Indian subject and thus comes with its own set of consequences and complications.

I noted in earlier chapters how the schizophrenic subject caricatures the rifts in man's relation to knowledge, for example, by believing that he is the architect and controller of all reality. As opposed to this, in India, there is an absence of subjectivity structured by man and his relation to knowledge. Thus, instead of being constituted by historical agents of labor, life, and language, people are constituted by the material forces of intentions, desires, intense affect, landforms, etc. There is instead, in the context of this absence of relation between self and knowledge, the structuring of the subject as constituted by and through intense affect and radical enmeshment. For example, a person can be "the afflicted" and "the curer" and can shift between these positions amongst many others. This structuring, instead of reflecting the historicity and centrality of the human subject, exposes the fragility and instability of subjectivity itself (at least in this social formation) by revealing its multiplicity, permeability, and transience. While this subject is managed by institutions and molded by discourse, it is not pinned down by them; it can wriggle its way out from under several positions to occupy other ones. Apart from the ephemeral positionalities of the "dancer-curer" and "the afflicted", Indian myths and legends reflect these shifting subjectivities which culminate, in the most extreme form, in the unshakable belief in reincarnation, where death is not final and the after-life has a mobility – you can be dead today and not tomorrow, a man today and a woman tomorrow, or even an animal or a tree in your next incarnation. More importantly, one can be both the father and the son, the mother and one's wife, and, according to some interesting stories, the child of two different sets of parents *at the same time* (children who say they remember their families from older births). In these cases, the son can literally be the father of the man.

The most significant consequence of this absence of a similar relation between man and knowledge in India is the non-existence of the *unthought* (Foucault, 1994). In Chapter 3 I had inspected how, resonating with the emergence of the *unthought* (later unconscious) on the horizon of Western knowledge, the schizophrenic personifies the tension between the opacity of the *unthought* and the clarity of the *cogito*. In response to the appearance of the *unthought*, the modern Western neurotic subject makes peace with the uncertain and the unknowable – the "Other" in one's self (Roberts, J. personal communication, October 10, 2017). The normal reflexive glare of the episteme, the luxury of language, and even the dissonance of uncertainty all lead the neurotic to be able to have a coherent sense of unity and interiority. The schizophrenic, on the other hand, is tortured by the *unthought* – he either attempts an absorption into complete certainty or is drowned in the terror of utter uncertainty.

This existence of the *unthought*, this "Other" in one's self, makes the epistemic focus on interiority understandable, in that we must attempt to figure out our motivations, fears, and desires to be truly known (self-knowledge); we must attempt to reach the "Other" if only through language. This concept of being not known to one's self and a consequent absence of focus on making clear the contents of one's psyche – in other words, the fixation with interiority – is not a priority among most people in India and I have found it to be missing not only in rural Uttarakhand but also among most people I know personally. The Western neurotic has struck a bargain with the uncertain and the unknown, whereas the schizophrenic obsessively tries to solve it (Roberts, J. personal communication, October 10, 2017). The Indian slippery subject is not structured through a cut of this nature. Instead, the "Other" that I did find in the Indian subject was desire, intention, or suffering of *others* – the spirit or deity or intentions that defined their wants, fears, and motivations. But this deity, ghost, or intention, this "Other", unlike the *unthought*, is not opaque. When people in Uttarakhand spoke of making the spirit or the ghost "speak" during the *jaagar*, the entities were privy to their own wishes, vengeances, and desires, and could communicate them, whether it was the need for a sacrifice or a lamb kebab. The "Other" in, or rather *on*, the Indian subject does not suffer the romance of the opaque, and the jouissance of the unreachable. While in the West, the "Other" is inside and opaque (the unconscious); in the Indian subject it is outside and transparent – a completely different entity altogether. The puzzle is not to know what is on the inside (relation to self-knowledge) but to resolve the demands on the outside.

We noted that the schizophrenic exaggerates the two extremes of the *unthought*; while the neurotic must figure himself out, the schizophrenic personifies this cut in the most radical of ways. An example of such exaggeration is a typical delusion that is common in the West – the unshakable belief that one's body is bugged, or people are listening through the walls, or that one is controlled by demons inside him/her. In all these cases, we can observe the effects of the *unthought* as they play out in the schizophrenic's obsession with something always opaque and hidden but also forever present – the bug or the demons. While there is absolute certainty that s/he is being watched or heard, the source mostly remains hidden or inside (a bug *inside* their brain, a camera in their teeth). But the *unthought* is not an Indian epistemological occurrence and so a similar play of omnipresent opacity is absent. Delusions of this variety are not easily found in India. For example, "A" was a young girl brought to the hospital during my clinical internship in Delhi; she suffered persistent delusions and hallucinations that a camera was following her and watching at all times. While both terrified and enthralled, she explained lucidly that instead of being hidden, this camera was right in front of her face and she could see it. It was situated outside (not in her) and it was visible. People in Uttarakhand believed that the voices they heard could be a dead relative giving them advice and guidance, or an entity that needs something from them. These entities were always from outside, existed outside or *on the person*, were sometimes visible, and their desires and fears were transparent. None of these "delusions" point to the presence of any form of opacity. These *Others* sometimes controlled their fears and desires much like the *Other* defines ours, but there is no fight against an unexpressed emotion or an unknown fear; instead there is negotiation with known friends and unruly enemies.

Apart from dissimilarities in the nature of the "Other" and the constitution of the subject, there is another interesting difference in the presentation of madness in the West and in India. Hallucinations, bizarre delusions, and strange behavior are common among the two cultures, but there is a peculiar quality about the schizophrenic that is encountered neither in India, nor, more interestingly, in the Western neurotic – the *trema*. Sass (1994) explains that, much like epileptic seizures, schizophrenic breaks are many times preceded by an aura, an uncanny feeling called *trema*, a term coined by psychiatrist Klaus Conrad (Sass, 1994). The person feels that the world has undergone a strange, ineffable change: "Reality seems to be unveiled as never before, and the visual world looks peculiar and eerie – weirdly beautiful, tantalizingly significant, or perhaps horrifying in some insidious and ineffable way" (Sass, 1994, p. 44). This period before the arrival of acute psychotic symptoms is filled with a bizarre feeling that everything is either unreal or extra-real – but always subtly different – an "ungrounding" and an "unworlding" (Sass, 1994). While the Western neurotic retains the episteme's inward orientation, he is also grounded in the absolute uncertainty of the "Other", essentially averting this feeling of unreality and the delicate, all-encompassing shift in the texture of the universe. This grounding in uncertainty, peace with the opacity, this resting in the cut, and remoteness from the "Other" – provides a reliable and safe connection with reality. "I can't *know* who I am but must try to find out" is a stable project of our times.

The schizophrenic, on the other hand, with the hyper-reflexive inward glare that turns background processes into objects, begins to question the implicit assumptions of others and self, and eventually experiences an "ungrounding" from the shared reality, which otherwise requires a certain numbing or de-sensitivity. S/he must know and solve the puzzle of this uncertainty and cannot be grounded or "worlded" through the "Other". Laing had also written about the schizophrenic's doubt over own and others' realness and substance – ontological insecurity. He also conceived this difference between the neurotic and the schizophrenic in terms of the

The slip and the sane 145

neurotic's preoccupation with gratification and the schizophrenic's with existential preservation. As noted in Chapter 3, in the modern episteme, the being is no more dependent on the Cartesian *cogito*, and the schizophrenic, in his absorption with complete certainty or uncertainty, does not have the grounding in the *unthought* either; instead s/he is doomed to oscillate. This "ungrounding" where he is neither tethered to the thought nor the *unthought* then translates to the characteristic *trema*. S/he roams the expanse of Western thought and, much like a nomad, has no home in either self or knowledge, and no certainty in uncertainty.

At the other end of the world, in the absence of an inward reflexive glare (the intensive triangulation of desire) and the cut of the *unthought, trema* or this ungrounded feeling of unreality and "unworlding", is distinctively absent in Indian subjects. While the people I spoke with referred to bizarre behavior (running naked in public), hallucinations, verbosity and apathy, and even a loss of control over the body – at no point did they even remotely allude to a feeling similar to *trema*. There was no mention of unreality or the feelings of sensing a subtle, omnipresent change. There was no "ungrounding" and "unworlding". The Indian subject, then, is not grounded in the "Other" (the cut inside to be rescued by language) but in *others* (intensities and enmeshment) and this groundedness remains unquestioned. The subject positions might be nomadic and slippery but the external and prolific trajectory of desire and the absence of a preoccupation with interiority renders his/her relation to the external world firm and stable.

The slipperiness I am writing about, when looked at through the lens of Western knowledge, appears to be pathological. Many words have been used to define the experience of unfixed and unstable boundaries, the foremost of which is "disintegration". The diffusion and scattering, both internal (structural) and external (relational) that is so normal for the rural Indian subject is a marker of pathology for the Western one. In *Schizophrenia and the Need-Fear Dilemma* Burnham, Gladstone, and Gibson (1969) talk about internal disintegration as an integral part of the schizophrenic psyche; there is a "tendency of many schizophrenic patients to diffuse, split, and otherwise scatter their adaptive efforts among many relationships because of their inability to contain and to integrate their intense conflicts within single relationships" (p. 6). The radical enmeshment, materiality, slipperiness that constitutes the rural Indian subject is inherently schizophrenic for many Western authors who characterize schizophrenia as an anomalous need for external structure and the absence of an internal one (Burnham, Gladstone & Gibson, 1969). This rhetoric reeks of a philosophy birthed in an individualist tradition that considers a boundaried existence to be normal, and that values a fixed subjectivity where excessive reliance on external structures and susceptibility to internal diffusion is pathologized, while integration is romanticized. The regulation of one's behavior from without rather than within (autonomy versus heteronomy) is deemed healthy, and acceptance of the family's version of reality as opposed to one's own is considered another marker of the schizophrenic repertoire, (Burnham, et al., 1969). The concept of disintegration presupposes that there is a stable contained individual with a coherent, fixed internal structure to begin with. The schizophrenic and the rural Indian, in their volatility and their explosive, unstructured, slippery, and exteriorized connectivity question this very conceptualization of the normal structure that romanticizes separate identity and reality-testing between inner and outer events. Thus these stable and boundaried people are missing in a place where one can catch hallucinations from each other, transfer intentions and ill-will through a morsel of bread, and have physical repercussions through mental desires (a differentiation real only to us).

Conclusion

To quickly summarize, through comparisons with the modern Western subject and his relation to knowledge, I tentatively flesh out some of the following properties of the post-colonial rural Indian subject: 1. an extensive, exterior trajectory of desire, 2. the "Other"/s as outside and transparent, 3. lack of an inward reflexive or hyper-reflexive glare which ensures the absence of *trema*, and 4. a slippery structure that allows multiple subject positions and non-binary choices.

To further clarify the nature and structure of this slippery form of subjectivity, in the next chapter I explore how it plays out in the girl-child and her negotiations with contradictions. In observing her birth and growth, and her challenges and triumphs, the effects of this slippery subjectivity can be discerned more easily.

6
CASE AND POINT
The girl-child's story

In the absence of a concrete definition, we examined the slippery subjectivity of the post-colonial Indian subject by tracing its effects. We observed how the position of "the afflicted" is not necessarily an individual; for that matter, most of the time it's a whole family, if not a community; moreover, he/she/they do not consistently remain "the afflicted". Unlike the mentally ill or the delinquent, the afflicted position can move between people, within people, and within families and communities. Nowhere is the display of this type of structure more conspicuous than in the formation of the subject structure of the girl-child in India. Thus, it is through a case study of her negotiations that I will drive home the point that the structure of the modern Western subject (stable, fixed, and intensive, with an opaque core) is unlike that of the rural Indian one (slippery, mobile, and extensive, with a transparent core) which will further allow for a critique of the problematic import of the Global Mental Health Movement. In the following pages, I bring these differences to fruition by conducting a thorough analysis of how the slippery subjectivity is reflected in her gendered being.

The reason the Indian girl-child stands out as a glorious example of these fluid subject positions is due to her life-long relationship with contradictions, and her negotiation with what many theorists have considered the cause of psychological pathology. It is thus important that, before I venture into what constitutes her, the role of contradictions in madness be made clear. The concept of contradictions shows up time and again in the literature on schizophrenia. The following pages present a brief description of the omnipresence of contradictions in literature on insanity.

The persistence of contradictions

Rooted in Enlightenment thought that appreciates rationality and embraces reason, psychology has for long considered contradictory thinking to represent a defect. Paradoxical thinking has been associated with unsophisticated cognition, immaturity, and even insanity in psychological literature. It is, then, no surprise that schizophrenia and contradictions are natural bedfellows. Whether it is the confrontation of the opacity of the *unthought* with the clarity of the *cogito* or the oscillation of Man's positions between empirical and transcendental extremes, there is in the modern episteme a tension between opposites and a play of paradoxes: "Indeed, it turns out that these dualities so basic to schizophrenia come very close to a set of contradictions and paradoxes that are no less basic to modern thought" (Sass, 1994, p. 326). A cursory study of schizophrenia and psychosis will reveal to anyone the long-standing relationship between mental disorders and contradictory thought. Whether it was the mother's inconsistent messages (Bateson, Jackson, Haley, & Weakland, 1956) or the presence of contradictory affect (Sass, 2007a), ambiguity and paradoxical thinking are considered either precursors to or markers of pathology. From Sass to Bateson, Laing, and others, the following pages reveal the persistence of contradictions in the literature on schizophrenic's behavioral and emotional repertoire.

Bateson and the double-bind

Originally an anthropologist, Bateson, along with Don Jackson, Jay Haley, and John Weakland published "Towards a theory of schizophrenia" in 1956, which introduced the concept of pathologies produced by double-bind messages and inconsistent communication patterns. The concept of the double-bind, removed from the complexity and context Bateson adorned it with, soon gained both popularity and notoriety. Bateson's seminal paper presents a theory of schizophrenia more complex than the simple idea that the schizophrenic is created in the face of a no-win communication pattern. Under inconsistent communication and failure to discriminate metamessages, the heart of this theory lies in the mother's anxiety and her attempts to assuage this anxiety through different means. Moreover, a true double-bind is far from simple and is based on four conditions: the presence of a negative conjunction based on punishment, the presence of a contradictory message which is more abstract than the first one, the necessity of a response from the child (intensity of the relationship), and the inability of the child to point to the said contradiction in messages.

What is of interest to us is that the prevalence of contradictory messages of different communicational modes creates an impenetrability not just towards the meta-messages of the mother (or primary caregiver) but an unknowability at the heart of the self – the child has to deceive *itself* utterly in order to ensure his survival. It has to be unaware of the mode of the message, whether the message was metaphorical, literal, playful, etc., for to be aware is a threat to his psychological survival. Between the contradictory messages of acceptance and avoidance – some verbal, others non-verbal, some literal, others metaphorical – Bateson et al. (1956) believed that the child develops different ways to respond to meta-messages, in turn leading to paranoid, hebephrenic, or catatonic schizophrenia.

Our interest lies not so much in whether Bateson's etiological understanding is accurate; instead it is important to notice that contradictions have always been associated with schizophrenia, in this case, at the micro (family) level. It is essential to remember that Bateson maintained that the double-bind was not only restricted to the families, neither was it a sufficient condition to produce schizophrenic individuals. Normally, people can move through communication modes with ease; they understand metaphor and play as they can access meta-messages and are able to infer context. As we have previously noted, the hyper-reflexivity of the schizophrenic's consciousness does not allow him the luxurious ease of communication; the focus is not on context or meaning, but instead on structure and sound. A playful comment and a sarcastic jab might not be evident to the schizophrenic, or an innocuous statement might seem full of vitriol if they focus on structure, sound, and the feel of a sign instead of meaning and context.

Other theorists, like Burnham, Gladstone, and Gibson (1969), have similarly stated that inconsistent and vague messages from the family are to be blamed for an incoherent structure of experience. They point to the schizophrenic's vacillation between the needs of others at one end and the fear of others at the other. Similarly, Laing talks about the contradictory demands of autonomy versus relatedness and the schizophrenic's failing attempts to negotiate these extremes. Oppositional dyads and schizophrenia seem to partner up with ease in Western thought.

The Kretschmerian paradox

While Bateson's double-bind implies a causal relation between schizophrenia and contradictions, Sass focuses on the contradictory expression and experience of emotions in non-paranoid forms of schizophrenia: "Many such patients, *at the very same moment* and *on the subjective plane*, experience *both* diminishment *and* exaggeration of certain kinds of emotional or affective response" (Sass, 2007a, p. 353). The first contradiction lies between the appearance of certain emotions and their subjective experience. The traditional assertion that flat affect, paucity of speech, and deadpan facial expressions are representative of an impoverished internal emotional life have been challenged by both phenomenological and physiological research, and autobiographical accounts. Research instead shows that some patients who appear to have flat affect may have higher affective response than non-patients, irrespective of whether they are on medication or not (Earnst & Kring, 1999). They further suggest no correlation between blunting of affect and subjective report of moods. Similarly, autobiographies of schizophrenics sometimes point to a paucity of emotions and at other times "portray such persons as having abnormally *intense* emotional or affective responses" (Sass, 2007a, p. 352). But such schisms don't just exist within the expressions of emotion.

Sass (2007a) cites the German psychiatrist Ernst Kretschmer, who not only spoke of both hypo- and hyper-emotional states present in schizophrenics and schizoid personality types, but also posited that these states are always present and at the same time: "the temperament characteristic of schizophrenia and schizoid personality, involves two opposite, aspects or tendencies: on the one hand, hypersensitivity, tenderness, nervousness, or vulnerability; on the other hand, an underlying numbness, indifference, or lack of sensitivity" (p. 354). Thus, the patient doesn't simply shift between two extremes but always lives them at the same time. Sass resolves this paradox by differentiating between the concepts of affect (general), emotion (targeted, object-oriented, cognitive), and mood (pervasive, less targeted). Therefore, he asserts that schizophrenic patients indeed experience emotional contradictions but in a peculiar manner. They experience hyper-arousal of affect and hypo-arousal of emotions, which means that while there is an increase in non-emotional forms of affectivity ("quasi-emotions"), there is at the same time a diminishment of real and targeted emotion.

Sass and Bateson's writings display how schizophrenia is intricately related to contradictions. Sass (1994) alludes to the place of contradictions in modern art and literature, and how these discordant states are reflected in the schizophrenic. We can also recall here contradictions inherent in the rigidity of schizophrenic language as juxtaposed with its fluid verbosity – both a result of "ungrounding" of the word from representation and meaning due to hyper-reflexivity. In contrast to Bateson and Kretschmer's assertions, which are restricted to family dynamics and phenomenological experience (the interpersonal), the explorations in Chapter 3 were concerned with how the schizophrenic personifies the extremes of the empirico-transcendental doublet and gets absorbed in the clarity of the *cogito* and the opacity of the *unthought*, thus exaggeratedly playing out the modern epistemological contradictions (the epistemic). Thus, whether at the micro-level of a family or the macro-level of epistemic shifts, contradictions and schizophrenia seem to be inseparable in some ways.

This brings us to an essential premise of this chapter where I investigate the young Indian female subject's response to contradictions and her resistance to pathology, in turn revealing something indispensable about the formation of her subjectivity. An in-depth examination of the Indian girl-child and how her birth and life are riddled with contradictions, further demonstrates how slipperiness is essential to the mitigation of pathology. This unique structure of hers, along with other factors like the discourse of "radical enmeshment" and the contagious and mobile nature of intense affect, allows me to generalize and extend the nature of this type of gendered subjectivity to many other post-colonial subjects. In the following pages I will begin by examining the forms of contradictions that she has to navigate and then move on to explore why, contrary to Western theories of schizophrenia, she does not succumb to a psychotic breakdown. I use the term "girl-child" because it has a special significance for me; when I was growing up it was this expression that was plastered over billboards and shouted through radios and television in appeals against female feticide – it exists deeply and shines brightly in the Indian collective consciousness.

In-betweeners: the girl-child's story

This story is about how the Indian girl-child's gendered subjectivity is fraught with contradictions and how she moderates and resolves these contradictions to avoid crisis. I first examine the incongruities that inform the experience of the girl-child from the moment of her birth and then explore how she comes to term with her "unwanted-ness" in a culture that persistently makes her aware of how undesired she is. The resolution of her unwanted-ness is complicated by the realization of the control her body exerts, specifically a certain unrestrained, unstable, destructive power that makes her a dangerous object. We will understand the development of female subjectivity in the context of these dual and seemingly contradictory messages – "you are helpless, unwanted, and a liability" on the one hand, and "you are powerful, an asset, and a goddess" on the other.

Emerging into unwanted-ness

In India, similar to a few other nations, son-preference is a norm that guides parenting behavior. The desire for a son can sometimes take the form of mild neglect of the girl-child and, in other cases, physical abuse. At times it takes the extreme form of murder: female feticide and infanticide are problems so prevalent that the government has made it illegal for doctors and ultrasound technicians to reveal the gender of the fetus, which has in turn led to the growth of black markets where illegal ultrasounds and abortions (of the female fetus) thrive. According to the 2001 Indian census (Agnivesh, Mani, & Koster-Lossack, 2005), the gender gap in India is so wide that even a projection of estimated 35 million "missing" girls is conservative (newer estimates increase the number to 50 million). Figure 6.1 is an example of public-service messages on billboards across the country.

The neglect or abuse is most obvious when the girl is not educated, while her brother goes to college, when she is fed only after he is satisfied, when she has to wear his old clothes, when she has to manage household chores while he plays with his friends, and when all her needs are overshadowed by those of her brother's. Further, the birth of a girl is many times compared to a curse because of the amount of dowry the family has to generate for her wedding – she is nothing but a bad investment.

It should be noted that there are indeed a great number of people who desire the birth of a girl, which could lead us to naively assume that these privileged few grow up unaware of the tribulations of feeling vestigial. But

FIGURE 6.1 A "Save the girl-child" billboard

the structuring of subjectivity is not that simple, especially in India where family does not end with your parents and siblings. Even for a child who is cherished in her immediate family, the public-service announcements of "save the girl-child", "educate the girl-child", "girls are important", "girls are a blessing", "killing the girl-child is illegal", etc. that cover billboards, radio, and television broadcasts scream out another story. There is an internalization of the narrative of prohibition – why would there be prohibitions against female feticide if there wasn't desire after all? Why would these ubiquitous messages exist if families didn't want to get rid of their little girls? This narrative is strengthened by extended family and community members who don't always share her parents' enthusiasm. The fact that there is a need to vehemently announce that the birth of a girl is desirable ensures that girls who grow up amid these announcements are aware that they were unwelcome, and internalize it early on.

Further, there are public-service announcements that plead for her protection and focus on her fragility ("she is someone's wife, mother ...") and thus implicitly convey to her a sense of helplessness. Now she feels not only undesired but also a liability (to be protected and paid for through a dowry) and utterly inept at helping herself. The messages are inescapable. Even in the absence of overt cues like physical neglect, every girl-child is founded by her unwanted-ness at some level. The discursive structuring of the subject is equally, if not more, dependent on covert and subtle messages as it is on deliberate inculcation into a narrative.

All these factors lead to the girl-child being subjected to the implicit and explicit discourse of "unwanted-ness" – she is born among the institutions that prohibit her annihilation and she has to incorporate a basic anxiety about her undesirability into her sense of being. To understand how inescapable this feeling is, we again have to recall the open borders of the Indian family matrix which involves the extended family, neighbors, and friends who are deeply involved in child rearing – they raise you and dictate your position in the culture. Child rearing in India is a communal task and it isn't strange to see a woman in a crowded bus passing her newborn child to absolute strangers who take care of it while she purchases tickets or just relaxes for a minute. The reason this behavior is not absurd is because the boundaries between family/non-family, individual/society (and as we will observe later, male/female) remain blurred. As we will soon see, I posit that it is this blurring of boundaries that saves the girl-child from obvious pathology in adulthood.

The Laxmi and the Kali: emerging into power

Irrespective of what someone's religious affiliations are, a profound awareness of mythology is unavoidable in India. When it's not being used as a beating stick by fundamentalists, Hinduism, through its myths and stories, occupies a subliminal space between being a religion, a philosophy, and a way of being that permeates daily lives in the same manner that most lived philosophies do. Sudhir Kakkar once keenly observed that everyone in India is a Hindu-Hindu, Muslim-Hindu, Sikh-Hindu, Christian-Hindu, Buddhist-Hindu, etc. In the 1990s you didn't have to be a practicing Hindu to religiously watch *Ramayan* and *Mahabharat* on public broadcast every Sunday, and it was common for people who did not own televisions to flock at that one rich neighbor's house. The legends and tales of the great epics have been sown into the fabric of our experiences; most people grow up with stories but most Indians grow *through* them. It is the omnipresent and subtle cultural markers of Hinduism rather than its isolation in temples that makes its influence all the more prevailing, nuanced, and even insidious.

My specific focus here is on the myths and narratives surrounding goddess tales. While the girl-child grows under the oppressive presence of her own helplessness and undesirability, she also grows along with images, motifs, and stories about various goddesses who exude unbounded power. Many local sub-traditions believe that the feminine energy is the primary, primordial force (Shakti) out of which everything else develops. Other traditions that do not emphasize the primacy of the feminine still believe that the feminine is the force that breathes life into all matter. The famous poet Ramprasad's words convey with clarity the primacy of the feminine personified by goddess Kali: "By her own desire to create, She differentiates Herself into a male and female whose subsequent union creates the world" (Dalmiya, 2000, p. 250). On the day of *Kanchke*, a north Indian festival, little girls are worshiped in the form of goddesses. They go from house to house, where their feet are washed, their bodies worshiped, and they return home with their pockets full of delightful sweets and a little money. *Durga puja* in Eastern India is the ten-day-long festival with processions that celebrate the victories of warrior goddess Durga (in her various forms). In the mountains of North India, where you might not find a person for miles, small goddess shrines (as seen in Figure 6.2) still seem to crop up on the edge of cliffs – she is everywhere. Diwali, probably India's most popular festival, is all about welcoming Laxmi into one's home.

FIGURE 6.2 A small goddess shrine in the mountains

Birthed and reared in this backdrop of intensely powerful and ubiquitous goddess images and stories of feminine triumphs, the girl-child becomes a subject. As she attempts to figure out her unwanted-ness, she also has to come to terms with a certain peculiar sense of power that is visible in various goddesses' narratives. The arrival of a girl in the family through birth or marriage is supposed to signify the arrival of luck and prosperity, as relatives and neighbors who mourn her birth will also in the same breath say *Laxmi aayi hai* ("You have been graced with Laxmi"). Public announcements and cultural prohibitions make her aware of how unwelcome she is, while the stories of Laxmi inform her that she has a place in everyone's heart and home. As opposed to the messages that portray her as helpless, the goddess she is also worshiped as conveys to her a sense of immense power. On one hand she is either subtly or overtly made to realize her status as a liability, whether it's through the "protection" of her *honor* or the immense burden of dowry. On the other hand, she is colloquially christened and compared to Druga, which translates as the one who is invincible. Movies repeatedly portray her with the *apla naari* trope (the helpless women) but just as regularly use the Kali trope (the unstoppable destroyer). The subtlety of these incongruent messages never allows her to respond to them directly, and their ubiquity ensures they are equally inescapable. These last two characteristics turn this situation into a classic Batesonian double-bind. Thus, along with the realization of unwanted-ness and helplessness, a diffused sense of power and desirability co-emerge in our young female subject.

The girl's body locates itself in a position of power not just through identification with goddesses; she also notes that the first sanctions on her little body are made by other women – mothers, aunts, neighbors, and strangers. While the training of bodies and minds is a mark of any self-respecting disciplinary system (Foucault, 2006), in India the body is perpetually and peculiarly managed by "honor" (often leading to the notorious honor killings we read about), and the keepers of that honor are frequently other powerful women. The ideas of honor and disgrace are intimately and specifically attached to the girl-child's body which is why placing restrictions on her is not just the prerogative of the family but of the community. The girl-child, through prohibitions, realizes very early how family and community honor are intricately attached to the control of her body. Love and acceptance might be heavily conditional on whether or not she deviates from the norms of "honor".

This early control of the body and the realization of how destructive it can be to the family and community carries with it the most important realization – that the body is a site of unrestrained, unstable, and destructive power that has to be controlled and limited to ensure community survival and social peace. Prohibitions, sanctions, and restrictions bring with them the recognition of a terrible but great material force with physical ramifications. It does not matter whether her body is actually the place of power – the prohibitions are enough to lead her to experience and create it as such. I would suggest that at some point in becoming a subject through these motifs, myths, and images, the girl-child realizes that she might be unwanted and helpless, but she is *at the same time* immensely powerful and an asset (like Kali) – she is an unwanted subject and a dangerous object – a Molotov cocktail that can be thrown in a smoothly functioning upper-caste community to obliterate all that they hold sacred.

Interestingly, while most would consider the boy's position as that of perpetual comfort and privilege, he is actually positioned as being in a place of lack – he does not possess something that another does. As mentioned earlier, with the fear and prohibition around the ability to decimate the community's honor, the female subject comes into the realization of her authority. The boy witnesses the control and sanctions on the female body and similarly comes into the realization of its power to destroy others *and* him. He has to come to terms with lacking this agent of destruction – he *lacks* the body that can obliterate the community with one small gesture, but, as we will soon observe, gender binaries are not immovable positions in India.

Resistance to crisis

Family theories of schizophrenia maintain that incongruent messages by family members, disjunctions in meaning, blurring of age–sex boundaries in the family, etc. are some of the causal mechanisms behind psychological pathologies (Mischler & Waxler, 1969). Recent years have seen a decline in these explanations and the "schizophrenogenic mother" has almost completely been discarded. Despite that, as we observed earlier, the presence of incongruent communication and contradictions in the etiology and presentation of schizophrenia have survived theoretical shifts.

Given the extensive literature that relates to madness and contradictions, I am forced to wonder about the female subject's response to the complications generated by familial, cultural, and social demands. Why does the girl-child, who is bombarded with incongruent communication and meta-messages from her family (including extended family) and contradictory motifs and myths from the community, not succumb to a pathology of some sort? How does she mitigate the crisis when research shows (Romme & Escher, 2012) that early childhood trauma, which includes both subtle emotional neglect and obvious abuse, increases the susceptibility of a person developing psychosis in adulthood? Moreover, many theorists have assumed a child's awareness of his/her unwanted-ness to be a definite precursor to pathology. Laing (1990) attributes ontological insecurity, which is essential to a schizoid presentation, to being unacknowledged in early childhood. Similarly, Winnicott (1960) emphasizes the importance of a good-enough mother whose basic presence is essential for the baby to achieve autonomy and develop a coherent sense of self. The girl-child is now in a classic double-bind – she cannot respond and she cannot escape. She is simultaneously a powerful asset *and* also a helpless liability, undesired and at the same time openly welcomed. Why does she not develop a psychotic structure? The answer lies in the absence of fixed subjectivity, and the culture's acceptance, nay production, of non-positional/multi-positional subjects. This slippery subjectivity and its effects are clear in her negotiations.

Unlike the Western industrialized world (which generated the family-process theories of schizophrenia), Indian culture, which is violently heterogeneous, with over a 100 major languages, provides and *creates* ample space for contradictions and chaos. Contradictions and non-duality are a part of the cultural fabric, as is evident in the paradox of goddess Kali who symbolizes both birth and death: "Kali is both a wife and a mother. But she is also an immodest, aggressive, and grotesque wife and a terrifying, violent, and self-absorbed mother .... Consequently, Kali comes to symbolize the paradoxical dyads: passivity/aggressiveness; traditionality/unconventionality; beautiful/grotesque; tender/terrifying" (Dalmiya, 2000, p. 243). Indian scientists worshiped their favorite gods before launching the Mars orbiter *Mangalyaan*, and the Indian mind imperturbably accepts the co-existence of evolution and myths of creation. British colonizers were known to deride the Indian intellect by calling it feminine because to them irrationality marked a woman's way of being. This blurring of boundaries between binaries like subject/object, genders, and species, etc. is the reason why the female subject, fraught with contradictions, can still manage to exist in in-between spaces. The girl-child can overcome dualities because they do not exist for her. Her subjectivity, not fixed, can hold complex permutations and multiple shifting positions. This ability to contain and tolerate ambiguity makes the female subject resilient to pathology.

She is not caught in the schizophrenogenic double-bind because she is a "slippery subject" and thus not bound by binary choices – born in ambiguity, thriving on contradictions and reveling in what seems, to us, chaos. I already wrote about the features of this form of subjectivity, and in the girl-child we can clearly observe how it mitigates pathology. This characteristic of the Indian subject is reflected in the famous Indian psychoanalyst Girindrasekhar Bose's (1949) clinical vignettes. Bose observed in his practice that he would come across many men with an unconscious desire to become women. According to him, the reason the boy desires castration to fulfill his wish of becoming a woman is due to his identifications with the mother (and mother surrogates), and this is reflected in the games children play where little boys wear dresses to enact the role of the wife (Bose, 1949). What is significant is that his cure for such a patient was to help him imagine being a woman (with a woman's desires) and then shift back into being a man, and so on until "he was relieved of his symptoms" (Hartnack, 1990, p. 930). As Bose (1948) concludes in the end, for his male patients a successful identification with the wife had to be followed by the same with his mother. This is not altogether surprising: the gender binaries in India are not tightly compartmentalized; after all, India does have a heavy cultural presence of the Hijra population that harbors an incredible diversity in ways of being and loving. In 2014, the Indian Supreme Court recognized this community as the official third gender. Before the discourse around homosexuality, trans-genderism, and the gender spectrum ever became popular in the West, India had the ubiquitous presence of a number of different variations of multi-gendered people who occupied public space.

Bose's case presentations reflect the culture's comfort with and acceptance of multi-positionality and fluid structures where neurotic patients could be cured by being asked to shift into both male and female roles and assume their desires. The slipperiness here was evident in the ability to inhabit two seemingly binary subject positions, sometimes at the same time, to ease the neurosis. In the last chapter I also discussed a similar lack of pathology and ease with multi-positionality while discussing the absence of identity crises post-liberalization in India. These amorphous boundaries are what enable the female subject's graceful escape from a crisis of subjectivity. It seems, just like Bose's patients, that she is able to slip through and move between various positions of being undesired and worshiped at the same time. The contradictions do not bind her since they do not exist for her; as already observed, the Indian psyche is highly comfortable with paradoxes.

Conclusion

This slippery subjectivity welcomes multiple and contradictory narratives, as reflected in the girl-child's response to and comfort with the unresolved contradictions that structure her. It allows for non-binary choices (she can be both the victim and the destroyer) and what looks like her resilience to pathology is actually not resilience at all. She, like the rest of the Indian subjects I wrote about in the last chapter, does not need to resolve, deny, or collapse incongruities. One must be structurally fluid, live in the in-between of transient subject positions and be able to slip into these locations to be immune to the onslaught of ambiguity and the anarchy of paradoxes. This brings to light the question of whether psychology has something to offer to a people so differently structured. These differences cannot be captured by phrases like collective and individualistic, but exist at a more fundamental level – a difference in the discourses that build us, the visibilities that shape us, and the contradictions that structure us. The next chapter attempts to tackle this concern to examine whether different theories of knowledge and structures of subject render psychology irrelevant.

7
NO COUNTRY FOR PSYCHOLOGY

As I write this, the World Health Organisation's 2018 mhGAP (mental health gap) forum is preparing to open tomorrow in Geneva. This year's theme is "Accelerating Country Action on Mental Health" and the forum "provides an opportunity for diverse stakeholders to discuss progress on WHO's Mental Health Action Plan 2013–2020" (mhGAP Forum, n.d.). Sessions include discussions on e-mental intervention and crisis as an entry point for scaling up mental health services. The website states that there is a pressing need to provide mental health services to those in low-income countries as they lack the resources to help themselves. It confidently assures us that, with care and medication, depression and schizophrenia, among other mental and neurological conditions, could be treated, and people could lead normal lives. As I bring this book to its conclusion, it will become evident from my theoretical and empirical assertions that the confidence is misplaced and the assurances are empty.

To do this I will first briefly note how the two cultures and their different epistemologies converge in some ways and differ in others. Doing this is essential to critique the ongoing march of seemingly benevolent psychiatry. That said, I do not aim to bring any kind of forced consistency in the narratives of the East and the West; I am not sure that is possible or even desirable, or if the East and West ever exist as the monoliths we make them out to be.

The schizophrenic and the slippery

Before I conclude the differences between these ways of being, I would first want to point to some similarities in these two cultures. First, for both schizophrenic thought and Indian rural discourse, language is about more than representation and signification. The former takes an inward turn to side-step meaning, and focuses on the structure of a word, the feel of a sound, or the shape of a grapheme. The latter believes words to have quantifiable and physical effects on things, whether they are curses of their ancestors, the sighs of a suffering parent, the unfulfilled vocal promise of a pilgrim, or the protective chants of a mantra. Second, the Western epistemological tension between a historically constituted man and a sovereign subject which is caricaturized by the schizophrenic resonates in some ways with the implicit discourse of "radical enmeshment". This discourse conceives a similar appreciation for radical determination through others, that is, the idea that people are constituted through other people and forces, and that their fate depends on the actions, desires, and intentions of others. It also implies that people are simultaneously radically agentic, in that their actions and desires have repercussion for others, both now and in the lifetimes to come. Thus, both the modern Western and the rural Indian, in very different ways and with dissimilar results, display a certain recognition of deep interconnectedness and historicity.

The common thread that runs through the Indian female subject, Deleuze and Guattari's nomadic subject, the rural Indian subject whose afflictions are contagious, and the modern Western schizophrenic subject, is that they are all shifting and not reified. We already noted how this applies to the first three, but it equally holds true for the modern Western schizophrenic. It is not Lacan's divided subject that oscillates wildly between the epistemic poles of modern knowledge; instead this is the tragic fate of the schizophrenic. He must bear the cost of this perpetual motion, implying yet again a mobility, a slipperiness, and a nomadic construction. This mobile structure of subjectivity is what connects the modern Western schizophrenic to the rural Indian one. The operations, movements, and pitfalls of desire might be different in the two cultures but these two subjects are united by their ability to sustain and slip through multiple subjective positions. The schizophrenic is annihilated by the persistent transience but the rural Indian subject frolics through the arena of eternal contradictions. It seems that Deleuze and Guattari may have been right in suggesting that the schizophrenic as a clinical entity is not the natural repercussion of the schizophrenia process but instead is a product of the response of others.

The differences between them are just as intriguing as the parallels. I first interrogated the conditions that gave rise to and sustained schizophrenia, and then critiqued the semantics and evidence underlying it. In India I found people who displayed symptoms that are integral to schizophrenia – psychosis – but had a different understanding and corresponding experience attached to it. I noted four major differences. First, the experience of seeing things and hearing voices did not necessitate distress as has been normally reported in the psychiatric literature. This was exemplified in the woman who spoke of her mother wanting to dance with her hallucinations or the hotel manager who talked, without alarm or worry, about his experience of "leg lock". Ethan Watters, in his book *Crazy Like Us*, similarly speaks about three families in Zanzibar and their experience of living with a schizophrenic family member. Distress, he shows, is often worsened by the stigmatization and incessant criticism of the schizophrenic individual, but more importantly he states how research points to a counterintuitive finding. Contrary to what most psychiatrists had predicted, the presence of the biomedical model in the US, Germany, and Turkey did not reduce stigma but instead worsened it, and furthermore it increased subjective distress and mistreatment by others. Additionally, narratives of spirit possessions which Western psychologists claimed were conducive to stigmatization, seemed to prevent exclusion, ill-treatment, ridicule, and forceful control from others (Watters, 2010).

Second, the symptoms could be transient instead of chronic; a psychotic break was usually short-term as opposed to the schizophrenic disorder that swallows decades of people's lives in the West and in Indian cities. Third, there was no relation between childhood and adult event trauma and psychotic expressions as some recent psychological theories have suggested. For that matter, trauma theory is facing scrutiny for its homogenization of all extreme suffering as psychologically traumatic and its lack of attention to material conditions or prevalent local discourses which do not fit the language of PTSD. This *tyranny of meaning* necessitates that resolution of individual and collective suffering happens through verbalization. Craps (2010) and Young (1997), amongst others, have opposed this imposition of language. While Craps (2010) writes about the monoculturalism of trauma theory and comments on the inadequacies of the South African Truth and Reconciliation Commission in post-apartheid Africa, Young (1997) focuses on unearthing the epistemological practices, historical narratives, and discursive conditions that sustain trauma theory. Human suffering might be universal but PTSD, with its characteristic symptom presentation, is not. This does not imply that those theories are not accurate or helpful; on the contrary, some of the work done by the Hearing Voices foundation has shown immense promise. It has helped to counter the pessimism that has surrounded schizophrenia from the time of Kraepelin (Kraepelin & Diefendorf, 1904), who himself believed there was a definite disease process that was permanent and progressive. It only means that explanatory frameworks are not universal, in that the presentation of similar symptoms does not necessitate similar causes across the world.

Finally, the content of the hallucinations was not necessarily negative as has been traditionally observed in the Western industrialized world. The hallucinatory experience of a wedding procession with music and of hearing voices of beloved dead relatives resonates with Luhrmann et al.'s (2015) findings concerning neutral and positive hallucinatory content in India and Ghana. Luhrmann et al. (2015) showed how the experience of psychotic phenomena in indigenous cultures varies across the world. Upon monitoring the phenomenological experience of hearing voices (auditory hallucinations) of patients in India, Ghana, and the US, they found that amount and quality of distress experienced by voice hearers was highly culture-specific:

> participants in the US were more like to use diagnostic labels and report violent commands than those in India and Ghana, who were more likely than the Americans to report rich relationships with their voices and less likely to describe their voices as a sign the sign of a violated mind.
>
> *(Luhrmann et al., 2015, p. 41)*

In my investigation of schizophrenic subjectivity, its exaggerated personification of the rifts in modern epistemology came to the fore. In a peculiar sense, the ability or inevitability of the schizophrenic subject's oscillations brings him closer to the structure of the Indian post-colonial subject than to the divided subject of psychoanalysis. Similarly, a relative disinterest in interiority (the *contents* of the psyche and their meaning) also marks the Western schizophrenic and the Indian subject, but not the neurotic one.

To summarize, a brief description of the dissimilarities between the subjects of Western modernity and the Indian social formation would be that the former is intensive, in that his structure and orientation is primarily inward (neurotic – contents, schizophrenic – processes), while the latter is extensive, in that his structure and orientation are outward. The material connectivity (of desire) is inward in the former due to the social institution of nuclear families (having to triangulate its desire and make binary choices), but outward in the latter due to the social institution of joint families (having multiple positions for desire to connect and make multiple and contradictory choices). The former is built through inward glare (hyper-reflexive for schizophrenic, and reflexive for neurotic) and the latter through outward "radical enmeshment". The former's tragic beauty lies in its loss – an opacity even from itself – the *unthought*. The latter's downfall and subsequent salvation is in its exposed transparency.

Personalizing experience with globalized psychiatry

In light of these similarities and differences, the question we need to answer now is whether the psychiatric discourse can be universal and objective, and whether it can apply to subjects that are structured so differently. Is psychology's occupation of foreign lands and distant territories of thought valid? My tentative answer would be that psychiatry and psychology have not shown a better prognosis or a better explanatory framework, even in their own cultural context, than the rituals and beliefs that our participants held concerning *seeing things or hearing voices*. This is especially true considering the evidentiary chaos surrounding schizophrenia as noted in Chapter 2. What is disconcerting is that the call for action to provide mental health services across the globe, with a special focus on low- and middle-income countries has been growing stronger. The principles that underlie this call are human rights concerns and faith in evidence-based treatments. This movement insists on a shift of burdens on mental health professionals to non-specialist task forces (Das & Rao, 2012), an increase in pressure on local governments to raise spending on mental health issues, the sensitization of communities, and fostering partnerships with local organizations.

China Mills and Suman Fernando (2014) chart the progress of the Global Mental Health Movement and question its underlying ethics. The term "global" comprises not just "supraterritorial processes and connections" in terms of spatiality, but also an "irreducible global quality" (Das & Rao, 2012). The very notion of a Global Mental Health Movement essentializes the construct of mental health as global, and mental illness as organic dysfunction. The concept of "treatment gap" begs us to pay attention to the lack of resources that low- and middle-income countries face in dealing with mental disorders but it doesn't question the universal nature and prevalence of mental disorders in the first place. According to Das and Rao (2012), the economic burden of mental disorders measured primarily by the Disability Adjusted Life Years (DALY) is problematic and overestimates the same. This push to scale up the efforts comes from two sides: The World Health Organization, and the Movement for Global Mental Health. According to Mills and Fernando (2014), "Such a view – reducing complex matters of living, behaving and thinking to 'mental' health and disorder developed in a particular socio-cultural context" (p. 188) has received rightful critique from many groups, especially at a point when the validity and efficacy of psychiatric treatment and diagnosis is under scrutiny in the global north itself.

Psychologists and activists alike have questioned the increasing globalization of mental health as a concept, and called for a need to decolonize it. Since many non-governmental organizations that operate in the global south are funded by sources in like transnational corporations in high-income countries, suspicions regarding their allegiance are expected and should be interrogated. This is reflected in unregulated drug sales in the global south where emphasis on intake of psychotropic drugs competes with unavailability of life-saving medication. At the same time there is the concern that, as multilateral agencies loan large sums to low- and middle-income countries for medication, it increases the economic dependence of poor countries on the global north (Shah, 2006). Louise Tam (2013; as cited in Mills & Fernando, 2014) uses the example of neurasthenia to show how diagnostic categories could turn issues of oppression into apolitical, private issues of family dynamics, and translate into psychological jargon the "experiences of racial profiling, classroom segregation, worker disablement, and poverty" (p. 192). This further results in the replacement of local ways of dealing with suffering with global ones which are not only inapplicable but also unsustainable in terms of resources. As Mills and Fernando (2014) suggest, the interwoven nature of our historical, cultural, geopolitical locations complicates our understanding and brings about a need to recognize "different lived realities of suffering worldwide, to imagine different relationships between medicine and madness, and to map ways to responding to distress that are not necessarily psychiatric" (p. 196).

The foundations of psychology

It is not only the nature and conceptualization of mental disorders and mental health that are garbed in an objective and universal rhetoric. The underlying assumptions that gave birth to psychology itself are historically situated and culturally defined. These ethical assumptions prescribe that not only is man primarily motivated by self-interest but also that psychology's aim must be to analyze an "individual's private experience and personal needs" (Mustakova-Possardt, Basseches, Oxenberg, & Hansen, 2014, p. 24). As has been repeatedly stated by Foucault, the foundations of the "value-free" discipline of psychology were economic, and, more importantly, moral. I am not interested in scrutinizing psychology's claim to objectivity, since the recent replication crisis has already managed that; instead what I want to emphasize is that the fundamentals of this "science" do not translate cross-culturally and across class structures. Thus, not only is the structure of the subject dissimilar, but the values inherent in the discourse of psychology emerge solely from Western middle-class society, thus making its export unfeasible at many levels. Talk to a person in rural India about the issues of personal rights and private space, and you will be met with uncomprehending stares that will make you question the individualist values that psychology is founded on. Watch people conduct a *jaagar* with their community and the assumptions regarding resource scarcity and natural competition that have so defined Western thought (Mustakova-Possardt, Basseches, Oxenberg, & Hansen, 2014) are put into question.

This is not to say that Indians live in collectivist bliss, but the cause of their intersubjective violence and the conditions of their misery are premised upon a different set of values. And let me assure you, there is plenty of senseless violence and misery, but the moment we dislodge psychology from its historical seat and consider it an objective science distanced from the context that birthed it, we allow it to run wild to wreak havoc on those it pretends to understand and intends to control. One cannot divorce psychology and the concept of mental health from the neoliberal ethic that sustains it.

We only need to look at the theories on trauma and resilience to find evidence for this. A recent emergence in the psychology of trauma has been the shift to study human resilience and post-traumatic growth, but as Schwarz (2018) writes, this conceptualization of resilience also has neoliberal roots and a causal logic based in universalizing tendencies. Pointing to Chandler's (2014; as cited in Schwarz, 2018) work she notes that a useful conceptualization of resilience will be contextual and sensitive to local realities, but in its current form even resilience reproduces "power imbalances and discrimination within our society" (Schwarz, 2018, p. 529). In personalizing concepts such as resilience, in that they become strengths and weaknesses dependent on and inherent in an individual, such discourses create further alienation and uphold the idea that psychological distress is a personal problem to be addressed in one person, and resilience is also a personal quality. Knowing what we know now about the form of resolutions common in rural India and temples like Balaji, these views of personal strength and resilience fall flat. This acquits the social systems that are at least partially responsible for creating conditions that produce psychological distress in the first place. Thus, even when psychology shifts its gaze from treatment-focused approaches, it can only go so far. Overall, most of the mainstream understandings of psychology either follow the computer model (cognitive behavioral theories) or an economic one (an individual's personal resources that make him resilient, the depletion of resources, competition between life circumstances and division of resources), and its foundations are riddled with the ethico-moral assumptions of Western modernity.

This dependence on Western values leads psychology to prioritize meritocracy, individualism, and materialism, and resultantly implies that since we can all create a materially satisfactory life, any problem that emerges is a problem within the person (Mustakova-Possardt et al., 2014). As opposed to this, amongst the people in rural Uttarakhand, the cause and resolution of the problem is sought outside the person. This is especially significant because research in the West itself has critiqued how these foundations, like that of crude materialism that rejects the importance of anything not directly apprehended, is the cause of much anxiety (Hanson, 2009; as cited in Mustakova-Possardt et al., 2014) and intergenerational human suffering. These assumptions are moral in nature and they imply that high stress is a natural by-product of the good modern life, which further leads people to accept its inevitability and resolve it through personal change and not social evolution. Its import to India without any scrutiny then leads to educated cities with their hospitals full of chronic schizophrenics who have spent 20 years receiving behaviorist interventions and forced yoga. Of course, we still have subversive pockets within the cities (at the Muslim shrines, Sufi dargahs, Hindu temples, etc.) plus most rural areas, where the schizophrenic is non-existent, but as Davar and Lohokare (2009) have pointed out, these pockets are under threat by global forces and local authorities. Make no mistake, the treatment of the afflicted is far from kind or easy; it is sometimes downright violent and can appear abusive. The question we are left with is whether being isolated in a system that: 1. drugs and discards individuals regularly, 2. has a rampant problem with physical and sexual assault in hospitals, 3. leads to life-long stigmatization, and 4. has especially poor prognosis, is any better than a chicken sacrifice and broom beatings?

In the previous chapters, we not only encountered different realities concerning the explanation of psychosis but also distinctly different ways of categorizing and experiencing suffering. Not only did I not find any relation between traumatic life events and psychotic symptoms, it appeared that distress was not a necessary repercussion of hallucinations. In light of this absence of distress, the absence of event trauma as an etiological factor, the inherent weakness and instability of schizophrenia as a psychopathological entity – a discipline whose underlying moral and ethical assumptions color its vision of health and disease – and most importantly the very different social formations that produce very diverse types of subjects (fixed versus slippery), I have come to believe that the Global Mental Health Movement is a misguided attempt backed by institutions with immense authority and repute, and that it will insidiously obliterate local discourses with unsustainable homogenous universal ones if it is not questioned or regulated. A difference of this magnitude cannot be wished away using culture-fair testing. The introduction of a treatment-based "therapeutic" approach which is rooted in a fixed type of subjectivity and prioritizes interiority, to a population that has an external trajectory of desire is not only useless but unethical. It just does not translate.

Our call for decolonization cannot be partial where psychological theories are developed in one place and then tweaked for another audience; a true critique is not only a critique of non-contextual psychology but of all ahistorical and apolitical forms of knowledge. We have to ask some difficult questions, like whether a focus on interiority and a preoccupation with psyche's contents is universal, and, if not, should we attempt to make it so? Is there really a need to turn the gaze inward and attend to one's past history or internal experience? Our answers might require us to chart through uncomfortable and uncertain places, both geographically and intellectually.

Conclusion

Madness arouses intense reactions amongst those in its presence, whether they study it, or encounter it themselves or in a loved one. From a vehement rejection of any meaning in madness to its devoted adoration in some traditions, madness brings us face to face with something completely alien yet disconcertingly familiar within ourselves, given its prowess to seduce and frighten simultaneously. It's a promise of freedom from the order of the *Other*, and a fear of enslavement by the chaos of the self. The mad might have been envied for their animal freedom, their inhuman strength, or even their creative disdain for civilization, but they can still be caught in the carnival of their own imagination and the prison of their dreadful delusions. I have concluded that these intense reactions the madman incites in us are partially a product of his crude exposé of our basic structures and the conditions that animate them. By focusing not on the content of madness but on its process and volatility, I was able to note its capricious nature, which speaks to the epistemic oscillations. As a homage to this unpredictability, I would like my closing remarks to be rather personal in tone.

The beginning of this venture was marked by an interrogation of the precarious conditions that anchor modern Western insanity. I use the word "interrogation" carefully and consciously, for at times this project felt like it was torturously tricked out of me and I was conjuring ideas whose existence I wasn't privy to till moments before I wrote them. It was when I peeled at the raised edges (those being madness, psychosis, schizophrenia) of the structure of subjectivity – an experience that felt more like a migraine and less like an academic undertaking for it was nauseating, agonizing, and intermittently enthralling – that the heart of this project was realized. The alienation of the modern West is my alienation; I did not emerge from its context but I am submerged in its repercussions. I recognize its fracture and I experience its thirst but I was raised by the product of its absence – the absence of the forever-present and the utterly unknown, the *unthought*. There is a dual loss here; first, the loss of certainty and then of the certainty of uncertainty. In some bizarre manner, I share this ungrounded homelessness with the schizophrenic. Maybe that is why this endeavor is riddled with open fascination and not distanced objectivity.

Married as I am (reluctantly so) to the pursuit of non-indulgence in narratives of progress or regress, I do not intend to simply demonize global imports and glorify the indigenous ones. Instead, it is my hope that by studying in detail the discontinuity of thought and by diagnosing the current epistemic constraints, I, or someone else, will be able to render transparent the prevalent discourses, delegitimize the accepted authority of certain institutions, and denaturalize the appearance of apolitical and ahistorical forms of knowledge. I don't remember Foucault's writings ever being particularly prescriptive but he did maintain that the role of the intellectual was to interrogate seemingly natural ways of thinking and to expose their violence by revealing their lack of neutrality. This seemingly passive approach, which is devoid of any revolutionary call to action, might strike some as strange, considering I have made direct accusations regarding the nature and effects of the Global Mental Health Movement and psychology itself. But this choice to uncover the "strangeness of the present" does not appear to me as an apolitical one at all, and neither is it passive. For the process of turning the obvious into the alien or the implicit into explicit might be schizophrenic, but it is also at the same time profoundly revolutionary.

REFERENCES

Adichie, C.N. (2014). *Americanah*. New York: Anchor.
Agnivesh, S., Mani, R., & Koster-Lossack, A. (2005, November 25). Missing 50 Million Indian Girls. *The New York Times*. Retrieved from www.nytimes.com.
American Psychiatric Association. (1952). *Diagnostic and statistical manual of mental disorders* (1st ed.). Washington, DC: Author.
American Psychiatric Association. (1968). *Diagnostic and statistical manual of mental disorders* (2nd ed.). Washington, DC: Author.
Andreasen, N.C., Nopoulos, P., Magnotta, V., Pierson, R., Ziebell, S., & Ho, B.C. (2011). Progressive brain change in schizophrenia: A prospective longitudinal study of first-episode schizophrenia. *Biological Psychiatry*, 70(7), 672–679.
Banal, R., Thappa, J., Shah, H.U., Hussain, A., Chowhan, A., Bharti, M., & Thappa, S. (2010). Psychiatric morbidity in adult Kashmiri migrants living in a migrant camp at Jammu. *Indian Journal of Psychiatry*, 52(2), 154–158.
Banerjee, M.N. (1944). Hindu family and Freudian theory. *The Indian Journal of Social Work*, 3, 180–186.
Barnes, M., & Berke, J. (1971). *Mary Barnes: Two accounts of a journey through madness*. London: MacGibbon and Kee.
Bassaglia, F., & Ongaro, F.B. (2018). A problem of institutional psychiatry: Exclusion as a social and psychiatric category. *International Review of Psychiatry*, 30(2), 120–128.
Basu, A.R. (2004). A new knowledge of madness: Nineteenth century asylum psychiatry in Bengal. *Indian Journal of History of Science*, 39(3), 247–277.
Bateson, G., Jackson, D.D., Haley, J., & Weakland, J. (1956). Toward a theory of schizophrenia. *Behavioral Science*, 1, 251–264.
Bentall, R.P. (1993). Deconstructing the concept of 'schizophrenia'. *Journal of Mental Health*, 2(3), 223–238.
Bentall, R.P., & Fernyhough, C. (2008). Social predictors of psychotic experiences: Specificity and psychological mechanisms. *Schizophrenia Bulletin*, 34(6), 1012–1020.

References

Bentall, R.P., Jackson, H.F., & Pilgrim, D. (1988). Abandoning the concept of 'schizophrenia': Some implications of validity arguments for psychological research into psychotic phenomena. *British Journal of Clinical Psychology, 27*(4), 303–324.

Berrios, G.E., & Markova, I.S. (2017). The epistemology and classification of 'madness' since the eighteenth century. In G. Eghigian (Ed.), *The Routledge history of madness and mental health* (pp. 115–134). London: Routledge.

Bhattacharya, A. (2013). *Indian insanes: Lunacy in the 'native' asylums of colonial India, 1858–1912* (Doctoral Dissertation). Harvard University.

Bhishagratna, K.L. (Ed.). (1916). *An English translation of the Sushruta Samhita based on original Sanskrit text* (vol. 6). Calcutta: Sanyal & Co. [www.rarebooksocietyofindia.org/book_archive/196174216674_10154370772061675.pdf.]

Bhugra, D. (2000). Migration and schizophrenia. *Acta Psychiatrica Scandinavica, 102* (407), 68–73.

Bhugra, D., & Bhui, K. (2002). Is the Oedipal complex universal? Problems for sexual and relationship psychotherapy across cultures. *Sexual and Relationship Therapy, 17,* 69–86.

Black, E. (2003). *War against the weak: Eugenics and America's campaign to create a master race.* Washington, DC: Dialog Press.

Bose, G. (1948). A new theory of mental life. *Samiksa, 2,* 109–205.

Bose, G. (1949). The genesis and adjustment of the Oedipus wish. *Samiksa, 3,* 237).

Boyle, M. (2002). *Schizophrenia: A scientific delusion?* Hove, UK: Routledge.

Braun, V., & Clarke, V. (2006). Using thematic analysis in psychology. *Qualitative Research in Psychology, 3*(2), 77–101.

Buchanan, I. (2008). *Deleuze and Guattari's Anti-Oedipus: A reader's guide.* London: Continuum.

Burnham, D.L., Gladstone, A.I., & Gibson, R.W. (1969). *Schizophrenia and the need-fear dilemma.* New York: International Universities Press.

Cantor-Graae, E., & Selten, J.P. (2005). Schizophrenia and migration: A meta-analysis and review. *American Journal of Psychiatry, 162*(1), 12–24.

Caraka. (1896). *Charaka-samhita: Translated into English.* Calcutta: Printed by G.C. Chakravarti.

Cardno, A.G., & Gottesman, I.I. (2000). Twin studies of schizophrenia: From bow-and-arrow concordances to star wars Mx and functional genomics. *American Journal of Medical Genetics, 97*(1), 12–17.

Caruth, C. (2001). An interview with Jean Laplanche. *Postmodern Culture, 11*(2): n.p.

Chalmers, D. (1995). Facing up to the problem of consciousness. *Journal of Consciousness Studies, 2*(3), 200–219.

Craps, S. (2010). Wor(l)ds of grief. *Textual Practices, 24*(1), 51–68.

Crick, F., & Koch, C. (1998). Consciousness and neuroscience. *Cerebral Cortex, 8*(2), 97–107.

Dalmiya, V. (2000). Loving paradoxes: A feminist reclamation of the goddess Kali. *Hypatia, 15,* 125–150.

Das, A., & Rao, M. (2012). Universal mental health: Re-evaluating the call for global mental health. *Critical Public Health, 22*(4), 383–389.

References

Davar, B., & Lohokare, M. (2009). Recovering from psychosocial traumas: The place of Dargahs in Maharashtra. *Economic and Political Weekly, 44*(16), 60–67. Retrieved from www.jstor.org/stable/40279157.

Deleuze, G., & Guattari, F. (1983). *Anti-Oedipus: Capitalism and schizophrenia*. Trans. Robert Hurley, Mark Seem, and Helen R. Lane. Minneapolis, MN: University of Minnesota Press.

Dennet, D.C. (1991). *Consciousness explained*. Boston, New York, London: Little, Brown and Company.

Dhar, A., & Siddiqui, S. (2013). At the edge of (critical) psychology. *Annual Review of Critical Psychology, 10*, 506–548.

Dorph-Petersen, K.A., Pierri, J.N., Perel, J.M., Sun, Z., Sampson, A.R., & Lewis, D. A. (2005). The influence of chronic exposure to antipsychotic medications on brain size before and after tissue fixation: A comparison of haloperidol and olanzapine in macaque monkeys. *Neuropsychopharmacology, 30*(9), 1649–1661.

Dowbiggin, I.R. (1997). *Keeping America sane: Psychiatry and eugenics in the United States and Canada 1880–1940*. New York: Cornell.

Earnst, K.S., & Kring, A.M. (1999). Emotional responding in deficit and non-deficit schizophrenia. *Psychiatry Research, 88*, 191–207.

Fadiman, J., & Kewman, D. (1979). *Exploring madness: Experience, theory and research*. Monterey, CA: Brooks/Cole.

Faith healing centers for mentally ill to be monitored. (2001, August 11). *The Hindu*. Retrieved from thehindu.com.

Fink, B. (1996). *The Lacanian subject: Between language and jouissance*. Princeton, NJ: Princeton University Press.

Fosse, R., Joseph, J., & Richardson, K. (2015). A critical assessment of the equal-environment assumption of the twin method for schizophrenia. *Frontiers in Psychiatry, 6*(2). doi:10.3389/fpsyt.2015.00062

Foucault, M. (1967). *Madness and civilization*. London: Tavistock.

Foucault, M. (1994). *The order of things: An archaeology of the human sciences*. New York: Vintage.

Foucault, M. (2006). *Psychiatric power: Lectures at the Collège de France, 1973–74*. Basingstoke, UK: Palgrave Macmillan.

Frances, A. (2010). Opening Pandora's Box: The 19 worst suggestions for DSM-V. *Psychiatric Times, 27*(3), 9.

Frances, A. (2013). Psychosis risk syndrome is back. *Psychiatric Times*. Retrieved from www.psychiatrictimes.com/dsm-5/psychosis-risk-syndrome-back.

Gaebel, W., & Zielasek, J. (2008). The DSM-V initiative "deconstructing psychosis" in the context of Kraepelin's concept on nosology. *European Archives of Psychiatry and Clinical Neuroscience, 258*, 41–47.

Green, H. (1989). *I never promised you a rose garden*. New York: Signet.

Gutting, G. (1989). *Michel Foucault's archaeology of scientific reason*. Cambridge, MA: Cambridge University Press.

Haldipur, C.V. (1984). Madness in ancient India: Concept of insanity in Charaka Samhita (1st century AD). *Comprehensive Psychiatry, 25*(3), 335–344.

Harley, H. (1921). Segregation versus hanging. *Journal of Criminal Law and Criminology, 11*(4), 512–527.

References 173

Hartnack, C. (1990). Vishnu on Freud's desk: Psychoanalysis in colonial India. *Social Research*, *57*, 921–949.

Hastings, T. (1856). Lunatic asylums in Bengal. *Calcutta Review*, *26*, 52.

Holland, E.W. (2001). *Deleuze and Guattari's Anti-Oedipus: Introduction to schizoanalysis*. London: Routledge.

Huford, I. (2016, October 2). Medicating a prophet. *The New York Times*. Retrieved from www.nytimes.com/2016/10/02/opinion/sunday/medicating-a-prophet.html.

Jablensky, A. (2005). Categories, dimensions and prototypes: Critical issues for psychiatric classification. *Psychopathology*, *38*(4), 201–205.

Jablensky, A. (2010). The diagnostic concept of schizophrenia: Its history, evolution, and future prospects. *Dialogues in Clinical Neuroscience*, *12*(3), 271–287.

Jones, P.B., Barnes, T.R., Davies, L., Dunn, G., Lloyd, H., Hayhurst, K.P., ... Lewis, S.W. (2006). Randomized controlled trial of the effect on quality of life of second- vs first-generation antipsychotic drugs in schizophrenia: Cost utility of the latest antipsychotic drugs in schizophrenia study. *Archives of General Psychiatry*, *63*(10), 1079–1087.

Jucaite, A., & Nyberg, S. (2012). Dopaminergic hypothesis of schizophrenia: A historical perspective. In J.S. Albert & M.W. Wood (Eds.), *Targets and emerging therapies for schizophrenia* (pp. 5–35). Hoboken, NJ: John Wiley & Sons.

Kakkar, S. (1982). *Shamans, mystics, and doctors: A psychological inquiry into India and its healing traditions*. Chicago, IL: University of Chicago Press.

Kellett, J.M. (1973). Evolutionary theory for the dichotomy of the functional psychoses. *The Lancet*, *301*(7808), 860–863.

Kendall, G., & Wickham, G. (1998). *Using Foucault's methods*. Thousand Oaks, CA: SAGE Publications Ltd.

Kennedy, M. (2010, August 10). India's mentally ill turn to faith not medicine. *NPR*. Retrieved from www.npr.org/templates/story/story.php?storyId=126143778.

Kirk, S.A., & Kutchins, H. (1992). *The selling of the DSM: The rhetoric of science in psychiatry*. New York: Transaction Publishers.

Koola, M. (2009). An interview with William Carpenter Jr. M.D. *The Resident's Journal*, *4*(3), 1–5.

Kraepelin, E., & Diefendorf, A.R. (1904). *Clinical psychiatry: A textbook for students and physicians. Abstracted and adapted from the 6th German edition of Kraepelin's Lehrbuch der psychiatrie*. London: Macmillan.

Kurosawa, A. (1983). *Something like an autobiography*. New York: Vintage.

Lahiri, J. (2003). *The namesake*. Boston, New York: First Mariner Books.

Laing, R.D. (1990). *The divided self: An existential study in sanity and madness*. London: Penguin Books.

Larkin, W., & Read, J. (2012). Childhood trauma and psychosis: Revisiting the evidence. In M. Romme & S. Escher (Eds.), *Psychosis as a personal crisis: An experience based approach* (pp. 61–69). London: Routledge.

Laws, K.R., & Al-Uzri, M.M. (2012). Semantic memory associated with negative symptoms in schizophrenia. In X. Anastassiou-Hadjicharalambous (Ed.), *Psychosis : Causes, diagnosis and treatment. Psychiatry – Theory, applications and treatments* (pp. 167–182). New York: Nova Science Publishers Inc.

Leff, J., Williams, G., Huckvale, M., Arbuthnot, M., & Leff, A.P. (2014). Avatar therapy for persecutory auditory hallucinations: What is it and how does it work? *Psychosis*, *6*(2), 166–176.

Lieberman, J.A., Tollefson, G.D., Charles, C., Zipursky, R., Sharma, T., Kahn, R. S. et al. (2005). Antipsychotic drug effects on brain morphology in first-episode psychosis. *Archives of General Psychiatry*, *62*: 361–370.

Longden, E. (2010). Making sense of voices: A personal story of recovery. *Psychosis*, *2*(3), 255–259.

Longden, E. (2013). *The voices in my head* [video]. Retrieved from www.ted.com/talks/eleanor_longden_the_voices_in_my_head/transcript?language=en.

Luhrmann, T.M., Padmavati, R., Tharoor, H., & Osei, A. (2015). Differences in voice-hearing experiences of people with psychosis in the USA, India and Ghana: Interview-based study. *The British Journal of Psychiatry*, *206*(1), 41–44.

Maj, M. (1998). Critique of the DSM IV operational diagnostic criteria for schizophrenia. *British Journal of Psychiatry*, *172*, 458–460.

Matei, V.P., Mihailescu, A.I., & Davidson, M. (2014). Is non-pharmacological treatment an option for certain schizophrenia patients? *Psychiatria Danubina*, *26*(4), 308–313.

McNally, K. (2016). *A critical history of schizophrenia*. Basingstoke, UK: Palgrave Macmillan.

Mendham, L. (Producer), & Farnham, J. (Director). (2017). *Why did I go mad?* [TV programme]. BBC. Retrieved from www.bbc.co.uk/programmes/b08pltgy.

Metzl, J.M. (2009). *The protest psychosis: How schizophrenia became a Black disease*. Boston, MA: Beacon Press.

mhGAP Forum. (2018). 11–12 October. Retrieved from www.who.int/mental_health/mhgap/forum_2018/en.

Mills, C. (2014). *Decolonizing global mental health: The psychiatrization of the majority world*. Abingdon: Routledge.

Mills, C., & Fernando, S. (2014). Globalising mental health or pathologising the global south? Mapping the ethics, theory and practice of global mental health. *Disability and the Global South*, *1*(2), 188–202.

Mischler, E.G., & Waxler, N.E. (1969). Interaction in families: An experimental study of family processes and schizophrenia. *Systems Research and Behavioral Sciences*, *4*, 328–330.

Miyamoto, S., Miyake, N., Jarskog, L.F., Fleischhacker, W.W., & Lieberman, J.A. (2012). Pharmacological treatment of schizophrenia: A critical review of the pharmacology and clinical effects of current and future therapeutic agents. *Molecular Psychiatry*, *17*(12), 1206–1227.

Morgan-Smith, K. (2019). Long Island woman loses case after being locked in mental facility for telling the truth about Obama following her on Twitter. *The Grio*, February 14. Retrieved from https://thegrio.com/2019/02/14/kamilah-brock-lawsuit-new-york-psych-ward.

Murray, R. (2016). Mistakes I have made in my career. *Schizophrenia Bulletin*, *43*(2), 253–256.

Mustakova-Possardt, E., Basseches, M., Oxenberg, J., & Hansen, I. (2014). Transforming a limited social function into a viable global action agenda. In

References 175

E. Mustakova-Possardt, M. Lyubansky, M. Basseches, & J. Oxenberg (Eds.), *Towards a socially responsible psychology for a global era* (pp. 21–46). New York: Springer.

Nagel, T. (1974). What is it like to be a bat? *The Philosophical Review, 83*(4), 435–450.

Nilolakopoulou, A., & Laucht, S. (2018). How many patients with schizophrenia do not respond to anti-psychotic drugs in the short term? An analysis based on individual patient data from randomized control trials. *Schizophrenia Bulletin*. doi:10.1093/schbul/sby095

Parnas, J. (2011). A disappearing heritage: The clinical core of schizophrenia. *Schizophrenia Bulletin, 37*(6), 1121–1130.

Patients freed; Karaikudi dargah asked to stop faith healing. (2001, August 13). *The Hindu*. Retrieved from thehindu.com.

Peterson, D. (Ed.). (1982). *A mad people's history of madness*. Pittsburgh, PA: University of Pittsburgh Press.

Porter, R. (2002). *Madness: A brief history*. New York: Oxford University Press.

Rachman, S.J. (1976). Schizophrenia and anti-psychiatry. In H.J. Eysenck & G. D. Wilson (Eds.), *A textbook of human psychology* (pp. 302–308). Netherlands: Springer.

Raguram, R., Venkateswaran, A., Ramakrishna, J., & Weiss, M.G. (2002). Traditional community resources for mental health: A report of temple healing from India. *British Medical Journal, 325*(7354), 38–40.

Ranganathan, S. (2014). Healing temples, the anti-superstition discourse and global mental health: Some questions from Mahanubhav temples in India. *South Asia: Journal of South Asian Studies, 37*(4), 625–639. doi:10.1080/00856401.2014.961628

Ranganathan, S. (2015). A space to 'eat, trance, and sleep': The healing power of Mahanubhav temples in Maharashtra (India). *Mental Health, Religion and Culture, 18*(3), 185–195.

Rao, M.A., Berry, R., Gonsalves, A., Hastak, Y., Shah, M., & Roeser, R.W. (2013). Globalization and the identity remix among urban adolescents in India. *Journal of Research on Adolescence, 23*, 9–24.

Romme, M., & Escher, S. (Eds.). (2012). *Psychosis as a personal crisis: An experience-based approach*. London: Routledge.

Rosenhan, D.L. (1973). On being sane in insane places. *Science, 179*, 25–258.

Rowe, D. (1980). Philosophy and psychiatry. *Philosophy, 55*(211), 109–112.

Saks, E. (2007). *The center cannot hold*. New York: Hyperion.

Sapolsky, R. (2014). What scientific idea is ready for retirement?. *Edge*. Retrieved from www.edge.org/responses/what-scientific-idea-is-ready-for-retirement.

Sass, L.A. (1994). *Madness and Modernism*. Cambridge, MA: Harvard University Press.

Sass, L.A. (2007a). Contradictions of emotion in schizophrenia. *Cognition and Emotion, 21*(2), 351–390.

Sass, L.A. (2007b). Explaining schizophrenia: The relevance of phenomenology. In M.C. Chung, K.W.M. Fulford, & G. Graham (Eds.), *Reconceiving schizophrenia* (pp. 63–96). Oxford: Oxford University Press.

Sass, L.A., & Parnas, J. (2003). Schizophrenia, consciousness, and the self. *Schizophrenia Bulletin, 29*(3), 427–444.

References

Schreber, D.P. (2000). *Memoirs of my nervous illness*. New York: New York Review Books.
Schwarz, S. (2018). Resilience in psychology: A critical analysis of the concept. *Theory and Psychology*, *28*(4), 528–541.
Scull, A.T. (1975). From madness to mental illness: Medical men as moral entrepreneurs. *European Journal of Sociology*, *16*(02), 218–261.
Scull, A.T. (1979). *Museums of madness: The social organization of insanity in nineteenth-century England*. London: Allen Lane.
Sechehaye, M., & Rubin-Rabson, G. (1979). *Autobiography of a schizophrenic girl: With analytic interpretation: Reality lost and regained*. New York: Grune & Stratton.
Seikkula, J., Aaltonen, J., Alakare, B., Haarakangas, K., Keränen, J., & Lehtinen, K. (2006). Five-year experience of first-episode nonaffective psychosis in open-dialogue approach: Treatment principles, follow-up outcomes, and two case studies. *Psychotherapy Research*, *16*(2), 214–228.
Shah, S. (2006). *The body hunters: Testing new drugs on the world's poorest patients*. New York and London: The New Press.
Siddiqi, M.Z. (1959). *Studies in Arabic and Persian medical literature*. Calcutta: Calcutta University Press.
Sloan, T.S. (1996). *Damaged life: The crisis of the modern psyche*. London: Routledge.
Somasundaram, O. (1987). The Indian lunacy act, 1912: The historic background. *Indian Journal of Psychiatry*, *29*(1), 3–14.
Spitzer, M., Weisker, I., Winter, M., Maier, S., Hermle, L., & Maher, B.A. (1994). Semantic and phonological priming in schizophrenia. *Journal of Abnormal Psychology*, *103*, 485–494.
Spivak, G.C. (1988). Can the subaltern speak?. In C. Nelson & L. Grossberg (Eds.), *Marxism and the interpretation of culture* (pp. 271–313). Macmillan Education UK.
Szasz, T.S. (1970). *The manufacture of madness*. London: Harper & Row.
Torrey, E.F. (1973). Is schizophrenia universal? An open question? *Schizophrenia Bulletin*, *1*, 53–59.
Tranulis, C. (2012). Coerced treatment in psychosis: Implications of insight, duration of untreated psychosis and stigma. In X. Anastassiou-Hadjicharalambous (Ed.), *Psychosis: Causes, diagnosis and treatment. Psychiatry – Theory, applications and treatments* (pp. 229–239). New York: Nova Science Publishers Inc.
Tranulis, C., Corin, E., & Kirmayer, L.J. (2008). Insight and psychosis: Comparing the perspectives of patient, entourage and clinician. *International Journal of Social Psychiatry*, *54*(3), 225–241.
Van Dongen, J., & Boomsma, D.I. (2013). The evolutionary paradox and the missing heritability of schizophrenia. *Neuropsychiatric Genetics*, *162*(2), 122–136.
Watters, E. (2010). *Crazy like us: The globalization of the American psyche*. New York: Free Press.
Willig, C. (2003). Discourse analysis. In J.A. Smith (Ed.), *Qualitative psychology: A practical guide to research methods* (pp. 159–183). New Delhi: Sage.
Wilson, J. (2009, June 17). *Elizabeth Fraser talks about her lyrics* [(video]. Retrieved from www.youtube.com/watch?v=XTx8VnZBvDc.
Winnicott, D.W. (1960). The theory of the parent-infant relationship. *International Journal of Psychoanalysis*, *41*, 585–595.

Woods, A. (2011). *The sublime object of psychiatry: Schizophrenia in clinical and cultural theory.* Oxford: Oxford University Press.

Yelich-Koth, S. (2017, June 26). Schizophrenia deconstructed. Retrieved from www.madinamerica.com/2017/06/schizophrenia-deconstructed.

Young, A. (1997). *The harmony of illusions: Inventing post-traumatic stress disorder.* Princeton, NJ: Princeton University Press.

Yuhas, D. (2013). Throughout history, defining schizophrenia has remained a challenge (Timeline). *Scientific American.* Retrieved from www.scientificamerican.com/article/throughout-history-defining-schizophrenia-has-remained-challenge.

Zuk, G.H., & Zuk, C.V. (1995). Freud's theory of paranoid delusion based on the Schreber case contrasted with related theories. *Contemporary Family Therapy, 17* (2), 209–216.

INDEX

abuse 44, 63, 152, 157; *see also* trauma
academic imperialism 85–86
accidents of history 16
active participation in healing 93
activity, benefits of 91
Adichie, Chimamanda Ngozi 79–80
adolescents 138–139
affect 50, 109–112, 150; *see also* intense emotions
affective arousal 50
afflicted, the, as subject 123–126, 130–131, 137–138, 140, 142
afflictions 95–99, 101–126
agency 43
agitation 95, 97, 99, 105
alcoholism 140
alienation 68, 74, 75, 77–81
alternative communities 38
Al-Uzri, M.M. 71
ambulatory schizophrenia 36
American Journal of Psychiatry 38
American Psychiatric Association 23, 31, 32
Americanah (Ngozi Adichie, 2014) 79–80
ancestors 101–104, 109, 113, 114
ancestral revenge 101–104, 109, 118

ancestral/paternal land 100, 107, 112, 113, 115, 117–118
anger 113
animality 13
annihilation 153
anosognosia 42
Anti-Oedipus: Capitalism and Schizophrenia (Deleuze and Guattari, 1983) 129, 131
anti-psychiatry movements 23, 35–39
antipsychotics 10, 40–41, 43
apparitions 96
appetite 88, 98
appropriation, cultural 90
Ardhanarishvara 135
arranged marriages 115, 133, 138
art 49–50, 58, 74–75
Arthashastra 92
asociality 50
associations, loosening of 73
astrology 101, 104, 114, 138
asylums: and catatonia 34; history in India 89–90; history in the West 15, 16, 19, 20; private 18; rise in inmates 21; and the symptoms of insanity 34
attachment styles 44

Attenborough, David 35
attenuated psychosis risk 43
attenuated psychosis syndrome 27
auras 79, 121, 144
authority: appeals to personal 26; asymmetrical 15, 19; clinical 30; diagnostic 32; societal systems of 38
Autobiography of a Schizophrenic Girl, The (Sechehaye & Rubin-Rabson, 1979) 49–50, 55, 62–63, 67
autonomy 17, 146, 149
avatar therapy 73–74
Ayurvedic approaches 86–94, 112

"bad child" 123
Balaji temple 116, 117, 118–122, 124
Banerjee, M.N. 132
baraat 95–96
Barnes, Mary 73
Bassaglia, Franco 38
Basu, Amit Ranjan 89–90, 91
Bateson, Gregory 8, 148–149, 150, 155
batwara 128
Beers, Clifford 55, 57
behavioral therapy 20
benevolent clinicians 4
benign voices 43
Bentall, Richard 24
Benthamism 17
Berke, J. 73
betrayal 99, 102, 105, 110–111, 113
Bhattacharya, Anouska 91
Bhela 87
Bhugra, D. 81, 133
Bhui, K. 133
bile (*pitta*) 87, 88, 112
bimaristans 92
binary choices, absence of 134–135, 136, 153–154, 158
biographical approaches 39, 43, 60, 73, 150
biological markers 23, 27, 28
biological reductionism of schizophrenia 39
biological understandings of madness 4, 32, 38–39

biologization 27, 42
biology 24–26, 53
bio-medical model of psychosis 4, 5, 9–10, 59, 162
biopsychiatry 20
bizarre behaviour 97, 99, 108, 145
bizarre delusions 32, 144
black magic 111, 135
bleeding 98, 112
Bleuler, Eugen 12, 22, 25, 26, 27–28, 34, 46, 73
blindness 98, 135
bodily sensations, hyper-awareness of 50
body of the girl-child 155
body schema, stable 77
body-without-organs 132, 135
bolna 105
Bond, Ruskin 83
bonds and connections, broken 101, 102, 106–107, 115, 123, 128–129; *see also* connectedness; interdependence; radical enmeshment
Bose, Girindrasekhar 158, 159
botanical taxonomic classification 24–25
bottom-up approaches 9
boundaries, unstable 145, 146
boundaries/definitions of madness, widening 21
bourgeois society 15, 17, 121, 122
Boyle, Mary 16, 17, 18, 19, 20, 21, 26, 28, 35, 46
Brahmanans 87
brain: brain tissue loss 41, 71, 72; Indian history of madness 87; insanity as brain disorder 20; location of mental functions in 19
Braun, V. 9
Brief Psychiatric Scale 93–94
brief reactive psychosis 32
British Psychological Society 9–10
Brock, Kamilah 32–33
broken bonds and connections 101, 102, 106–107, 115, 123, 128–129
Burnham, D.L. 17, 145, 146, 149

Index

Cantor-Graae, E. 78
capitalism 132, 133, 134
Caraka 87, 88
caricaturization 63–64
Carothers, John 36
Carpenter, William 29, 31
Cartesian divide 14, 67, 70, 87–88
castration 36, 158
catatonia 25, 32, 33, 34, 50
catching a fright 83–84, 124
categorical thinking 71
causes of afflictions 101–104
causes of psychosis 54
causes of schizophrenia 32
Chalmers, David 52
chanting 120
Charaka Samhita 84, 86–87, 89, 112
checklists 23
Cheetam, Mark 23
chemical imbalance theory 38–39, 41
child rearing, communal 153
chlorpromazine 38
civil rights movement 32, 37
Clarke, V. 9
classical subject 51
classification of insanity 21–27, 31, 87–89, 95
cleanliness 91, 122
clinical judgement 21, 30
clinician training 29
clozapine 41
cogito 48, 66–70, 76, 142, 145, 148, 151
cognitive behavioral theories 166
cognitive processes 64, 70–74
colonialism 2, 6, 89, 90, 91
commands 53–54
community interventions 42
compulsive thinking 65, 99
concept formation 23
conditions of possibilities 6
confinement of madness 13–14, 90, 91
conjunctive synthesis 132–133, 134
connectedness 71, 106, 110, 113–117, 131, 136, 146; *see also* interdependence; radical enmeshment
Conrad, Klaus 144

consciousness 49–50, 67–69, 77, 81, 87, 98
consciousness studies 51–52, 53
contagion 120, 121, 136, 138, 151, 161
contingencies 109
contradictions 134, 136, 147, 148–151, 157, 158
control, lack of 14, 64–65, 71, 125, 143, 145
convulsions 98, 99, 107, 120, 125
Cooper, David 37, 38
coping response, schizophrenia as 37
counter-culture movements 37
Craps, S. 162
Crick, F. 51
criminality 35–36; *see also* deviant behaviours
critical theory 6
critical thinking 29
cultural change 138, 139
cultural consistency 81
cultural fair assessment 5
cultural identity 81
cultural outsider positions 77–81
cultural psychology 115, 130
culturally relevant approaches 10
culturally sensitive psychology 4
cure versus panacea 14
curers 125, 140, 142

daan 109, 117–118, 123
Dalmiya, V. 154, 158
dance 99, 107, 115
dancer-curers 125, 140, 142
Das, A. 164
Davar, Bhargavi 4, 93, 167
Dayabhanga 92
decolonization 8, 10, 164–165, 168
definitions of insanity 87
degenerates 36
dehumanization 7
deities: dancer-curers 125–126; explanations of afflictions 101, 102, 104; history of madness in India 87, 88; and the land 99; local deities' choice of curers 126; and opacity 143; random possessions 126;

resolutions 118; stickiness 124; and trance 107
Delay, Jean 38
Deleuze, Gilles vi–vii, 5, 6, 8, 54, 129, 131, 132, 133, 134, 136–137, 161
deliberative styles of acting 73
delinquency 36, 123, 139
delirium 14, 73
delusions: adaptive 44; bizarre delusions 32, 144; certitude and indifference 55–56; content of 43–44; in diagnosis of schizophrenia 32; of enlightenment 67; and language 60; as metaphors for past experience 73; and the mind-body split 14; non-literal interpretations of 55–56; protective elements of 23; subjective assessments of 32–33; and subjectivity 53, 143–144; therapeutic process 43
dementia paralytica 20, 26
dementia praecox 12, 17, 21, 22, 27, 28, 31, 32, 34, 35–36, 46
demons 87, 88, 143
Deniker, Pierre 38
Dennett, Daniel 52
depression 81, 95
deprivation 10
derealization 49
Descartes, Rene 70
deserving/undeserving 18
desire for the prohibited 134
desiring-production 130–137
de-stigmatization 42
detachment 48
deterritorialization vi, vii, 135
devbhoomi 99
deviant behaviours 35, 37, 38, 95, 99, 114, 116, 140
deviants 18, 19, 20
Dhar, A. 10
diagnosis: diagnosis by exclusion 32; dimensional models 33; dimensional models of diagnosis 33; versus formulation 43–44; history in the West 16, 24, 26–27;
iatrogenic effects 22; in India 104; objectivity and validity 38; of schizophrenia 32; technical-rational discourse 29
dialogue, therapeutic 43
Diefendorf, A.R. 17, 18, 22, 34, 35, 36, 40, 67, 162
Disability Adjusted Life Years (DALY) 164
discourse 9, 28, 57, 59, 76, 78, 109, 142, 153
discursive economy 9
disease entities 23, 39
disinhibition of semantic networks 72
disintegration 145–146
disjunctive synthesis of recording 134
dislocation of being 80
disorganization 32, 49
displacement, sense of 78
dissociation 14, 62, 107
dissociative identity 34
dissonance 136, 142
distancing 80
distress 8, 10, 95, 97, 103, 122, 162
distress communities 93
divided subject 74, 161, 162
divinity, and materiality 13–14
Diwali 154
Djinns 135
doctors: and asylums 19; authority of the 15; in India 100; mad doctors and medicine 16–21
Donaldson, Kenneth 29–30, 42
dopamine-dysregulation hypothesis 27, 39, 41–42
doshas 89
double-bind 8, 129, 148–149, 155, 157
Dowbiggin, I.R. 36
dreams 101, 104–105, 119
drinking 140
Druga 154
dry throat 98
DSM 26
DSM-I 22
DSM-II 23, 31
DSM-III 23, 32, 39
DSM-IV 32
DSM-IV-R 32

Index

DSM-V 26, 27, 29, 31, 32, 34, 43
dual positioning 55–56
DuPont family 16
duration of untreated psychosis 42–43
Durga puja 154
dysfunctional families 38, 44

early-intervention approach 42–43
East India Company 90–91
echolalia 62
echopraxia 63
economics 52
ego 70
elders, family 132
emotional distress 95
emotional regulation 18
emotional shock 97, 102, 108
emotional support 106
empirical evidence, lack of 28
empiricial science 32, 33, 35, 52–53
empiricist discourse 28
empirico-transcendental doublet 54–57, 65–67, 151
encephalitis lethargica 34
endogenous (consitutional) insanity 87
Enlightenment 67–68, 90, 148
environment, relations with 18, 40
epileptic seizures 98, 144
epiphenomena 59
episodic memory 71
epistemology: and language 57–66; of modernity 46–82; psychiatry in India 90; and schizophrenia 7, 12, 29, 40, 50–52, 151; Western hyper-connectedness 72–73
Equal Environment Assumption (EEA) 40
Escher, Sandra 43, 108, 157
essential self, madness exposes 3
essentialism 9
ethical problems 17, 43, 44
ethnicity 32, 36–37
etiology of schizophrenia 35, 37, 87, 149
eugenics 36
Euro-centricity 6
evangelicalism 17
event trauma 7, 162

everyday living, simple 93, 94
evidence-based treatment 164
evolutionary advantages 44
exclusion from society 13, 116, 162
execution 36
existential preservation 37, 53, 145
exogenous (accidental) insanity 87, 88
extended family 105, 106, 111, 114, 153

facial expressions 150
Fadiman, J. 63, 69
Fairburn, Chris 2
faith-healing 1–2, 92–93
false perspective 50
false positives 32
false self 37
familial duties 102, 105
families, involvement in healing 93, 94, 106
family, Indian 128, 132, 133, 137, 153, 155
family backgrounds 38
family-process theories of schizophrenia 157
fear 87, 89, 96, 103, 111, 144, 155
female feticide 129, 151, 152, 153
female subjectivity 151, 155–156, 161
feminine energy 154
Fernando, Suman 164, 165
fetishes 36
film 74–75
financial problems 98, 102, 106, 112
Fink, B. 74, 76
first-break approach 42–43
first-person narratives 54, 69
first-person studies of consciousness 51–52
fixed subjectivity 132–133, 139, 146, 157
flat affect 50, 150
food 87, 88, 90
forced detention 91
forced sterilization 36
forced treatment 43, 44
forces 53–54, 64–65
forms of thought 72, 82, 112
formulation (versus diagnosis) 43–44

Fosse, R. 40
Foucault, Michel vi–vii, 3, 5, 6, 9, 13–15, 16, 19, 23, 25, 26, 28, 30, 34, 46, 47, 50–52, 53, 56, 57, 59, 62, 64, 65, 66, 67, 68, 70–74, 85, 108–109, 117, 122, 123, 134, 139, 142, 155, 165, 169
fragility of being 70
Frances, A. 32
Fraser, Elizabeth 58, 61, 62
freedom of choice 42
Freud, Sigmund 8, 54, 132
fright (*ghabrahat*) 96, 101, 103, 108, 110, 111, 123–124
fright-prone person 123–124
fugue 34
fundamentalism 11

Gaebel, W. 26, 27
Garfield, President 36
gender 134, 135, 136, 151, 158
gendered subjectivity 151
general affective syndrome 27
general psychotic syndrome 27
genetics 23, 26, 39, 40, 116
George III, King 16
Germany 21, 26, 35
ghabrahat (fright) 96, 101, 103, 108, 110, 111, 123–124
ghosts: attachment to land 104; ghost encounters 88, 96, 101, 103, 109, 114; hauntings 100, 118, 121, 124; history of madness in India 83, 84; more mischievous than deities 104; narratives 105; and opacity 143; radical enmeshment 115; stickiness 110, 116, 124
gift-giving 109
girl-child in India 147, 151–159
Global Mental Health Movement 5, 6, 8, 147, 164–168
global South 85, 165
globalization 138, 139, 164–168
globalization of mental health 10
god, knowledge of 67
goddesses 99, 126, 129, 151, 154–157
gods 103; *see also* deities

grandiosity 33, 55
Green, Joanne (Hannah) 65–66, 69
grey-matter loss 41, 71, 72
grief 89
grounded self 69
groundlessness 62; *see also* ungrounding
Gruenberg, E.M. 31
Guattari, Félix vi–vii, 5, 8, 54, 129, 131, 132, 133, 134, 136–137, 161
Guiteau, Charles 36
Gutting, G. 51, 53, 57, 62

Hadfield, James 16
Haldipur, C.V. 87, 88
hallucinations: auditory hallucinations 43; avatar therapy 73–74; certitide and indifference 55–56; cultural variations in 10; in diagnosis of schizophrenia 32; of enlightenment 67; ghost encounters 84; grandness 55; in India 144; as metaphors for past experience 73; and the mind-body split 14; non-literal interpretations of 55–56; not necessarily distressing 162; positive content 162; protective elements of 23; rural northern Indian perspective 95; spirit possessions 84; tactile 97, 112; therapeutic process 43; and trauma 44; and unthought 143; *see also* hearing voices; seeing things
Hanuman (god) 120
Harley, Herbert 35–36
Harry Potter 58–59
Hartnack, C. 158
Hastings, T. 91
hauntings 100, 118, 121, 124
head injuries 34
headaches 98
healing, indigenous approaches to 92–94
healing spaces 94
hearing sounds 95
hearing voices: benign voices 43; bio-medical model of psychosis

10; Djinns 135; of family members 102, 143–144; heterogenous experiences of 2; interdependence 113; and the land 100; mind-body duality (lack of) 88; not necessarily distressing 103, 122, 162; resolutions 105; rural northern Indian perspective 94–99; and schizophrenia in the West 43
Hearing Voices movement 43, 55, 60, 73, 162
heart 87, 102, 111
hebephrenia 25, 36
hematoxicity 41
heredity 36, 53, 92
heritability 40
Hijra 158
Himalayas 83, 84, 100
Hindu, The 1
Hindu astrology 104, 114
Hindu laws 92
Hindu myths 29, 135, 154
history as way to diagnose the present 109
history of madness: India 86–94; in the West 12–45
Hoffman, Monica 43
Holland, E.W. 136
homosexuality 36
honor 155
hope 43
hospitals: emergence of 14–15, 20; in India 90, 92; involuntary hospitalization 43, 44; sterility of 122
Huford, Irene 44
human rights 164
human sciences 52, 141
humanistic traditions 5
humanitarianism 15, 16, 19
humanization 14
humors/elements 87, 89
Husserl, E. 56
hyper-awareness 70, 81
hyper-cognition 70–74
hyper-connectedness 72–73
hyper-consciousness 47
hyper-focus 78
hyper-priming 72
hyper-reflexivity 48–50, 52, 56, 59, 61, 65, 74, 76, 81, 144, 149–150, 162
hyper-sensitivity 150
hypo-arousal of emotions 150
hysteria 14, 22, 34

I Never Promised You a Rose Garden (Green, 1989) 65–66, 69
iatrogenic effects 22, 34
ideas of reference 54
ideational styles of acting 73
identity formation 138–139, 140–141
idleness 17–18
illegal detention 91
illegitimate use of the conjunctive synthesis 132, 134
immigration 77–81
immune systems 44
implicit styles of thinking 4, 109, 117, 131, 135–136
impotence 54
impure foods 87
inappropriate affect 89
incarnations 142
India-Pakistan partition 81
indigenous approaches in India 10–11, 92–94
indigenous discourse around madness 85
indirect priming tests 72
individualism 113, 114, 115, 133, 138, 140, 145–146, 166–167
individual/society binary 153–154
industrial revolution 17, 18, 114, 157
infertility 98, 112, 134
inner speech 65
insecure attachment 44
insight 38, 42, 44, 67
Institution of Psychiatry 90
institutions: alternatives to 38; in India 90; rural northern Indian perspective 117–122; *see also* asylums
intense emotions 109–112, 121, 122, 124, 131, 134, 135, 145, 150

Index

intentions 103, 109, 110, 111, 113–114, 115, 121, 122
interdependence 101, 102, 103, 106, 113–117, 130, 161
inter-generational causes of affliction 101, 106, 167
interiority 60, 76, 77, 90, 95, 112, 113, 126, 134, 143, 162, 168
internal control 17
International Classification of Diseases (ICD) 23, 26, 31
inter-rater reliability 32
interview methods 8
intimacy, desire for 50
introversion 95, 97
involuntary hospitalization 43, 44
ipseity 49
irritability 95, 98
isolation 38, 53, 116
Italy 38

jaagar 105, 106, 107, 115–116, 117–118, 122, 124, 125, 166
Jablensky, A. 33
Jaspers, Karl 47, 48, 69
jaw, clenched 98, 135
jealousy 113
Jefferson, Lara 63, 69
joint families 132
joy 87
Jucaite, A. 42
Julie 64
Jung, Carl 34

Kahlbaum, Karl Ludwig 34
Kakkar, Sudhir 122, 154
Kali 155–157, 158
Kant, Emmanuel 23, 51, 52
kapha (phlegm) 87, 88, 112
Kapoor, Ekta 128
Kashmiri migration crisis 81
Kellett, J.M. 44
Kendall, G. 85, 109, 117, 127n1
Kennedy, M. 2
Kewman, D. 63, 69
Khilji, Mahmood 90
kindness 91
Kingsley Hall 38
Kirk, S.A. 20, 21, 26, 28–29, 38, 39

kisi ki hai lagna 103
Klein, Melanie 54, 61
knowledge 141–146; *see also* epistemology
Koch, C. 51
Koola, M. 29
Kraepelin, Emil 12, 17, 18, 21, 22, 25, 26, 27–28, 34, 35, 36, 40, 67, 162
Kretschmerian paradox 149–151
Kurosawa, Akira 74–75
Kutchins, H. 20, 21, 26, 28–29, 38, 39

labor 13, 17–18, 91
Lacan, Jacques 8, 74, 76, 77, 161
lagti hai 110
Lahiri, Jhumpa 79
Laing, R.D. 37, 38, 53, 55, 60, 64, 70, 73, 149, 157
land 99–100, 104, 107, 110, 111, 115–116, 118, 123, 126, 131
language: alienation through 74; of behaviour rather than identity 141; disorder of 29; effect of speech on material reality 98, 103, 112; and epistemology 58; of formulation 43–44; more than representation and signification 85, 161; of possession 116; of psychiatry 37–38; and psychosis 75–77; and schizophrenia 57–66, 149; stickiness of affect and word 109–112; and subjectivity 9; terminology of schizophrenia 27–30; texture of 58; and the traumatic subject 74; un-grounding of 57–66; verbalization 58, 74, 85, 117, 162; vocalization of ghost narratives 105
Laplanche, Jean 76
laughter 118, 120, 136
law of the father 74, 76
Laws, K.R. 71
lawsuits 22
Laxmi 154–157
Laxmi, Dama 2
Leff, J. 73

"leg lock" 98, 112, 135, 162
liberalization 138, 139
life events 4, 108
life problems 95, 98–99, 112
life stories 73; *see also* narratives
life-long nature of illness 139, 162
linear causality 17, 116
literature 48, 57, 61
local healers 93
Lohokare, M. 93, 167
Longden, Eleanor 55
lower castes 93
LSD 38
lucidity 67
Luhrmann, T.M. 162
Lunacy Acts 90, 91, 92

machines 131, 135
"mad woman" figure 119–120, 124–125
madness, overview of 3–6
Madness and Civilization (Foucault, 1967) 13–15
Madness and Modernism (Sass, 1994) 49–50
magic 90, 99–100, 111, 135
Mahanubhav temples 93, 99–100, 107
Maier, Hans 38
Maj, M. 32
male/female binary 134, 153–154, 158–159
Mallarmé, Stéphane 49, 62
"man," as object 50–52, 70, 81, 137, 141
mania 91
manic-depressive psychosis 38
mantras 105, 112, 120
marginalized populations 78
marriage, arranged 115, 133, 138
marriage restrictions 36
mass hysteria 118, 121, 124, 136
Massive Attack 58
masturbation 36
materialism 166–167
materiality: of affect 110; desiring-production 131; in India 84, 87, 100, 122; of intention 111; physical connections 116; versus physiology 116; stickiness 109–112, 121
McNally, Kieran 21–22, 23, 25, 27, 28, 31, 37–38, 46
Mead, Richard 19
meaning: faith in 73; meaning/representation 85; metaphorical meaning 60; and the traumatic subject 76; tyranny of meaning 162
meaning-based models of madness 4, 73–74
meaningful language 62–63, 64
medical management 19–20
medical model: history in the West 15, 19, 20; mad doctors and medicine 16–21; medical discourse of schizophrenia 29; schizophrenia 12, 38–39; somatization 19
medication 5, 10, 38–39, 41–42, 165
medicine, discourses of 9
meditative states 61
Mehandipur Balaji 118–122
memory connections 71–72, 125
mental health awareness, calls for 85
mental health services, calls for more 160, 164
mental illness, madness as 15
mental shocks 87, 89
mentalization 58, 131
Merleau-Ponty, C. 51
mescaline 38
meta-analysis 40, 44, 78
meta-awareness 50
meta-messages 148–149, 157
Metzl, J.M. 32, 37
mhGAP (mental health gap) forum 160
migration 77–81
Mills, China 164, 165
mind-body duality 14, 87–88, 90, 112, 134
misrecognition 47, 133
Mitakshara 92
modern art 49–50, 58
Mohini avatar of the Vishnu 135
moral control 18, 19

moral insanity 35
moral management 18–21, 46, 91
morality 14, 15, 35–36, 167
mothers 37, 148, 157
MRIs 39
multiculturalism 138
multiple positionalities 130, 137, 139, 142, 157, 159, 162
Murray, Robin 24
music 105
Muslim saint shrines 93
Mustakova-Possardt, E. 165, 166, 167
myths 33–35, 124, 135, 136, 154, 158

Nabokov, V. 93
Nagel, T. 52
Namesake, The (Lahiri, 2003) 79
Narasimha 135
narcissism 69
narrative of progress 29
narrative positioning 75
narratives 105, 116, 117, 123, 154
nasal discharge 88
National Public Radio 1
NDMA-receptors 41
need-fear dilemma 17
neoliberalism 166
nerve-language 62, 64–65
nervous disorder, insanity as 19
neurasthenia 165
neuro emotional integration disorder 27
neuroleptics 38, 40–41, 71
neurology 20–21, 39, 51, 71
neurosis 37, 68, 72, 73, 132, 144, 162
neurotic subject 142–143
neurotransmitter imbalances 4, 41–42
Neyer, Bernhard 37
Ngozi Adichie, Chimamanda 79–80
Nietsche, Friedrich 62
nomadic subject 129, 130–137, 161
non-self 70
nuclear family 132, 133, 162
Nyberg, S. 42

obsessions 89
oedipalized fixed subject 132, 137
Oedipus 133
offerings 109, 117–118, 120, 121, 122
Olanzapine 41
omnipotence 54, 56, 137
ontological insecurity 37, 144, 157
opacity 67–68, 74–77, 143, 144, 148, 162
Open Dialogue approach 43
Order of Things, The (Foucault, 1994) 25, 48, 50–52
organization 17, 32
Other 2, 6, 13, 18, 67–69, 76, 115, 142–144, 168
otherness 33, 38, 46–82, 129
outpatient clinics 20–21, 44
outsiders 78
over-activation of semantic networks 72
over-diagnosis 91
over-religiosity 99

pacification of patients 39
panacea 14
paradoxical thinking 148, 158
paranoia 22, 25, 31, 32
paranormal interpretations of phenomena 111, 121–122
parental neglect/abuse 102
parents 132; *see also* mothers
Parnas, J. 24, 33–34, 49, 76–77
passive voice 28
pathological co-dependence 130
pathological conceptions of psychosis 4, 10
pathologization of behavior 35, 42, 85
paucity of speech 62, 150
Payne, Arthur 91
perception, changes in 50, 67
permanent affliction 139–140
personal biographical approaches 39, 43, 60, 73, 150
personality 22, 87
personalization of desire 133–134
personalization of soma 132
perspectivism 49, 74

Index

perversions 132, 139
Peterson, D. 57
pharmacology 5, 10, 38–39
phenomenology 56–57
philosophy 19, 23, 39, 51, 52, 66–70, 141, 154
phlegm (*kapha*) 87, 88, 112
phobias 69
physical connections 131
physical consequences of affect 110
physical health 95, 98
physical malformations 34
physiological explanations 116
Pinel, Philippe 1, 15, 20, 21, 46, 121
pitr-bhoomi 100, 107, 112, 113, 115, 118
pitta (bile) 87, 88, 112
place 110
placebo studies 42
planets 103, 104, 133, 138
poisons 89
political beliefs 37
polygenic disorders 40
Porter, R. 19, 20, 26, 39
positivism 15, 52
possession 101, 116, 118, 121, 124
post-colonialism 6, 130, 132, 135, 138, 162
post-modern art 48
post-structuralism 6
poverty 18, 79
power dynamics 36–37, 92, 155, 166
power relays 15
powers of restraint 43
praecox feeling 48
prayer 93
priests 90, 109, 117–118, 126
privacy 114, 132, 166
private madhouses 18–19
prodromal phases 49, 79, 144
prognosis 42–43
projection 63
Psychiatric Power: Lectures at College de France, 1973–1974 (Foucault, 2006) 15
psychiatrization of distress 10
psychiatry: birth of 15, 19; claims of universal applicability 129; and the creation of classes of mentally ill 37–38; definitions of schizophrenia 22; diagnosis 16; discourses of 29–30; and eugenics 36; in India 9, 89–92, 141; mad doctors 20–21; narrative of progress 29; nature of psychiatric knowledge 30; in non-Western settings 85; personalizing experiences with globalized psychiatry 164–168; power of 37–38; prejudice in 36–37; and schizophrenia 7, 23–24, 30, 34–35, 76
psychic functions 22
psychoanalysis 35, 54, 70, 162
psychodynamic theory 130
psychologization of madness 14, 60
psychology: classification of insanity 25; cross-cultural coherence 10; dominance of mainstream psychological narrative 86; and a focus on interiority 134; foundations of 165–168; golden era of psychological science 15; in India 2; objectivity and validity 165–166; personalizing experiences with globalized psychiatry 164–168; as philosophy of mind 19; physiological explanations 116; and psychiatry 39; and sticky phenomena 111
psycho-pharmacological treatment 5, 10, 38–39, 41–42, 165
psychosis: Balaji temple 118, 124; contradictions 134; cultural variations in 10; and language 75–77; mainstream understandings of 7; prodromal phases 79; right to choose 44; and temple stays 94; and trauma 85–86
psychosis risk syndrome 27, 32
psychosomatism 87, 110, 111
psychotic symptoms, in diagnosis of schizophrenia 32
psychotropic drugs 39, 94, 165
puja 93, 114, 154

racism 33, 36–37
radical enmeshment 113–117, 122, 134, 135–136, 145, 151, 161, 162
Raguram, R. 93–94
Ramprasad 154
randomized controlled trials 41
Ranganathan, S. 93, 94, 99–100, 107
Rao, M. 139, 164
rapid modernization 138–139
Rashomon (Kurosawa, 1983) 74–75
rational-empiricist discourse 30
rationality 13, 18
reading rice 104–105
reality 23, 29, 30, 50, 55–56, 74, 144, 146
reality testing 27
reason, and madness 13, 14
recording 134
recovery 18, 44
reddish appearance 88
reductionist biological understandings 4
Reform movement 17, 19
rehabilitation 38
relativism 74
Renaissance 13, 50, 55, 62
Renee 49–50, 62–63, 67
repetitive phrases 62
repetitive thinking 97
representation 51, 57, 59, 60, 61, 64, 65, 70, 73, 85
research methods 8–9
resilience 166
resistance to crisis 157–159
restraint 43, 91
retroactive assessment of insanity 26
revenge 101–104, 109, 113, 118
reward and punishment systems 20
right to speak 19
rigidity 34
rituals 93, 102, 104–105, 106, 109, 113–114, 120, 164
river ghosts 83
rivers 104, 109, 110, 115, 124, 135
Roberts, J. 77, 142, 143
romanticization 3, 10, 57, 146
Romme, Marius 43, 108, 157
Rosenhann, David 38
Rowe, Dorothy 39

Rubin-Rabson, G. 49–50, 55, 62–63, 67
sacred ash 105, 111, 115
sacrifice 102, 109, 114, 117, 123
sages 88
saint shrines 93
Saks, Elyn 53–54, 56, 60–61, 72
sankat 92
Sanskrit 87, 92
Sapolsky, Robert 40
Sass, Louis 5, 47, 49–50, 52, 54, 55–56, 57, 61, 65, 68, 70, 73, 76–77, 79, 81, 144, 148, 149–150
schematic associations 73
schizoid personality 150
schizophrenia: abuse and anti-psychiatry 35–39; attempts to classify 21–27, 30–31; Balaji temple 118; causes of 32; and contradictions 148–151; as coping response 37; critical to psychiatry's authority 7; current theories 39–44; "discovery" of 12, 16, 27; evolutionary advantages 44; family-process theories of schizophrenia 157; historical overview 12–45; hyper-modern subject 46–82; and immigration 77–81; incurable nature of 14; in India 167; and institutions 30–33; and internal disintegration 145; and language 57–66; language of schizophrenia 27–30; objectification of 53, 54; as polygenic 40; and psychiatry 23–24, 30, 34–35, 76; and race/ethnicity 36–37; saner than the sane 38; schizophrenic cognition 70–74; and subjectivity 53, 129–146; sub-types 31, 32, 34, 36; and temple stays 94; transience of 141; and trauma 74–77
schizophrenia childhood type 23
schizophrenic paradoxes 50
schizophrenic process 136
Schreber, Daniel Paul 54, 60, 62, 64–65
Schwarz, S. 166

scientific discourse 28
Scull, Andrew 16, 17, 18, 19, 20, 21, 46
Sechehaye, M. 49–50, 55, 62–63, 67
seeing things: and the land 100; mind-body duality (lack of) 88; not necessarily distressing 103, 122, 162; resolutions 105; rural northern Indian perspective 94–99
Seikkula, Jaako 43
selective lucidity 60
self-affectation 49, 77
self-awareness 49, 64
self-evident ideas 29
self-harm 42, 107, 115, 121
selfhood, Western models of 17, 18
self-identity 115
self-improvement 17
self-knowledge relations 142, 143
self-mastery, as goal 17
self-objectification 77
self/other binary 134
self-referentiality 49
self-reflexivity 48, 51, 65, 68, 77, 78–79, 142
self-restraint 17
Selten, J.P. 78
semantic memory 71–72
semantic priming 72
Sen, Amartya 139
sensory heightening 80, 83–84
sepoy revolt 90, 91
sexual behavior 36
Shah, Firoz 90
Shakti 154
shamans 16, 90, 92
shared troubles 93
Shiva 135
shrines 92, 93, 99, 117–118, 119, 120, 154
Siddiqui, S. 10
side effects of medication 5, 40–41, 61
signs 57–66
sleep 88
slippery subjects 129, 130–141, 143, 145, 157–162
Sloan, T.S. 138

Snape, Severus 58–59
social causes of schizophrenia 40
social class 25
social constructionism 6, 9
social pressures, and schizophrenia 38
socially-constructed discourses of insanity 4
socio-cultural subjectivity 9, 39, 42, 164
socio-economic status 36
sociology 38
sociomoral concerns 93, 106
somatization 19, 20, 35
speech and schizophrenia 57–66, 71
spirits: Balaji 118, 121; detaching 122; explanations of afflictions 101, 103; history of madness in India 88, 98; and the land 100; and opacity 143; spirit possessions 109, 162; stickiness 110, 113, 114, 116, 124
spiritual concerns, and healing 93
spiritualism 20
Spitzer, M. 71, 72
Spivak, Gayatri 6
splitting 22
statistical methods 24, 31, 32
sterilization 36
stickiness 109–112, 116, 124, 131, 135
stigma 32, 42, 43, 85, 162
Stimmung 79, 80
story telling 75, 84, 105, 135
strange happenings 98–99, 109
stress 79, 167
structure of subjectivity 3, 8, 13, 129, 161, 168
stupor 33, 34
styles of thought 7
subalterns 6
subjective experience 2, 7, 26, 31, 50, 103, 111, 150
sublime 23, 30, 47, 76
subservience 63
subversions 63
suffering: cultural variations in 10; psychiatrization of distress 10; stickiness 110; suffering and revenge as

Index

cause of affliction 101–102; and trauma theory 162
surgery 89
survivors of psychiatry 39
Sushruta Samhita 89
symbolic: dominion over the 65; injury sustained during entry to the 74
symptoms: Balaji 121; as basis for classification 25; in diagnosis of schizophrenia 32, 34; fright (*ghabrahat*) 103; fundamental core versus fluctuating surface 33–34; objective symptom criteria 29; symptomatic relief 94
syphilis 20
Szasz, Thomas 22, 37–38

tabulating and recording madness 23
tacit processes 52, 78
"Teardrop" 58, 61
technical-rational discourse 28–29
temples 93–94, 99–100, 107, 116, 118–122, 124
terror 55, 56, 76
thematic analysis 9
theories of mind 19
therapeutic confinement 15
therapeutic process 43, 91, 167–168
third gender 158
thought disorders 23, 71, 72
tongues, speaking in 105, 107
totalization 76
trance states 93, 99, 105, 107, 115–116, 117–122, 123, 125
transcendence 52, 53, 56, 77, 148
transgenderism 158
transient affliction 139–141, 162
transvestites 36
Tranulis, C. 42, 43
trauma: and the girl-child 157; Global Mental Health Movement 162; and neoliberalism 166; and psychosis 10, 44, 73, 85–86; rural northern Indian perspective 107–108; and schizophrenia 74–77
trauma theory 4, 5, 166
treatment gap 10, 31, 164

treatment-resistant schizophrenia 41
tree weddings 138
trema 144, 145
trembling 98, 107, 115, 125
triarchic theories 87
Trilafon 61
truth-taking star 79
Tuke, Samuel 15
Tuke, William 17, 46
twin studies 40

unchaining of the mad 1
unconscious 67, 68–69, 73, 76
undifferentiation 32
unfulfilled desire 101–102, 110–111, 112, 121, 122, 123, 131, 135
unfulfilled duties/promises 102–103, 105, 109, 112
ungrounding 144, 145, 150
unproductiveness 18
unreality 49–50, 81, 144
unreason 13, 14
unthought 8, 48, 66–70, 76, 86, 142, 143, 145, 148, 151, 162, 169
unundertandability 47, 48, 69
unwanted-ness 151, 152–153, 154
unworlding 49, 79, 144, 145
upper castes 6, 9, 109, 130, 155
US 18, 20, 31, 36, 37
Uttarakhand: description of 84; *devbhoomi* 99; as site of research 7; as special place 99–100, 110, 114–115

vacant stare 34
value-free approach 14, 15, 165
vatta (wind) 87, 88, 112
Vedic texts 89
vengeful ancestors 101–104, 118
verbalization 58, 74, 85, 117, 162
vibuti 105, 107, 111, 115
violence 99, 110, 166
Vishnu 135
visibilities 117–122, 125, 129, 130
visions 67; *see also* seeing things
vomiting 88
Vonnegut, Mark 38

Watters, Ethan 162
ways of thinking 51, 78, 109, 169
wedding processions *see jaagar*
weight loss 98
whiteish appearance 88
Why Did I Go Mad (Mendham & Farnham, 2017) 78
Wickham, G. 85, 109, 117, 127n1
Willis, Thomas 19
wind (*vatta*) 87, 88, 112
Winnicott, D.W. 157
witchcraft 90
women, and schizophrenia 37

Woods, Angela 17, 18, 23, 24, 30, 32, 35, 47, 76
word associations 60
word salads 72
workhouses 18
World Health Organization 10, 31, 160, 164
writers 19

yellowish appearance 88
Young, A. 162
Yuhas, D. 31

Zielasek, J. 26, 27